Logistics Outsourcing ~ A Management Guide
Second Edition

Clifford F. Lynch

CFL Publishing
P.O. Box 770398, Memphis, TN 38177
(901) 415-6800, Fax (901) 415-6810
E-mail: cliff@cflynch.com   Website: www.cflynch.com

Cover by Lamar Caldwell
ISBN 0-9744167-1-1

Copyright 2004 CFL Publishing
P.O. Box 770398
Memphis, TN 38177-0398
E-mail: cliff@cflynch.com Website: www.cflynch.com

Dedicated to my wife, Annette, for her continuing support and encouragement.

Logistics Outsourcing -
A Management Guide
Second Edition

Clifford F. Lynch

Acknowledgements

As was the case with the first edition of this book, to a great extent, the work is nothing more than a collection of the ideas, thoughts, and actions of the thousands of logistics professionals I have met during my forty plus years in the industry. To all of them I extend my sincerest appreciation for adding to my base of knowledge, either knowingly or unknowingly.

Several of these deserve specific mention, however. Special thanks to Ken Ackerman and George Gecowets, two pioneers of our industry, who continue to give me a critique when I need it whether solicited or not; to Leslie Harps, Lisa Harrington, Mitch MacDonald, and Peter Bradley whose writings have contributed so much to the body of logistics literature, and to Cheryl McMains whose encouragement, patience and word processing skills turned hundreds of handwritten pages and notes into a real manuscript.

Finally, I never could have completed the task without the assistance and contribution of Jim Bierfeldt, Dan Boekelheide, John Christian, Carl Curry, Bruce Edwards, Bill Gates, Chris Kane, Craig Levinsohn, Scott McWilliams, Jeff Miller, Stephane Picard,

Elijah Ray, Cindy Riley, Herb Shear, Alex Stark, David Waits, and Andrea Webber. To all of you, I am deeply indebted.

Disclaimer

It is not the purpose of this book to print all the information that might be available on the subject of logistics outsourcing. Every effort has been made to make the information herein as accurate as possible, but it should be used only as a general guide. The reader is urged to study as much data and literature as is practical and tailor that knowledge to individual needs.

In some instances, names of logistics service providers and publications are cited. These citations are intended only as examples, and should not be construed as recommendations of particular companies, directories, or journals.

The sample contracts included are intended as suggestions only and are not to be construed as legal advice. Before entering into any contract for logistics services, competent legal counsel should be sought and the resultant advice followed.

- Clifford F. Lynch

About the Author

Cliff Lynch has been active in the logistics industry since 1958.

Before beginning his consulting career he was chief executive of Trammell Crow Distribution Corporation, now a part of the Exel organization. Prior to that he spent over twenty-eight years with The Quaker Oats Company, with more than half that time spent as the senior logistics executive.

Lynch holds an undergraduate degree from the University of Tennessee and an MBA from the University of Chicago.

He is a member and past president of the Council of Logistics Management, and has received numerous awards in the field of logistics. Among them are the CLM Distinguished Service Award, *Traffic Management Magazine* Professional Achievement Award, University of Tennessee Department of Marketing and Transportation Distinguished Alumnus, Chairman and President's Awards for Outstanding Contribution to the American Society of Transportation and Logistics, Salzberg Memorial Medallion, the AST&L Chairman's Award for Exceptional Service, and the AST&L Outstanding Transportation/Logistics Executive.

Lynch is a Certified Member of the American Society of Transportation and Logistics and is a member of the Editorial Review Board, *Journal of Business Logistics*; Editorial Review Board, *International Journal of Physical Distribution and Logistics Management*; Editorial Advisory Board, *Supply Chain Management Review*; Editorial Advisory Board, *DC Velocity*; International Warehouse & Logistics Association; and Warehousing Education and Research Council.

He has provided logistics management advisory services to companies throughout the United States, Mexico, China, and the Philippines with a special emphasis on outsourcing.

A longtime advocate of logistics education, he has authored numerous articles and has spoken at hundreds of conferences and seminars, as well as any number of colleges and universities.

His practice is based in Memphis, Tennessee

Contents

Compact Disk Appendices and other forms for individual use

Logistics Outsourcing ~
A Management Guide
Second Edition

Clifford F. Lynch

Introduction

Why Another Book on Logistics Outsourcing?

Few informed logistics professionals would suggest that outsourcing is not a meaningful force in their industry; indeed, this entire book and the one before are based on the premise that it is extremely important today and will become even more so in the future.

It would appear, however, that in some respects the growth in logistics outsourcing has continued to be more by accident than by design. While success stories are plentiful, less publicly, the industry also has been a victim of poor planning, lack of understanding, inadequate performance, or in some cases, abject failure.

1

Logistics outsourcing is still an emerging industry, and emerging industries often are characterized by false starts and business failures.

There are a number of reasons for this, but in my opinion, lack of understanding on the part of both client and provider, more often than not, is the major cause of difficulty and failure in logistics outsourcing relationships.

It is hoped that this book will make some contribution to that understanding and serve as a useful tool to those who are contemplating or implementing a logistics outsourcing relationship.

For the purposes of this discussion, logistics outsourcing will be defined as an arrangement whereby a logistics service provider performs services for a firm that could be, or have been, provided in-house.

In addition to a refining of the basic history and principles, there have been a number of developments in outsourcing that warrant attention.

For example, since the publication of the first edition, there has been much more emphasis on the outsourcing of supply chain management systems. The list of traditional logistics service providers now contains names of companies that were unheard of a few years ago. This subject will be discussed in considerable detail in this edition.

After years of discussion and writing about them, we finally have begun to see true global outsourcing arrangements. Up until recently, while there were any number of firms that had operations in foreign countries, in most cases their logistics activities were confined to the countries in which they were located and those in close proximity. Today, we routinely move products back and forth throughout the world. To some firms outsourcing has become as important internationally as it has been in the United States. This edition addresses these opportunities.

Finally, logistics service contracts are becoming more sophisticated and are placing more pressure on the relationships to provide process and cost improvements and share these benefits with the client. The chapters on contracts and gain sharing reflect some of the new thinking in the development of outsourcing contracts.

As was the case in the previous book, the term "third party," while one of common usage, will be referenced as little as possible. Logistics outsourcing is about subcontracting logistics activities to firms that are equipped to provide the services. Besides being numerically inaccurate, the concepts of third and even fourth parties only serve to cloud the relationships.

Chapter 1

A Brief History

Frank and Ernest

THAT'S FUNNY--ALL THE WRITING SUDDENLY STOPS AT Y2K B.C.

©1998 Thaves. Reprinted with permission. Newspaper dist. by NEA, Inc.

Outsourcing of logistics services is not a new concept by any means. While it has gained renewed emphasis in recent years, the practice can be traced back almost as far as one would care to research it.

In *Warehousing Profitably* author Ken Ackerman suggests that one of the first business logistics arrangements is described in *The Bible*, Genesis Chapter 41.[1] This is an account of the seven years of plenty during which the people in the land of Egypt accumulated crops for the predicted seven years of famine. The grains and other fruits of their labors were taken to storehouses for safekeeping.

One could argue that this also may have been one of the first outsourcing arrangements, since the grain was placed in storehouses owned and operated by Joseph for later re-distribution during the time of need.

In Europe, a number of logistics service providers can trace their origins back to the Middle Ages. The first commercial warehouse operations were built in Venice, Italy in the 14th century. Merchants from all across Europe used them as collection and distribution points. [2]

In the United States in the 1930's, Al Capone, in an effort to keep his associates out of harm's way, outsourced the smuggling of liquor from Canada to Chicago. Since most shipments were subject to hijacking and other unpleasantness, Capone minimized his risk through strategic alliances with fledgling ambitious and aggressive service providers.

In a nutshell, any person or firm who has ever subcontracted an activity has outsourced.

Through the 1950's and 1960's the outsourcing of transportation and warehousing was common. The relationships were primarily transactional and typically short term in nature. There were some long-term contracts involving large companies such as DuPont and Quaker Oats, but these were the exception rather than the rule. Most warehousing transactions were standard thirty-day public warehouse agreements.

Contract motor carriage was available, but not as we know it today.

During the 1970's, manufacturers put heavy emphasis on cost reductions and improved productivity. Longer-term relationships became more common, particularly in the warehousing area. Single tenant facilities were built and operated by warehouse companies in major markets of the U.S. Consolidation of facilities into larger operations became more and more frequent.

In 1971, Frederick W. Smith used a $4,000,000 inheritance and over $90,000,000 in other capital to acquire a Little Rock, Arkansas, used aircraft business. It was Smith's intention to provide an overnight delivery service.

In 1973, Federal Express, with 389 employees and 14 Dassault Falcon planes, began operations at the Memphis International Airport. By 2004, it employed almost 220,000 people located around the world and had a fleet of 643 aircraft and 70,000 vehicles. [3]

In the early 1980's, the services offered by the outside firms expanded rapidly. So-called value-added services included packaging, blending, systems support, inventory management, customized handling and other offerings which had not been available previously.

At this point, difficulties began to surface as some providers defined value-added services as whatever the client wanted them to be. They quickly found themselves unable to provide services they had agreed to because they did not have the resources or simply did not know how.

The most significant event of the decade took place in 1980 when common carriers of all modes, as well as intermodal, newly freed from stifling federal and state regulation, were able to enter into innovative, long-term relationships with customers; and true logistics partnerships began to surface. These alliances quickly brought about major improvements in both customer service and logistics economies.

The 1980's also brought with them a phenomenal number of mergers and acquisitions; and in many cases, firms found themselves with more warehouses and distribution centers than any one company ever wanted.

Consolidation of facilities became a necessity, and what better time to re-analyze the distribution systems and put the centers where they really ought to be.

Many of these new consolidated facilities were outsourced; and by 1990, there was an increasing interest in outsourcing *any* function that was not directly related to a company's core business.

In *Post-Capitalist Society*, Peter Drucker described outsourcing as a needed change in business philosophy. He wrote that this change:

> "means that the big business, the government agency, the large hospital, the large university, will not necessarily be the one that employs a great many people. It *will* be the one that has substantial revenues and substantial results – achieved in large part because it, itself, does only work that is focused on its mission; work that is directly related to its results; work that it recognizes, values, and rewards appropriately. The rest it contracts out." [4]

During the 1990's more and more firms came to realize that the real competitive edge was to be found in enhanced customer service and relationships, and many found outsourcing to be an effective method of accomplishing this. This was particularly true of smaller companies that could contract with logistics service providers that would offer service superior to that which they could facilitate on their own.

By 1999, the entire country was caught up in the potential and mystique of the Internet. Projections for Internet retail sales were staggering. The problem was that many, if not most, of the Internet retailers had invested enormous amounts in marketing and technology, and virtually none in distribution systems. This proved to be disastrous for many. During the Christmas season in 1999, nearly 50% of all online consumers experienced fulfillment problems.

Failure rates were even higher at Mother's Day in 2000. Perhaps we should have listened to Brian Ferren, then the Chief Imagineer for Walt Disney Company, when he said:

"Trying to assess the true importance and function of the Internet now is like asking the Wright brothers at Kitty Hawk if they were aware of the potential of American Airlines Advantage Miles."

Even though there was a tremendous amount of fallout in the retailers, as well as the providers that had been established to distribute products for them, some good lessons were learned.

Those that survived are both wiser and more conservative, and in 2003, $52 billion in Internet sales were distributed with reasonable dispatch. This was 22% more than during 2002. [5]

In addition, we saw small parcel carriers become a more formidable force in logistics pipelines. By 1999, UPS was delivering 12.4 million packages daily, and FedEx another 4.5 million. FedEx further expanded its ground operations; and by late 2002, had 297 home terminals serving the total U.S. population. [6]

It was also about this time, we began to see another wave of consolidation in the logistics provider industry, and users of these services found themselves dealing with different companies and individuals, as well as different cultures. The mergers of Deutsche Post/AEI/Danzas, Exel/Mark VII/Ocean Group, UTi Worldwide/ Standard, UPS/Fritz, Kuehne & Nagel/USCO, APL Logistics/GATX Logistics, and others introduced larger and, in many cases, foreign entities into the outsourcing equation. Many of these alliances were an effort to respond to the increasing global needs of outsourcing firms.

Technology offerings have expanded significantly; and during the new decade, more and more users began to rely on their provider to handle complex technologies, including warehouse management systems, transportation management systems, and the so-called supply chain event management systems.

The December 2003, issue of *Logistics Today* listed over 200 firms offering warehouse and transportation management systems.[7] Many of these firms did not exist in the late 1990's, but others are the more traditional providers such as Schneider Logistics with a sophisticated transportation management system, and Menlo Worldwide Logistics weighing in with a warehouse management system.

Finally, the tragic events of September 11, 2001, shocked an already weak economy into almost a standstill. The downturn spread through almost every industry group, and it became absolutely critical that firms rethink their missions and re-establish connections with their customers. Like other firms, logistics service providers suffered, but most of the major firms survived.

Indeed, some became stronger, because with the increasing customer service and economic pressures, firms once again began to concentrate more on what they did best – their core competencies; and outsourcing held its own as an effective vehicle for helping to achieve these changing business goals.

And there still is plenty of room for growth. Even with the increased emphasis on outsourcing, only about 12 to 14 percent of the relevant logistics services in the United States are outsourced. In Europe, where outsourcing has a longer history, the percentage is more than twice that.

As intense competitive pressures in the marketplace persist, streamlining and downsizing also will continue, no doubt resulting in a steadily increasing interest in outsourcing arrangements.

At the same time, as logistics service providers gain efficiencies and sophistication and increase their service offerings, this interest will manifest itself in new, even more creative alliances, particularly in the area of technology.

Perhaps the most important outsourcing lesson learned during the turmoil of the late 1990's and early 2000's was that the complacent, reactive provider was fast becoming obsolete. To survive in the changed and, most believe, improved environment, the provider must be pro-active, flexible, and clearly focused; and the outsourcing firm should deal only with those that are.

Chapter 2

Why Outsource?

*Give light and the people will find their own
way.*

- Scripps-Howard motto

There are as many reasons for outsourcing as there are firms
who do it. Many of these are unique to specific firms and
industries, but in a broad sense there are several readily
identifiable advantages to subcontracting logistics services. No
priority has been assigned to these since relative importance will
vary by firm and circumstance.

Return on Assets

First of all, outsourcing allows the user firm to improve its
return on assets. By reducing the not insignificant investments in
warehouse facilities, materials handling, order picking,
transportation equipment, and information technology, returns

can be enhanced significantly. While it is true that most firms capitalize leases, the fact of the matter is that the majority of logistics contracts are relatively short-term and allow reasonable termination arrangements. Most importantly, the user firm does not have to make the capital outlay.

This capital, in turn, can be invested in those ventures that fall into the core competencies or basic businesses of the user firms, whether they be manufacturing, marketing, or distribution.

Personnel Productivity

Utilization of personnel can be more effective since by emphasizing the core business, the productivity of the employees can be improved greatly. Often there will be fewer people to train in fewer skills, thereby increasing the level of expertise.

Take for example, the case of a major grocery manufacturer that, a few years ago, operated a large manufacturing and distribution facility on the same site. For new employees the entry-level route was through the distribution center as an order picker or forklift operator. All job openings in the facility were posted, and every time a higher paying production position would become available, those at the lower levels would apply for it, often successfully.

The end result was a warehouse that functioned more as a school for forklift operators than as a distribution center. Because the company never achieved true warehouse operations efficiency, the center was a prime candidate for outsourcing.

The personnel productivity advantage often is difficult to measure, but can be real, nonetheless.

Flexibility

Flexibility is another key outsourcing driver for most firms. As new markets and new products are developed, many times it is impossible to predict future logistics needs accurately.

Likewise, as existing market and product characteristics change, logistics needs change as well. New customer service requirements, ordering methods, and competitive offerings and services all influence a firm's logistics practices; and the use of a contract provider greatly reduces the risk of misplaced or outdated facilities and equipment.

There have been a number of empty buildings around the country located in markets for services or products that became obsolete. The building boom generated by the Internet bubble is a classic example. Several 500,000 plus square foot, fully automated facilities were left empty after only a few months of operation.

In the case of mergers and acquisitions, if the firms have outsourced logistics services, it is much easier to combine operations and take full advantage of logistics synergies. Often logistics cost reductions can be one of the major motivators of the transaction.

This was effectively demonstrated by a major firm that had maintained twelve to fifteen distribution centers for a number of years. After two acquisitions in quick succession, the company found itself with almost two hundred warehouses, in some cases, two or more in the same city.

Because the majority of these were public or contract warehouses, consolidation was greatly enhanced; and within two years, the total number of distribution locations was down to twenty. Logistics costs were reduced by millions of dollars annually.

If these facilities had been owned and/or operated by the firms themselves, it would have taken years to achieve the same savings if, in fact, they could ever be realized at all.

Labor Considerations

While labor issues can be somewhat delicate depending on the user firm's own labor environment, these considerations should not be ignored when considering outsourcing, particularly in the warehousing area.

If you are operating in a union climate and your own facilities are organized, the advantages to utilizing a facility that is non-union or even one that has a different union sometimes are obvious.

The key word here is caution. All appropriate labor agreements should be evaluated carefully by competent legal authority. Labor unions are well aware of outsourcing advantages, and in some cases, have taken measures to protect their members.

With the outsourcing of hundreds of thousands of jobs to India and other foreign countries, the term outsourcing has taken on a negative connotation to many. While this is quite different from logistics outsourcing, the very mention of the word can raise a red flag.

This caution is not intended as a deterrent but a reminder that thorough research will minimize the risks and protect the projected benefits.

Cost

To many firms considering outsourcing, operating costs will be the most important consideration. Surveys conducted on the reasons for outsourcing almost always find it to be in the top three determinants. [1]

In addition to capital savings, the outsourcer will expect the outside facilities to operate at a lower cost or achieve savings that could not be generated internally.

Obviously, this is important and is often the case; but the sophisticated firm sometimes will find this not to be true. If a company has an efficient, well-managed distribution system, outsourcing it may not reduce operating costs.

Subcontracting, however, may add to the value of the system, and this should be the primary cost consideration. While the absolute dollars spent may be more, the value received often can more than offset the premium. A Mercedes Benz costs more than a Ford Taurus, but that does not necessarily make it a bad investment.

Most important of all, when comparing the cost of your firm's performance of a logistics function to that of the provider, be sure to capture your total cost. The results may be surprising.

Management and Political Considerations

In the modern business environment, managing any function is difficult, particularly at the middle management level. More often than not, there is an ongoing pressure to reduce costs and improve productivity with fewer resources.

People are more difficult to manage and some have work ethics that often are not compatible with the goals of the organization.

Just as the firm wants to invest in its core competency, its managers should focus on it as well. Logistics and personnel issues require significant amounts of attention and resources; and outsourcing facilitates managing the basic business and leaving the solution of distribution problems to others.

It is far easier to manage one, or a limited number of, providers than it is to manage the individual functions internally.

This is not intended to be a text on corporate politics, but one would be naïve to ignore them. All too often, managers see their primary survival technique to be that of recommending how others could manage their function better, or in some cases, how they themselves could manage it better than the incumbent.

Outsourcing removes the logistics function from the corporate political spotlight and enables the logistics executive to manage it in a more orderly, less political, and more productive fashion.

Customer Service and Specialized Services

In today's environment of error-free, prompt deliveries and unique business and consumer requirements, customer service has to be the most important consideration for any firm.

This focus on increased customer satisfaction in both the business-to-business and business-to-consumer markets has resulted in many changes in logistics practices and service approaches. These changes are likely to continue and must be addressed in a timely fashion if the firm expects to remain competitive.

Specialized services are becoming the rule, rather than the exception. Although some logistics service providers have been able to serve the needs of various industries efficiently, a number of firms have gradually evolved into businesses which offer specialized services for specific industries. This, of course, shortens the learning curve, encourages expertise, and removes the inefficiencies from the system.

"Just In Time"

The automotive industry provides a good example of the potential for outsourcing. "Just In Time" techniques have been utilized in this industry for a number of years, and many of the associated functions have been performed by outside providers.

One carrier-based contract logistics firm handles warehousing, transportation, and assembly for several major automobile manufacturers. The provider has the ability to acquire parts from hundreds of vendors in a myriad of geographic locations, move them into one warehouse, process the orders, and deliver to destination plants within two-hour time windows.

Another warehouse-based provider has a similar arrangement. Through an electronic data interchange network, trucks are dispatched to parts suppliers. Parts are collected and delivered to a cross dock where they are consolidated and shipped to twelve different assembly plants in North America. The parts are never warehoused or inventoried at the plants.

This JIT delivery system schedules next-day arrival fifteen to thirty minutes prior to the time the parts are needed for manufacturing. While they are en route, a sophisticated system monitors each part and its expected arrival time.

While JIT techniques have been utilized in the automotive industry for some time, the more recent introduction of the retailing and grocery industry's version has enhanced awareness of the outsourcing option.

Order Consolidation

Efficient Consumer Response (ECR), sometimes called Quick Response (QR) or Continuous Replenishment Process (CRP), is designed to link all segments in the product pipeline into a smooth flowing stream of products.

Vendor Managed Inventory (VMI) is another variation of the same theme, utilizing a "pull" rather than a "push" inventory system.

In the grocery industry, Collaborative Planning, Forecasting and Replenishment, or CPFR, links customer demand with replenishment scheduling. This joint planning, if successful, can lead to a smooth flow of products through the entire length of the pipeline.

All designed to reduce inventories in the system, these techniques result in smaller, more frequent shipments. Rather than handle these small shipments from their own facilities, grocery manufacturers have turned to the contract logistics companies. With a multiple client base and sophisticated systems the providers are able to combine these shipments into truckloads, reducing freight and handling costs, and even further enhancing the cost reductions in the ECR process.

One food manufacturer eliminated its network of privately owned and operated distribution centers and outsourced the entire system to firms with sophisticated consolidation programs.

Although consolidation has been a factor in the food business since the 1960's, the early programs were very simplistic manual operations. Today, the leading logistics firms have systems that combine orders into truck or container loads by customer and requested arrival date, route the shipments, and electronically tender them to the appropriate carriers.

One major logistics provider ships 500 – 1,000 trailers of consolidated product daily. Such consolidation programs, in addition to providing superior service, have produced consistent reductions in transportation costs of thirty to fifty percent.

Programs of this type would be virtually impossible without the logistics service providers.

Packaging

Outsourcing also has facilitated the changing landscape of consumer goods retailing. Buying one of anything can be almost impossible in many of the "club" stores.

In a high volume manufacturing plant, the combining of two or three packages of the same item by banding or shrink wrapping causes tremendous inefficiencies. Manufacturers are tooled up to put twelve, twenty-four, or forty-eight packages in a case, seal it, palletize it, and move it to storage or the dock, untouched by human hands.

If the customer packaging requirements were all the same, the issue could be dealt with. The difficulty arises when Wal-Mart wants three tubes of toothpaste shrink wrapped together, Costco wants two tubes, and Target wants a toothbrush thrown in. Much of this labor-intensive work is outsourced.

At the provider's facility, the original cases are opened, and inner packages are grouped together according to customer demands, using small shrink wrap tunnels or other combining techniques. They then are placed back in the original case, or some other form of display module, and shipped. While this is tedious, it is considerably less disruptive and less expensive than attempting to customize packages at the manufacturing plant.

Order Fulfillment and Electronic Commerce

It is an irrefutable fact that the Internet and electronic commerce have had an enormous impact on logistics service requirements.

While the concept of order fulfillment is not new (our grandmothers' Sears Roebuck catalogs would effectively demonstrate that), the direct consumer contact with manufacturers through the Internet has resulted in more precise and critical communications, information, and customer service requirements.

Residential deliveries are required more often than not, presenting an entirely new set of challenges.

Many manufacturing firms simply do not have the expertise to establish and manage these delivery and communications systems as well as a dedicated outside firm and are turning to these providers to provide the necessary customer-focused services.

In addition, an efficient order picking facility is expensive to equip and maintain, and sales volumes can fluctuate wildly – a classic case for outsourcing.

Here, selection of the best-qualified provider will be critical. Sophisticated order fulfillment is not for the faint-hearted. Be sure that the providers are in the business for the long haul. There have been several conspicuous examples of those who were not.

The most important thing to remember in electronic commerce will be that there is direct exposure to the ultimate consumer at a number of stages in the process and that good rapport must be protected at all costs. The selected provider must be one that will focus on, and nurture, customer relationships for its clients.

Information Technology

For firms engaged in electronic commerce and even those who are not, the increasing demands for new information systems and resources often can be met more efficiently and economically through outsourcing.

When resources within the firm are scarce, or logistics systems development has a low priority, there can be significant advantages to utilizing a provider that has the necessary systems in place, or the ability to develop them. Additionally, there are literally hundreds of firms that offer warehouse and transportation management systems, as well as other supply chain management technology. Such firms can be included in outsourcing arrangements with transportation or warehousing specialists, assuming they add some value to the process. The technology available is quite impressive, and the outsourcing firm can acquire such capabilities as carrier selection, route optimization, order/shipment visibility, freight payment, load planning, and asset tracking, to name a few.

Caution must be exercised, however. Again, care should be taken to ensure that the provider is well-capitalized and has the resources and expertise to maintain existing systems, as well as enhance them as needed. The important thing to remember about information technology is that, in and of itself, it has no value. The real value is in the information and decision-making tools it enables. It must enable reporting metrics, operational efficiencies, visibility, and the integration of processes. Peter Drucker said, "The computer can handle only things to which the answer is 'yes' or 'no.' It cannot handle maybe. It's not the computerization that's important then; it's the discipline you have to bring to your processes." [2]

Global Capability

As firms seek to expand into worldwide markets, outsourcing can be an extremely effective method of establishing foreign distribution centers, and/or arranging for, and making international shipments. There are a number of excellent freight forwarders, for example, that can provide sophisticated logistics services throughout the pipeline. Many U.S.-based logistics managers simply do not have the expertise necessary to be effective in the international logistics arena, and will find outsourcing a valuable tool.

Managing a domestic logistics network can be challenging enough. Combine those issues with customs, security, terrorism, foreign cultures, currency, and language, and the task becomes formidable indeed.

The Logistics Service Provider

Another important reason for outsourcing is the increasing maturity of the logistics companies themselves. No longer is the industry characterized by smaller, unsophisticated companies. Today's successful integrated logistics service provider is a dynamic firm, utilizing a combination of systems, facilities, transportation, and materials-handling techniques. It is managed and staffed with logistics professionals, and in many cases has true global capabilities.

Quite often, it is better qualified than its clients to perform the product distribution function, and can contribute knowledge to the process that many logistics managers simply do not have. The *McKinsey Quarterly* aptly referred to outsourcing as moving from "economies of scale to economies of skill." [3]

Conclusion

There are, of course, some inhibitors to outsourcing. Some logistics managers have reservations about outsourcing, particularly in the areas of confidentiality, control, and security. Others do not have the confidence that providers can be trusted with important customer contacts and relationships.

Every firm that considers outsourcing will have its own unique reasons for doing so and must qualify its own advantages and disadvantages. Whatever they may be, they should be analyzed and researched as thoroughly and realistically as possible by managers that are thoroughly educated in the industry. Managers considering outsourcing should ask themselves four questions:

(1) Is logistics a core competency of our firm?
(2) If not, are we exceptionally good at it?
(3) Will outsourcing add true value to our logistics process?
(4) Can we become comfortable with the risk of turning over control and customer relationships to an outside firm?

If the answer to the first two is yes, serious consideration should be given to retaining the function in-house. Conversely, if the answer to three and four are yes, outsourcing can be a viable option.

Implemented and managed confidently and properly, outsourcing can be a powerful logistics tool.

Chapter 3

What Should Be Outsourced?

The data suggests that businesses are now recognizing that most functional areas are too business-critical not to consider outsourcing.

- The Outsourcing Institute

There is no standard response to the question, "What should be outsourced?" Exactly what the firm should outsource will depend on individual needs and strategies. Some will choose to contract for the entire logistics or supply chain function. More often than not however, certain individual, or combinations of, areas will lend themselves to outsourcing better than others.

A study by Georgia Tech, FedEx and Cap Gemini Ernst & Young identified the twenty most frequently sub-contracted logistics services as: [1]

- Outbound Transportation

- Inbound Transportation
- Freight Bill Auditing/Payment
- Rate Negotiations Warehousing
- Warehousing
- Shipment Consolidation/Distribution
- Cross-Docking
- Order Fulfillment
- Return/Reverse Logistics
- Product Returns and Repair
- Customs Clearance
- Customs Brokerage
- Information Technology
- Consulting Services
- Carrier Selection
- Inventory Management
- Procurement of Logistics
- Selected Manufacturing Activities
- Product Marking, Labeling, Packaging

Other important areas include:

- Fleet Management
- Order Entry/Processing
- Product Assembly/Installation
- Customer Service
- Inventory Ownership

Certainly, as the industry continues to mature and client strategies and requirements change, there will be others; but an understanding of these will greatly facilitate the outsourcing decision.

Transportation

The contracting for transportation services is so common that many tend to forget that they are outsourcing. In its simplest form, transportation is the movement of products (or people) from where they are to where they need to be; and most firms use transportation providers to perform this function.

Certainly, there are many efficient manufacturer- and distributor-owned truck fleets (although very few private railroads or airlines), but for-hire transportation is the choice of most firms.

The United States has one of the finest transportation networks in the world, and most transportation carriers are well equipped to take advantage of it.

Motor Carriage

By far, the most popular form of freight transportation is the motor carrier. In the U.S., truck transportation is decisively the most dominant mode, accounting for well over half the volume, and more than three quarters of the freight dollars spent. [2] The value of goods transported in 2002 was $6.2 trillion. [3] This is more than the gross national products of Britain, France, China, Italy, and Mexico combined!

Truck transportation is the most reliable of the ground modes and tends to provide fairly rapid delivery, even over long distances.

Since the 1980 regulatory changes and the resulting competition in the business, costs have remained fairly stable with most increases in rates tied to rises in the cost of fuel, and more recently to increasing insurance costs, the cost of government-mandated truck engines, and the impact of driver hours of service rules.

Both truckload and less-than-truckload service are readily available in most areas. Often, in addition to the traditional carriers, a diversified logistics service provider will offer truck transportation as part of its overall logistics services.

Likewise, motor carriers have become very creative in their logistics offerings, and in many instances, provide warehousing and other non-transportation services. Most offer electronic data interchange.

One major manufacturer that had operated its own truck fleet for a number of years converted the entire function to a contractual dedicated fleet provided by an outside carrier. By doing so, the manufacturer was able to eliminate hundreds of employees and thousands of pieces of trucking equipment.

Costs were reduced, service improved; and since the project was handled with some sensitivity, many of the displaced employees were able to obtain positions with the new provider.

A major automobile manufacturer outsourced the transportation management of one of its major divisions to a leading motor carrier, known for its logistics innovation and creativity. The arrangement was a complex one, involving 3,500 suppliers, over 1,000 destinations, and 16 distribution centers; yet in the first two years of the new program, transportation costs were reduced by ten percent annually, amounting to tens of millions of dollars.

Home Depot, working with J. B. Hunt Dedicated Contract Services, redesigned their northeastern transportation network. By combining equipment, drivers, and traffic lanes, empty miles were reduced, efficiencies were increased, and year-over-year cost per load was reduced by nearly 10%. [4]

Such success stories are not uncommon in the outsourcing of trucking operations. There are significant opportunities for improving costs and service in most industries.

Rail

While rail transportation usually is considered an entity unto itself and is not a factor in most logistics outsourcing decisions, it is an important mode and deserves mention.

Railroads operate over 125,000 miles of track in the United States and are used primarily for the movement of bulk commodities such as grain, ore, chemicals, and coal. Over forty percent of the railroads' total tonnage is coal. [5]

While some consumer goods, including automobiles, still move by rail, this has become more the exception than the rule. Motor vehicles and equipment account for only two percent of rail tonnage.

It is interesting to note that while many have tried, few rail carriers have successfully offered a broader, integrated logistics service. Expansion to other areas of logistics has always seemed to be just beyond their grasp. Those that do exist tend toward more specialized rail-oriented services. In fairness, however, there are some carriers that have successfully integrated rail performance and information systems.

For example, Union Pacific Corporation and Daimler Chrysler formed a new company to track three million Chrysler shipments annually. Through use of the Internet, the new company, Insight Network Logistics, was established to assist Chrysler in gaining logistics efficiency through planning, control, and visibility. [6]

BNSF Logistics, using the technology of i2 Technologies, Inc., manages networks, load plans and shipment status for clients of its Supply Chain Solutions operating unit. [7]

Intermodal

One important growth area for the railroads has been in intermodal movements. There are two basic types of intermodal concepts; i.e., TOFC, or trailer-on-flatcar, and COFC, container-on-flatcar.

TOFC is utilized by motor carriers that ship trailers by rail to reduce fuel and driver costs. United Parcel Service, for example, is a major user of this service.

COFC is used primarily in connection with import and export movements on containers from and to the ports. It is not uncommon to see entire trainloads of containers moving from the major ports to domestic destinations.

Air Freight

Both domestic and international air freight transportation are available from passenger and cargo airlines or through air freight forwarders. While many firms deal directly with airlines, the bulk of the air cargo moves through freight forwarders.

Express and Small Package Shipments

While technically not a mode of transportation, because of its importance to order fulfillment operations and electronic commerce, small package movement has become an extremely important logistics consideration. With today's critical delivery cycles for small consumer or business-to-business shipments, both reliable air and ground package transportation availability have become a necessity.

While there are a number of small package carriers available, by far the most volume, both internationally and domestically, is handled by FedEx and UPS. And it is no longer just about purple and white airplanes and brown trucks. While most of UPS' revenue still comes from moving packages, 8% of it comes from their Supply Chain Solutions business, UPS' fastest growing division. [8] SCS has provided logistics solutions for everything from cash register repairs in Paris to spark plug distribution in the United States.

Water

One of the transportation assets that many tend to ignore unless in the bulk shipping business is the 25,000-mile navigable waterway system in the United States. Sixty percent of the country's grain exports and 20% of the coal moves by barge. It is by far the most economical mode of transportation. One barge has the capacity of 15 rail cars or 60 fifty-foot trailers.

Many shippers of bulk commodities own their barges and towboats, but common carriers and terminals are available for those firms wishing to utilize them. The total waterways "population" of 4,000 tug and towboats and 28,000 barges moves almost 800 million tons annually. [9]

Obviously, the mode of transportation that is the most optional to the firm when considering outsourcing is motor carriage, but it is important to understand where and how the various other forms of transport factor into logistics decisions.

Freight Bill Auditing and Payment

The outsourcing of freight bill auditing and payment (FBP) is not a new concept; but as the need for more sophisticated and timely information has grown, the contracting for this activity has become more popular and better understood.

The freight bill payment firms themselves have become much more progressive and experienced and offer an impressive array of processing and informational services. Because they serve a number of clients, they have achieved a critical mass that enables them to keep abreast of the latest informational technology; and often they are able to provide more reliable information than the client firms themselves.

The basic concept is simple. The client directs its carriers to send all freight bills to the freight bill payment company for processing.

29

When the bills are received, either electronically (EDI) or manually, they are entered into the computer system. This gives immediate visibility to the bill itself.

Once the bills are entered, they are audited, or checked for accuracy. Experienced auditors will verify, either manually or electronically, depending on the circumstances, such things as:

- Validity of the bill itself (Did it go to the right party?)
- Weight
- Accessorial charges
- Use of correct tariff, classification, discount, etc.
- Extensions
- Mileage, origin, and destination accuracy
- Proper application of tariff rules
- Duplicate payments

When the bills have been checked for validity and accuracy, the charges are coded according to client specifications, then reconciled with the original data input.

From there the bills are organized for payment, funding requirements are identified and communicated, and checks are written and mailed.

Outsourcing this activity can reduce costs, both in personnel and systems; but one of the major advantages is the availability of information on an almost real time basis. As a matter of routine, management reports are generated to provide payment detail and summaries by such categories as carrier, origin, destination, hundredweight, and account codes. However, since the entire bank of freight data is in the payment firm's system, almost any inquiry can be made and answered.

The leading freight bill payment firms provide clients secure access to their data via the Internet. Through an Internet report writer, the client not only can research one or more bills by such parameters as pro number, carrier, date, or customer; but the logistics manager can develop management summaries in statement, chart, or graphical formats.

Since all the transportation cost data is in the system, it can be manipulated to answer analytical kinds of questions, as well. For example, it is possible to re-rate shipments or assign new shipping locations and review the resulting costs.

Typically, freight bill payment companies also provide other related services such as loss and damage claims processing, vendor and carrier compliance reporting, traffic management, contract development and review, and carrier rate negotiations.

While the outsourcing of freight bill payment is an excellent vehicle for the firm to divest itself of bothersome clerical and accounting functions and to collect valuable information, caution should be exercised when selecting a provider.

According to Delaney, there are two reasons why inferior freight payment companies are inferior. They do not provide good service and they do not know how to manage money. [10] In order to understand the latter, it is important to understand how the money is handled.

Typically, a freight bill payment company will require a client to advance funds before freight bills are paid. Once the client is notified of the amount needed to pay a week's freight bills, for example, it will execute a wire transfer of funds to the payment company. Obviously, for a large FBP company (or even a small one) this can be a significant amount of money, depending on the size and volume of the clients.

This cash then resides in the bank account of the provider until its checks are actually cashed by the carriers. This time period, averaging about a week, plus the cash constitute what is called the "float." During periods of high interest rates, the float was invested in short-term instruments, and the interest was a valuable source of revenue. This income enabled the FBP companies to be very liberal when quoting fees for the actual services they performed. (If interest rates are high enough, a company could almost afford to process freight bills for nothing just to generate the float.)

Delaney's point was well confirmed in the early 2000's when interest rates dropped significantly.

The following example illustrates the impact of interest rates on the float.

Assumptions:
- Value of freight bill $500
- Interest rate   5%
- Float time   5.5 days
- Annual bills paid   20 million

Formula:

$$\frac{\text{Amount per bill X Interest rate X Float Time}}{365} = \text{Float per bill}$$

$$\frac{\$500 \text{ X }.05 \text{ X } 5.5}{365} = \$.38$$

Value to Provider:
20 million X $.38 or $7.6 million annually

When short-term interest rates dropped to 2%, the calculation became

$$\frac{\$500 \text{ X }.02 \text{ X } 5.5}{365} = \$.15 \text{ or an}$$

annual value of $3 million.

Of course, not all freight bills are for $500. Some are lower, and some are higher. These calculations show, however, why some FBP companies found themselves with minimal float income and non-compensatory transaction fees. Several bankruptcies occurred, and it was determined that in more than one firm, the owners of the business had lived lavishly off the float. The negative results were criminal charges, irate carriers, and clients that had advanced funds for bills that had not been paid, only to still be liable for the charges.

The positive result was an industry that is wiser, more responsible, and prices services according to the cost of providing them.

Be cautious, but remember that most of those companies left standing are worthy of consideration.

Carrier Rate Negotiations

Carrier rate negotiations often are conducted by outside firms, and freight bill payment companies are well qualified to perform this service. The availability of information is the key factor in their selection.

One large industrial distributor has hundreds of locations across the country; and typically, each had negotiated freight rates with carriers. The logistics manager instinctively knew that if the entire transportation network were presented as one entity, it would be possible to obtain lower rates. Since his own time and resources were limited, he turned to a freight bill payment firm for assistance.

The first step was to transfer all freight bill payment to the new vendor. As the payment firm began to pay bills, at the same time it started to build the foundation for an effective bid package. Eventually, requests for bids were sent to forty-five carriers. The packages included:

- A contract designed to meet legal and business requirements.
- Special circumstances.
- History, origin, and destination of shipments.
- A list of items, their classifications, descriptions, and freight class.
- A bid summary sheet.

Each carrier was asked to relate its bid, in the form of a discount, to a set rate structure, providing for easy comparison and analysis of bids.

All carriers responded; and after an extensive analysis, it was determined that the total freight bill could be reduced by twenty-five percent.

Nine months after the first bill was paid, annual cost reductions of two million dollars had been identified. [11]

Warehousing

In addition to being one of the first logistics functions to be outsourced, warehousing has become one of the most frequently sub-contracted areas.

Initially, most of the warehousing arrangements involved simple, short-term agreements, usually thirty days, and services provided were very basic. Products were unloaded from trucks or rail cars and placed into storage where they were held until the warehouse operator was directed to load them back out.

Other than elementary receiving, inventory, and shipping documents, there was little record keeping and few, if any, special services.

Over the years, the industry has matured; and now there are hundreds of large, efficient warehouse service providers available to the firm interested in outsourcing the function. A number of these providers operate square footage well into the millions.

Single-tenant and multi-tenant facilities are available under both long- and short-term arrangements. The warehousing client can choose from global, national, regional, or local firms, or from carriers such as air and motor that also operate warehouses.

As in the outsourcing of truck transportation, success stories in warehousing are plentiful. Advantages to outsourcing warehousing operations were identified in Chapter 2, and many firms have capitalized on these opportunities.

One major food company distributed products through a network of thirty warehouses, some privately operated and some managed by outside providers. Over a period of time, this network was downsized to a total of ten, all operated by logistics service providers.

Cost and service both were improved.

An industrial equipment manufacturer contracted for a 240,000 square foot warehousing operation housing approximately 37,000 stock-keeping units. Orders are filled with lift trucks equipped with radio frequency data terminals from which the operators receive picking instructions.

On-time shipment reliability consistently is over ninety-nine percent. Both productivity and economics exceeded client expectations.

A variety of related services is available from the warehouse provider, many of which have been very progressive in providing total logistics solutions. This is important in that most firms that outsource warehousing are looking for a broader range of services. There are exceptions such as production leveling storage, special promotions, and labor negotiation stockpiling; but for the most part, the sub-contracting of the warehousing function is only part of a total solution.

In addition to basic storage and handling, some of the services offered by the warehouse-oriented logistics firm are:

- Transportation
- Consolidation
- Cross docking
- Consulting/solutions
- Pick and pack
- Light assembly
- Packaging and kitting
- Reverse logistics; return and repair
- Order processing and fulfillment
- Information technology
- Inventory management

As Allen, Langley and Columbo confirmed, many of these services are contracted for frequently, and are provided by most of the warehouse-based logistics firms. [12] Some of the carrier-based firms offer them as well, but they tend to be identified more with the warehouse providers.

Consolidation

Discussed in Chapter 2, shipment consolidation is not so much a logistics function as it is a means to an end. It has proven to be a very effective method of improving service to the customer while holding distribution costs to a minimum. It has been particularly successful in the consumer goods industry. While not a new concept, it has been re-branded and now often is referred to as shared services.

One unique example is provided by Kuehne & Nagel Logistics. K & N combines the shared service concept with an elaborate form of cross docking for the delivery of store supplies and fixtures to retail outlets. They receive separate shipments of various materials from multiple suppliers and combine them into finished displays delivered directly to the stores. [13]

Cross Docking

As the reliability of information and transportation service have improved, cross docking has become an effective and efficient method of moving goods through the distribution facility. Again, it is to some extent, a means to an end, but one that can be achieved through outsourcing.

In its purest form, the coordination of the inbound flow of products from suppliers and the outbound flow to various destinations enables the warehouse operator to move products through the system with very little actual storage.

In the final analysis, it is dependent on good information, reliable transportation service, and the matching of supply and demand; but some firms have managed the concept quite effectively. Wal-Mart and Sam's Club, for example, utilize logistics service providers to cross dock goods from suppliers to individual stores with a high degree of success.

Another argument for outsourcing this activity is the physical facility itself. While not absolutely necessary, cross docking works best in a narrow building with truck doors on either side.

Many firms will not have a building of this type readily available or have an interest in investing in one.

Order Fulfillment

The explosion in electronic commerce has had a major impact on the entire economy and presents entirely new sets of challenges in distributing products.

Never before has there been such a large number of transactions directly with the consumer, with such critical service requirements. Order fulfillment has taken on a new meaning and the volume of transactions is such that in some cases, massive fulfillment facilities are required.

While some firms are reluctant to outsource the function since they want to control the critical customer service dynamics, one must be careful not to let the fulfillment function overshadow and complicate the basic business. If a firm's core competency is manufacturing, it might do well to leave the order fulfillment to someone else.

Order fulfillment is really a combination of the other logistics functions such as warehousing and transportation, but it emphasizes them in very different ways.

Physical facilities often will require extensive and expensive systems of conveyors and racks, as well as computerized control.

Order volume is high and often seasonal, and order entry systems must be reliable and fast, and provide for a two-way dialogue with the customer.

One 500,000 square foot facility in Memphis, Tennessee is fully racked and contains over six miles of conveyors. Shipping capacity is 100,000 orders per day.

Residential delivery will be commonplace, and new kinds of carrier relationships will be necessary.

More often than not the facility must operate twenty-four hours per day, seven days per week.

These operations will challenge the logistics service provider, but if the activity is planned, implemented, and managed properly, it lends itself to outsourcing more so than most other distribution operations.

For the manufacturer or distributor, one way to keep ahead of the learning curve will be to outsource the function to someone who understands it.

The client basically contracts for a state-of-the-art fulfillment operation with a proven track record. Because of the volatility of this business, however, finite due diligence will be absolutely critical as outsourcing decisions are made. The modern, Internet consumer is very intolerant of slow, inaccurate product delivery. The days of ordering the Dick Tracy Two-way Wrist Radio and waiting four to six weeks for delivery are gone forever.

One of the recent and more interesting success stories in order fulfillment involved the growth of one provider and the demise of another. The following account was written by Alex Stark of Kane Is Able, a Scranton, Pennsylvania warehouse company, and provides an excellent illustration of how a client, a provider, and a lot of imagination can solve a logistics problem.

EJ Footwear: Stepping Into the 21st Century

On October 1, 1882, a four-story factory on the corner of Washington and Henry Streets in Binghamton, New York, stood idle. On October 1, 2001, a 450,000 square foot building in Baltimore lay empty. This is the story of the connection between these two buildings, a story driven by changes in technology and in the marketplace.

The Binghamton factory was home to the Endicott Johnson Corporation, one of the largest and most integrated shoe

38

manufacturing companies in the world. It stood idle that October day because factory employees were solemnly attending the funeral of Horace N. Lester, the factory's owner. Horace Lester had been a prominent man in the city. He was a former mayor of the city, a senior officer of the Binghamton Savings Bank, president of the YMCA, and co-founder of the Lester Shoe Factory. But it is perhaps because of his Endicott Johnson factory that Horace Lester left his greatest legacy.

Horace Lester's factory marks the dividing line between two worlds: the slow, methodical, hand-crafted shoe making business it was before his innovation, and the shoe manufacturing *industry* it became. During his lifetime, Mr. Lester and his generation helped to transform the entire shoemaking process. These entrepreneurs were the visionaries who utilized new machinery and technological advances to make the shoe industry into a multi-billion dollar, global enterprise.

The Baltimore facility was home to Webvan, the "Internet Grocer" and one of the most spectacular of the "dot-com" failures of 2001. Webvan had leased the building as a distribution center for home delivery of groceries in the Baltimore-Washington metro area. It lay idle because Webvan's river of funding had finally run dry.

Webvan is the story of entrepreneurs who tried to change the way consumers shop. Unlike Horace Lester, however, Webvan was never able to use technology to lower the price of the product to consumers. When Wall Street money was flowing freely, Webvan had an open budget to spend on facilities and technology. No expense was spared by Webvan when investing in its distribution centers. The billion-dollar brainchild of Louis Borders (founder of Borders Books and Music chain), Webvan tried unsuccessfully to rewrite the rules of retailing in late 1990s.

Webvan, in much the way Endicott had done 150 years before it, possessed a revolutionary idea – selling merchandise with the assistance of new technology. Webvan's idea: selling grocery items over the Internet and having those purchases delivered to the customer. Webvan's plan was calculated and well-financed, but no matter how many state-of-the-art, automated warehouses (each the size of seven football fields with over four miles of conveyor belts) they built, the company never proved that its plan was viable.

With all the factors that led to Webvan's crash, there is one that stands above them all. In its audacious attempt to seize the online market, Webvan overlooked the consumer. Webvan's ambition to be larger than Amazon.com blinded them from performing the simple task of satisfying the customer day in and day out. In addition, in the fast paced world of instantaneous electronic communication, Webvan simply could not afford to have its idea catch on slowly. Unfortunately for Webvan, consumers were slow to adopt this new model.

In comparison, Endicott unknowingly possessed the luxury of having its merchandizing idea during a completely different era in history. As the industrialization of the 19th century began to displace skilled artisans, the erosion of specialized craftwork led to a growing division of labor and, consequently, great resistance and conflict. However, this change took a period of a few decades to unfold, as one technological advance led to another. So as Endicott succeeded over time, Webvan closed down because it did not have enough time to generate interest. As a result, Webvan has ceased to exist while Endicott Johnson is still going strong.

That is not to say the shoe manufacturing business has been easy, but Endicott has shown the ability to adapt to the market and to today's economic realities. At its height in the 1920s, Endicott Johnson employed over 20,000 people in its facilities in the southern tier of New York State. Unfortunately, as the 20th century wore on, Endicott Johnson began to lose its footing in an ever-tightening marketplace as the industry experienced the trend of moving overseas for labor savings. At the close of the century, the 112-year-old company saw three of its competitors forced to shut down operations completely.

In light of this changing economy, Endicott Johnson, which currently does business as Father & Son shoe stores, stood at a business crossroad. In 1999, the company received a 7.5-million-dollar loan from Paragon Capital. Paragon Capital, an asset-based lender based in Needham, Massachusetts, specializes in helping small- to mid-sized retail businesses grow and adapt within the changing economic landscape. With this vote of confidence, Endicott is looking to the future for new growth opportunities.

Endicott Johnson's evolution has now led the company to the power and potential rewards of e-fulfillment. Endicott hired a consultant in the spring of 2001 to advise management on the scope of this business service and to assemble a list of national providers. Most of the national providers were not cost-effective, so on advice from the consultant, the company contacted a few, strong regional providers. Kane Is Able, Inc., based in Scranton, Pennsylvania, caught Endicott's attention. As Endicott was turning the corner on a new avenue for growth, Kane, a northeast logistics service provider, was beginning to sharpen its focus on fulfillment. The timing worked out favorably for both companies. However, there was one final piece of the puzzle that needed to be in place, and this is where the story of these two idle facilities meet.

Just as technology played an important part in the transformation of the shoe manufacturing business in the 19th century, technology would again play a starring role in the next big move for Endicott. In order to have an efficient fulfillment business, the right equipment is essential. Kane was able to take advantage of the liquidation of Webvan's state-of-the-art conveyor and carousel systems and put them to use for the benefit of EJ Footwear. The equipment had been installed and tested in the Baltimore facility but never put into operation. Kane's challenge was to take a system designed for the packing of grocery orders and convert it into a full-scale sortation and distribution system for shoes.

In the summer of 2001, Endicott Johnson contacted Kane to provide their fulfillment needs. With the fall of Webvan and with all its modern warehouse facilities closing, Kane was able to propose a deal giving EJ the full benefit of the top-end equipment but passing on to EJ the cost savings Kane achieved on the sortation system by buying it for pennies on the dollar.

Kane next approached the company who installed the equipment for Webvan to dismantle and then reassemble the machinery 200 miles away in Pennsylvania. The immense structure was meticulously broken down in to component parts and shipped to Kane utilizing approximately 300 trailers of Kane's freight line division. This complex logistical initiative was completed in the weeks surrounding Thanksgiving of 2001.

The pick-to-light technology of the Diamond Phoenix carousels, Buschman conveyor sortation systems, high bay and flow racking provides a state-of-the-art distribution center for Endicott. The management of the over five million pairs of shoes is continuously tracked in real time using software that uniquely supports all of Endicott's shipping and receiving requirements. This sophisticated operation ensures that all orders will ship the day they are received for maximum efficiency and turnaround.

And that takes the story to the present day where the final touches are being applied to the fulfillment center at Kane. The Endicott-Kane partnership stands on the cusp of a truly exciting venture employing 21st century skill for a shoe company who has its roots deeply embedded in the 19th century.

Reverse Logistics

Reverse logistics has been defined as "the process of planning, implementing, and controlling the efficient, cost-effective flow of raw materials, in-process inventory, finished goods and related information from the point of consumption to the point of origin for the purpose of recapturing value or proper disposal." [14]

This definition encompasses not only reverse movements for the purpose of recycling containers and materials, but for repair and refurbishing, as well as merchandise returns. Since reverse logistics is not an activity that many firms can or want to do well, many turn to outsourcing as a solution to this "unnatural" logistics process.

And it is a more complex logistics process than many realize. Some industries are more concerned about reverse logistics than others, depending on the volume of returns they experience. As shown in Figure 3-a there is a huge variance across various industries.

Whatever industry a firm is in, there is ample justification to consider outsourcing this activity.

One function commonly outsourced, particularly by computer or small appliance manufacturers and distributors, is that of return and repair.

When a product needs repair or refurbishing, rather than return it to the manufacturing facility which is not equipped to recondition products efficiently, firms have selected outside parties to perform this service. In many cases, a logistics service provider will be the vendor of choice.

FedEx, for example, has a program in which customers of a computer manufacturer return products in need of repair to FedEx. FedEx, in turn, provides the transportation and sub-contracts with another firm to perform the actual repairs.

Toshiba and UPS have an interesting arrangement. Consumers with laptop repair needs can take their computers to any one of

Industry	Percent of Returns
Magazine publishing	50
Catalog retailers	18 – 35
Greeting cards	20 – 30
CD-ROMs	18 – 25
Computer manufacturers	10 – 20
Mass merchandisers	4 – 15
Electronic distributors	10 – 12
Printers	4 – 8
Auto industry (parts)	4 – 6
Consumer electronics	4 – 5

Source: USF Processors/Reverse Logistics Executive Council, University of Nevada, Reno

Figure 3-a: Percentage of Products Returned for Selected Industries

over 3,000 UPS Stores, and it will be shipped to the UPS repair center in Louisville. The work is done by UPS Supply Chain Solutions using certified technicians. [15]

In both cases, the service is provided efficiently and expeditiously, a good example of each party in the pipeline doing what it does best. With the growth in electronic commerce and order fulfillment, the role of reverse logistics in the distribution of products has increased dramatically.

As Rogers and Tibben-Lembke pointed out, it is not unusual for a direct catalog retailer to experience return rates above 35 percent, with an approximate mean level of 25 percent. Since Internet sales are, in many respects, simply electronic catalogs, it is not unreasonable to expect online retailers to have similar experiences. [16]

Many of these retailers, both online and conventional, have turned to logistics service providers that are specialists in the product return or reverse logistics areas.

Early on, with annual returns in the hundreds of million dollars, K-Mart turned to GENCO Distribution System to handle the returns to its 2,000 plus stores. Using a network of four return centers, GENCO handled all the product returns from these stores, processing not only the physical products, but necessary information, as well. [17]

Another example, also involved GENCO and retailer, Best Buy. By eliminating two of four return centers and outsourcing to GENCO, Best Buy has experienced faster processing times, a reduction in non-working inventory, and more timely and accurate information. [18]

Many other companies have established similar programs, outsourcing to providers for whom reverse logistics has become a true core competency.

International Shipments and Operations

With over five hundred pages of customs regulations for import shipments alone, most firms turn to a licensed customs broker for the handling of imports and exports.

Well versed in the regulations as well as the politics, a customs broker provides valuable assistance in clearing customs, determining accurate classifications and duties, and arranging for transportation.

Services are available from traditional customs brokerage firms or, in some cases, international logistics service providers.

As firms become more global in their operations, however, they may want to turn to one or more of the major freight forwarders or international logistics service providers for other services as well. A survey by the Foundation for the Malcolm Baldrige National Quality Award revealed that 95% of the CEO's surveyed identified more globalization as their top challenge over a three- to five-year horizon. Eighty percent identified improving the performance of their global supply chains as a top challenge. [19]

In addition to understanding the customs issues of the countries with which the firm is concerned, there will be a myriad of other issues as well; i.e., culture, labor, regulations, etc. In order to deal with all the international complexities, outsourcing is almost "non-optional."

A case in point involved an American specialty chemicals firm with manufacturing facilities in the southern part of the country. As their volume grew in the European and Russian markets, they realized that their main focus had been on sales and product innovations with very little attention to the supply chain.

As a result, they turned to UTi Worldwide who conducted an analysis of their techniques and costs. As a result of improvements recommended by UTi, the company was able to reach these markets more effectively; and at the same time, savings of 30% of total supply chain costs were realized.

On the import side as well, international service providers can perform valuable services.

A driving factor in Kuehne & Nagel's 2001 acquisition of USCO Logistics was the ability to gain full access to the North American contract logistics market. One important element was the company's network of multi-client distribution centers, which provides flexible logistics solutions for customers with changing distribution needs. Shared warehousing allows customers to pay only for the space and service they need, and as their business expands or contracts, logistics costs parallel the revenue stream. In addition, the new Kuehne & Nagel network throughout the United States allows foreign clients to position inventory closer to their customers.

Kuehne & Nagel now is able to provide one-stop shopping for current or future customers looking to grow in the United States. Here is an example of how one European company took advantage of Kuehne & Nagel's integrated service capabilities.

Minerva U.S.A., Inc., the North American subsidiary of one of the world's leading olive oil manufacturing and trading companies, had to move quickly when the company landed a major retail chain account at the end of 2002. The new account was expected to substantially increase the volume of Fort Lee, New Jersey-based Minerva, a subsidiary of Minerva S.p.A., Genoa, Italy.

The company had six months to procure the raw materials, manufacture the product, finalize packaging and labels, make all logistical arrangements, import the product, and begin shipping it to the new account.

Recognizing that its customer was taking a risk by using a single supplier to produce and deliver a large volume of private-label olive oil, Minerva sought to design a logistical solution that would deliver the highest levels of service at the lowest possible cost.

The company examined all logistical possibilities, including shipping product direct to the chain account's distribution centers, and evaluated a range of distribution networks with different combinations of distribution centers. Minerva, which had historically worked with a freight forwarder, carrier, and multiple warehousing providers, knew that they had to make some dramatic changes and began thinking about an integrated solution.

After evaluating several logistics providers, Minerva selected Kuehne & Nagel to manage storage, shipping and delivery to the chain account's facilities via truckload and LTL distribution. Kuehne & Nagel already managed all aspects of the import transportation, U.S. customs brokerage, and container delivery. All products arrive in ocean freight containers for storage at Kuehne & Nagel centers in Miami, Los Angeles, San Francisco and Portland, Oregon.

Working with a single provider has helped streamline Minerva's logistics process. Minerva USA Vice President Stephane Picard says, "Instead of talking with five companies with five systems and five cultures, I talk with one. It's very harmonized, and has saved us a lot of time and hassle."

Information Technology

In the past, outsourcing firms have relied on their own technology and/or that of the traditional providers. With the continuing progress in the development of supply chain management systems, this no longer is the case.

Today it is not unusual to outsource technology to one firm and other logistics functions to another.

There are hundreds of vendors and systems to choose from, and they are utilized not only by the outsourcing firms, but the providers as well. The two most often mentioned are Transportation Management Systems and Warehouse Management Systems. A comprehensive TMS will provide the following functionalities:

- Asset Tracking
- Carrier Selection
- Claims Management

- Driver Management
- Freight Payment
- Load Planning
- Load Tendering
- Order and Shipment Visibility
- Package Delivery and Pickup Tracking
- Pickup Scheduling
- Rating
- Route Optimization and Reporting
- Shipment Consolidation

An effective WMS will provide for

- Cartonization
- Flow-through/Crossdock Capability
- Fulfillment
- Inventory Management
- Lot and Serial Number Tracking
- Order Management
- Order Visibility
- Picking/Put-away Capability
- Unit Load Management
- Value-added Services
- Warehouse Simulation
- Web-based Access to Tasks
- Web-based Inventory
- Yard Management

Often the outsourcing firm will ask a provider to install a particular system. For example, a major food and confection manufacturer needed to update its distribution centers to "right size" the capacity and allow for growth for the next five years. Additionally, this client wanted to establish "repeatable processes" across all of its distribution centers. It selected Red Prairie as the WMS solution for its new redesigned distribution centers, and was looking for a provider with the distribution and IT resources to implement a large distribution center and implement the installation of a complex "paperless" WMS.

A warehouse provider implemented a 585,000 square foot facility and worked in concert with Red Prairie and the client to implement and integrate the WMS system and SAP into the operation. The warehouse company provided project management, systems integration and operations management resources to successfully start up the operation. They implemented a labor management system and developed a series of operational reports using the data from this base. These reports provided the key productivity indicators that measured the effectiveness of the operations. The provider also utilized the business process teams to refine and improve the processes in the facility. One key success has been in the development of a slotting tool that automates the slotting of static pick locations based on the weekly download of forecast data from the client. This tool has dramatically improved case pick productivity, while reducing the amount of clerical time to support the analysis.

A major aerospace company installed a HighJump Software WMS and realized immediate benefits. Thousands of parts are needed for the building of a jet engine and using the WMS they are combined into kits and delivered to the assembly lines. Inventory accuracy has moved from 75 to 80% to a consistent 97.5 to 99%. The elapsed time between the first conceptual meeting and the total implementation was ten months.

Solutions

In the past, many logistics managers have been dependent on consulting firms to provide network analyses or solutions to other logistics problems. For example, a firm might contract with a consultant to determine the appropriate number and location of distribution centers. The logistics manager, armed with that analysis, then would start contacting logistics service providers in those cities, eventually selecting one or more of them to become a part of the new network.

Many of today's larger logistics service providers have in-house solutions or consulting groups and offer their services to clients or potential clients. For the firm considering outsourcing, these analyses can be very helpful.

They can answer the questions of how many, how big, and where, but the client must be careful that the study includes valid options other than just those offered by the provider performing the analysis.

There are a number of experienced companies providing such services. Ten years ago, Schneider Logistics, for example, assisted General Motors Parts Operations in solving a formidable problem – carrier contracting, freight management, payment and claims for 435,000 items shipped daily from 3,000 suppliers to four processing centers, to 18 regional parts distribution centers, and finally 8,000 dealers and distributors.

During the first two years, GM reduced its freight bill by 10 percent while adding 14 million miles of transportation annually, and decreased its carrier base from 1,200 to 600.

Schneider Logistics and others have continued to add sophistication and new technology to such analyses and today can provide almost any kind of supply chain analysis.

Site Selection

As network analysis has become more complex, some firms may want to outsource the process of selecting the sites for new distribution centers. Even when they have an organized real estate group, companies sometimes will turn to outsiders for assistance. These firms can assist in the modeling of the network, as well as selection of precise locations.

In addition to the economics, there are a number of factors that must be considered. Some of these are

- Land or Building Availability
- Zoning Regulations
- Availability and Cost of Utilities
- EPA Requirements; i.e., Water Retention, etc.
- Access to Transportation – Air, Rail, Highway
- Availability of Industrial Support Services
- Building Restriction, if any; i.e., Height, Setbacks, Landscape Requirements, etc.
- Fire Codes/Protection
- Availability and Cost of Labor
- Union Environment
- Unemployment Rate
- Tax Structures – Property, Inventory, Sales, Income, etc.
- Availability of Tax Abatements
- Educational Facilities
- Community Services; i.e., Commercial, Churches, Medical
- Availability of Special Financing; i.e., IRB, Incentives, etc.
- Location and Volume of Customers to be Served
- Origin of Products and Materials Flowing into Warehouse
- Unique Transportation Requirements

As with outsourcing other functions, be cautious. Much of the site selection analysis is provided by real estate firms, and it is important to make sure the selected location is indeed the best one – not necessarily the one where the provider has a large presence or listings.

Special Events

On occasion, there will be special projects or events so complex or time consuming that a firm simply doesn't have the resources to deal with them. An excellent case in point involved the global provider, Exel.

One of the world's greatest heritage motorcycle companies celebrated its 100th birthday on August 31, 2003. Starting out as a small business in a shed in Milwaukee, Harley-Davidson eventually developed into an expanding and successful company with a yearly production of about four million motorcycles. To celebrate its 100th birthday, Harley-Davidson staged "The Ride Home," a gigantic rally gathering bikes from all over the world to Milwaukee. There, a great birthday party was held, lasting from August 28 to 31, 2003, with over 200,000 guests and their bikes from all over the world attending.

Harley-Davidson's subsidiary, Harley-Owners Group (H.O.G.), caters to 550,000 Harley-Davidson enthusiasts worldwide. 17,000 of them are located in Europe (mainly Germany and Austria) and regularly meet in 68 regional locations. To celebrate the 100th birthday, H.O.G. offered full logistic services for all their members to ensure bikes arrived in the US in time for the party. H.O.G. turned to Exel to develop a customized solution to transport bikes in from around the world.

The time window started four weeks before the event and closed four weeks after. A lot of Harley-Davidson owners used the occasion to ride through the US. Also, bikers try to use the short season in Europe as much as possible, so they asked for the latest possible departure dates in Germany and for the option to pick up and deliver their bikes from or to various US airports.

Careful packaging was of vital importance to avoid any scratches and damage to paint, chrome and other parts of the valuable machines. Thus, Exel worked closely to cooperate with Harley-Davidson's main transportation agent, SKS, who has a very long and successful experience transporting motorcycles by truck in Europe. SKS was responsible for the pick-up and packaging of the bikes. The bikes had to be in a clean condition and their tanks filled to no more than one quarter of their capacity to conform to US import regulations. Also, battery cables had to be disconnected.

To provide the maximum service for every biker's individual budget, Exel offered two transport solutions: shipping by ocean and the fastest possibility – air freight. Both air and ocean freight are calculated by volume, so to get the lowest possible transportation cost, the bikes had to be packaged as space-efficiently as possible, meaning that windshields, mirrors or bulky handlebars had to be detached.

Deciding on air freight, Exel decided to go for an exclusive alliance with Lufthansa. Complete charters were reserved just for motorcycle transportation. To ensure that loading would go smoothly, several test loadings were made in 2002, together with both SKS and Lufthansa.

In the US, Exel took over the complete motorcycle logistics. Exel's Transportation Services team has worked with H.O.G. USA for many years and has a good basic knowledge of the motorcycle industry.

The service package for Harley-Davidson owners included the complete US import customs and the re-import to Germany. Transport and vehicle insurance was optional. Last, but not least, Exel also cooperated with a travel agency and reserved over 325 motel rooms with a view of the occupants' bikes.

Exel developed an innovative logistical concept that was tailored to the bike rider's needs. Not only the typical logistic requirements, but also all additional worries and needs regarding the bike's transport and their owner's requests cared for, resulting in a complete "no-hassles-no-worries-package" for both the client and the bikers.

Other firms may have similar logistics challenges with new product introductions, promotions, or other temporary situations. On these occasions they would be well served to at least examine the possibility of using a qualified logistics service provider.

Other Services

There is almost no end to the list of logistics services that can be outsourced; but increasingly, firms are focusing on outsourcing functions that are related to, but not a part of, the traditional logistics structure.

One of these is packaging – not the repacking activity discussed in Chapter 2 – but major primary packaging operations. Exel, for example, has a co-packing division whose sole function is to provide packaging services to clients who have such a need.

According to Adrian Gonzalez of ARC Advisory Group, "The merging of packaging and logistics can lead to significant reductions in supply chain costs and cycle times. Consumer goods giant, Unilever, has saved $20 million in an efficiency project that includes integrating its packaging and logistics." [20]

Another logistics-related function being outsourced by some firms is inventory financing. Some of the larger LSP's are offering such financing, usually with the help of other entities. UPS Capital, for example, utilizes a syndication of banks, and PB Capital and DHL, both parts of the Deutsche Post World Net Group, have developed a joint program. [21]

The advantages to the outsourcing firm are obvious. The elimination of hundreds of millions of dollars in inventory can go a long way toward the improvement of short-term financial positions. Although such offerings are limited and have been so since they appeared on the outsourcing scene in the early 1990's, they are available to those firms interested in the concept.

Conclusion

Certainly, there are other logistics functions that will be suitable for outsourcing, either as freestanding activities or as part of an overall logistics arrangement. Some of these may be more important to you than those discussed here; but whatever they are, they should be considered and decided upon with care and in a manner that is consistent with corporate logistics strategy.

Chapter 4

Developing a Strategy for Outsourcing

You've got to be careful if you don't know where you're going because you might not get there.

- Yogi Berra

Setting a goal is not the main thing. It is deciding how you will go about achieving it and staying with that plan.

- Tom Landry

In one of his brushes with re-engineering, Dilbert pleaded, "If you let me keep my job, I'll do the work of ten people. Specifically, it would be the ten people in our strategic planning group. They don't do much." [1]

When it comes to strategic planning for logistics outsourcing, Dilbert probably could do the work of twenty people. In spite of its impact on the logistics function and often the entire corporation, outsourcing frequently is undertaken with little regard for overall logistics strategy.

It is important to remember that outsourcing itself is not the strategy. It is a vehicle for achieving the strategy, whatever it may be. Keep in mind that outsourcing may not be appropriate for every firm. Do not enter into an outsourcing arrangement simply because it is written or talked about frequently, or because other firms in your industry are doing it. A sure recipe for disaster is to embark on a program that is not suitable, not understood clearly, or one that is marred by unrealistic expectations.

Major failures in outsourcing relationships occur when a firm outsources an activity its own personnel do not totally comprehend, and the provider promises to meet requirements that have not been fully defined, communicated or understood.

Senior Management Commitment

As with any other significant undertaking in the firm, it is absolutely critical that the outsourcing project have senior management support. When all or part of the logistics function is turned over to an outside party, a number of other disciplines can be impacted. Some functional managers will be more supportive than others, and in a few cases, they may be totally opposed to the concept. If they view the outsourcing arrangement as a threat to their careers, they must be convinced not only of the benefits to the corporation, but to themselves.

Usually, the logistics manager will be the project leader or champion, but he must have the full weight of the organization behind him to be effective.

Project Team

Once senior managers have committed to the project, it will be important to have the commitment and participation of other departments or functions that will be affected by the decision.

These of course will vary by firm, but in addition to Logistics, the groups most often impacted will be:

- Information Technology
- Production or Manufacturing
- Quality
- Sales and/or Marketing
- Merchandising
- Finance and Accounting
- Purchasing
- Human Resources

Ideally, some customer participation should be sought as well, either directly or through Sales.

Representatives from these or other departments must be part of the process and should comprise the study team. Not only is their input important to the success of the project, but they must support the decision, whatever it turns out to be. With most firms becoming more aware of total supply chain management, logistics managers who attempt to take major steps unilaterally are being naïve and are setting themselves up for failure.

An outsourcing project can be a true test of how effective a logistics manager can be with the supply chain management concept. For the project to succeed, he or she must have a consensus of all the functions in the chain. Rarely will he/she have responsibility for them all, and a satisfactory result can be achieved only by exceptional negotiation and sensitivity toward other function heads.

Hopefully, it goes without saying that when outsourcing supply chain management systems, information technology personnel should be driving the process.

Outsourcing Objectives

One of the first tasks of the study team should be to determine what the firm is attempting to accomplish through outsourcing. Objectives must be set, and many questions must be dealt with. They should go beyond "What will it cost?" and each question must be analyzed carefully. They will include:

- What problem are we trying to solve?
- What results do we expect?
- Is outsourcing consistent with the overall corporate strategy and mission?
- Will outsourcing be acceptable to the other functional groups?
- Is the timing right?
- What is the competition doing?
- Is it working for them?
- How will it affect the organization?
- Are there identifiable managers who can implement and manage an outsourced function? Who are they?
- Will outsourcing enable us to concentrate better on our core competencies? How?
- Will it help maximize our strengths and avoid our weaknesses? How?
- What are our customer service requirements?
- How will the decision impact customer service?
- Do we understand what we are trying to outsource well enough to do it?
- Are we simply trying to outsource an activity we cannot manage efficiently?
- Will outsourcing expose us to innovative logistics techniques and/or information systems?
- What are the risks?
- Are they acceptable?

Once these and other questions have been answered, the objectives have been set, and the activities to be outsourced have been identified, it will be necessary to establish a basis for comparison.

Assessment of Current Operations

For some managers, assessing current operations may be the most difficult part of the outsourcing process. In order to make an intelligent decision about providers, cost, and benefits, however, it will be necessary to conduct this audit. The project team must have a clear picture of current logistics operations, their capabilities, limitations, and cost, as well as future needs. When this has been completed, a set of benchmarks against which to measure the various options can be established.

Outsourcing should not be evaluated strictly on the basis of various provider proposals, but as an alternative to an internal solution, as well.

For most firms, the best way to develop the information will be to flow chart the entire logistics process. Each function represented on the study team should be consulted to make sure the flow is accurate and properly reflects the impact on other parts of the company. Pay particular attention to the information technology requirements. It will be necessary for the logistics provider to replicate the systems, or more appropriately, improve on them.

The flow chart can be used to determine strengths and weaknesses in the system. This will help in determining what improvements can be made through outsourcing, as well as which provider may be more suitable.

It is important to remember that all costs must be captured, both fixed and variable, direct and indirect. It is quite possible that some logistics expenditures, such as those for order processing or management time, may be difficult to quantify, but they cannot be ignored if valid comparisons are to be made.

If at all possible, it will be much easier to compare internal and outsourced costs if corporate costs can be determined by activity. Activity-Based Costing (ABC) assigns costs to specific activities or products, rather than traditional line item costing. [2]

Cost comparisons will be discussed in more detail in a later chapter, but in-house costs are a necessary part of the current situation assessment.

The data collection task can be a formidable one, but bear in mind, much of the information developed will be necessary to define the scope of work for the potential service providers. In other words, the task is not optional. It is unavoidable.

Including the Provider in the Planning Process

Many outsourcing relationships have been developed by traditional methods. The interested firm prepares a Request for Proposal which outlines the tasks to be performed and specifies the contents and format of the proposal. The RFP is presented to three or more providers who are asked to submit bids to perform precise tasks in precise ways. The contract then is awarded to the provider who demonstrates the best cost/benefit ratio.

It is recommended that in anticipation of the RFP, a preliminary Request for Information (RFI) be used to gather information about potential providers that are known to have experience in the client industry. Not only will these responses aid in narrowing down the list of providers who will be sent an RFP, but they will help identify a qualified provider to include in the planning process.

The RFP makes providers' proposals easier to compare and evaluate, but ignores the basic issue of determining the most cost- and service-effective logistics process. A true partnership or relationship suggests input by all parties, and the most successful ones have been those that were established through joint analysis and resolution of the logistics objective.

This may require qualifying logistics providers before the cost of their services is known, but a more satisfactory relationship can result from bringing a potential provider into the planning process early. As a matter of principle, some logistics providers will decline to respond to RFP's that they do not feel will maximize their assets, capabilities, and experience. They also will avoid those that appear to be just "fishing expeditions."

If a firm is going to enter into an outsourcing relationship, however, it makes infinitely good sense to leverage the provider's knowledge and expertise early in the process. After all, that is what the outsourcing process is all about.

Conclusion

The planning, analysis, and other activity mentioned in this discussion will be tedious and, in some cases, downright unpleasant. Collecting data will require valuable time and resources, and the entire process will require patience, perseverance, and persuasion in dealing with other functional groups. As difficult as it may be, however, it simply is not optional if an effective outsourcing relationship is to be realized.

There is no substitute for planning. Four centuries ago, the Spanish Jesuit, Baltasar Gracián, set the tone when he wrote:

"Think in anticipation, today for tomorrow, and indeed for many days. The greatest providence is to have forethought for what comes. What is provided for does not happen by chance, nor is the man who is prepared ever beset by emergencies. One must not, therefore, postpone consideration 'til the need arises. Consideration should go beforehand. You can, after careful reflection, act to prevent the most calamitous events. The pillow is a silent Sybil, for to sleep over questions before they reach a climax is far better than lying awake over them afterward. Some act and think later – and they think more of excuses and consequences. Others think neither before nor after. The whole of life should be spent thinking about how to find the right

course of action to follow. Thought and forethought give counsel both on living and on achieving success." [3]

And so it is with logistics outsourcing.

Chapter 5

Identifying Potential Providers

Logistics providers fit into different niches. While most sell themselves as being capable of all things, they normally are better at a couple of them.

- Richard D. Armstrong

If your company already is outsourcing some of its logistics functions, the information in this chapter may be redundant. If not, the identification of potential providers can be a formidable, but not impossible, task.

There are hundreds of firms offering a varying array of services for a variety of clients, and the industry is segmented in a number of different ways. It is important to understand this segmentation, even though in some cases it is rather basic.

Additionally, there are two broader categories of provider that should be recognized at the outset of the identification process.

Asset vs. Non-Asset

All logistics service providers can be divided into two basic classifications; i.e., *asset-based* and *non-asset-based*. As the term implies, *asset-based* providers own (or lease) trucks, warehouses, and other tangible property that are used in executing their clients' requirements. An example would be the warehouse-oriented companies such as Exel or Standard Corporation, now a part of UTi Worldwide.

Non-asset-based providers do not own a major portion of the assets used, but contract with other firms to provide all or portions of the services. One example of this type supplier would be an intermodal provider such as The Hub Group that buys high volumes of transportation capacity from the railroads and "re-sells" it to shippers at a higher price. Freight forwarders such as Danzas, Panalpina and Fritz Companies (UPS) operate in a similar fashion.

Another group of providers, some of which refer to themselves as facilitators, can be little more than brokers. Their major qualifications are knowledge and experience which they use to develop logistics systems for clients through negotiating with and sub-contracting to other providers.

The financial community sometimes uses the terms "non-asset" and "information-based" providers interchangeably. This can be misleading. While most information-based firms could safely be categorized as non-asset, not all non-asset providers are information-based.[1]

As with most logistics classifications, the line between asset- and non-asset-based firms is a little blurred. In many cases, a logistics provider will be a combination of the two. Perhaps the best way to classify them is through a "rule of predominance." If they own or control most of the assets they use to fulfill their missions, they are asset-based. If not, then by default they fall into the other category.

This has nothing to do with size or specialty. It is simply an ownership or control issue, and there are large and small firms of all types in both categories.

Whether the firm uses one or the other classification of provider will depend on need and preference, but one could argue that the best partner will be one that has a strong ownership of the process, either through asset control or otherwise.

Single Sourcing

While technically not a classification of logistics service companies, the concept of *single sourcing* plays an important role in supplier selection. Some firms will prefer to deal with one lead provider to either perform or contract for all the functions being outsourced. The lead firm can be asset- or non-asset-based. Usually it will fulfill those requirements that it is equipped to handle and sub-contract to other organizations those services it does not provide. The term strategic alliance often is used to define these arrangements.

The important advantage to the client will be the one focal point for all the activities. The lead provider will be responsible for the performance of the other firms in addition to its own.

The disadvantage is that there is no intimate relationship between the client and its full complement of providers. The very arrangement that simplifies communications and management can also be a detriment.

One group of outsourcing experts advocates single sourcing, but has said that it presents challenges that must be addressed at the outset to ensure a successful result. "The key is for the buyer to take responsibility for making the sole source approach disciplined and vigorous. The necessary components of this include:

-   Carefully defining the buyer's objectives and the services required.

- Establishing a framework (financial and other factors) that helps both parties know when the proposed solution is acceptable.
- Laying the foundation for the two organizations to productively govern the implementation and ongoing execution of the solution." [2]

On the other hand, Peter J. Rose, Chairman and CEO of Expeditors International, was quoted as saying, "No one provider is capable of offering one-stop shopping, and no one really wants it. You don't say, 'I want a shirt, a tie, four tires and a head of lettuce' in the same store."

Fourth Parties (4PL)

Intertwined with the asset versus non-asset and single sourcing concepts is the so-called fourth party or 4PL. The term actually was coined by a leading consulting firm that went so far as to copyright it. Its usage has been vague at best, and many practitioners have felt it is just one of the wretched excess of buzzwords and terms which abound in the industry.

The fourth party could best be defined as a BPO, or business process outsourcing provider. A qualified fourth party should be able to visualize a process and determine what will be necessary for success. When considering the fourth party option, the outsourcing manager should keep two things in mind; i.e., the provider must be totally neutral in its selection process and, in spite of the alleged origin of the term, should not assume that the term is synonymous with consultant. [3]

For example, UPS Supply Chain Solutions is considered to be a 4PL that manages the activities of providers it subcontracts to, in addition to the services that might be provided by UPS.

Integrated Logistics or Lead Providers

Some provider firms have gone far beyond their basic orientation and have become as skilled in other disciplines as in their core businesses. Similar to, if not the same as, 4PL's, they are sometimes referred to as *integrated logistics providers* or *lead logistics providers (LLP)*. (The term preferred by the author.) They offer total supply chain or logistics solutions, utilizing their own facilities and systems, or through strategic alliances with others.

In many cases, they will offer in-house consulting services and logistics network design.

Exel, Kuehne & Nagel, and other large providers, for example, function as LLP's, leveraging technology, transportation management, supply chain engineering, and/or warehousing along with other services provided by an established network of other providers.

Geography

The most basic segmentation of providers is by geography. Firms can be local, regional, national, domestic, North American, international, or global.

A *local* provider operates in one city or metropolitan area. This category would include one-city public or contract warehouses and local cartage companies.

A *regional* firm will operate in multiple cities but will concentrate its operations in a geographic region; i.e., Southeast, Northeast, etc.

A *national* provider is exactly what the term implies; i.e., a company that has operations not necessarily in every major market, but spread fairly evenly throughout the country.

Since none of the above offer services outside the United States, they also can be referred to as *domestic.*

A *North American firm,* while technically international, is simply a national firm that operates in Mexico and/or Canada, as well.

An *international* provider is one that operates in the United States and other countries, and a *global* firm is one that is perceived, at least, to have worldwide operations.

Basic Orientation

Logistics service providers also can be characterized by their basic orientation reflecting either the origins of their business or the areas in which they have elected to specialize. The five categories are:

- Warehouse-Based
- Carrier-Based
- Brokerage/Forwarder-Based
- Package Carriers
- Technology/Information-Based

While firms in each of these categories offer other services as well, they generally are known for their expertise in certain core businesses. Some examples are:

- Warehouse-Based	Exel
	Standard Corporation
	Saddle Creek
	Kane Is Able
- Carrier-Based	BNSF Logistics
	CRST Logistics
	Ryder Integrated Logistics
- Brokerage/Forwarder-Based	C. H. Robinson
	Fritz Companies (UPS)
	The Hub Group
	Expeditors International

- Package Carriers   DHL
FedEx
UPS Worldwide
United States Postal Service

- Technology/
Information-Based   Cass Information Systems
Continental Traffic Service, Inc.
i2
Intellitrans, Inc.
Manugistics
Schneider Logistics

Industries Served

Some providers specialize in certain industries such as grocery products, pharmaceuticals, cigarettes, chemicals, computers, and electronics. Others, while not advertised specialists, have come to be preferred by clients in particular industries.

The advantages to dealing with specialists are obvious. The knowledge and expertise they have in specific industries lend economies, efficiencies, and innovation to their operations; and in some cases, synergies and cost reducing services such as consolidation and shared services can be achieved only through using a specialist.

There are, however, excellent generalists in the industry as well. Many of them have learned to operate with as much skill in a variety of industries as some of the specialists have in one.

Sources of Information

At this point in the outsourcing planning process, the logistics manager should be ready to identify specific providers he or she will want to communicate with and/or investigate.

Word of Mouth

As with other business issues, the best sources of information will be from those who have had experience with the various providers. Conversations with colleagues, customers, and competitors, as well as attendance at various seminars and conferences can yield invaluable, accurate knowledge of the industry and specific providers. This will be particularly true in the complex area of information technology.

Whatever the user industry might be, the chances are there is another firm that has had outsourcing experience and is willing to offer advice and counsel and share thoughts. In the words of an old Chinese proverb, *A single conversation across the table with a wise man is worth a month's study of books.*

Trade Publications and Journals

In addition to provider advertising, the leading trade journals all provide heavy coverage of outsourcing developments. Numerous articles and accounts of user experiences can yield valuable information and contacts.

Some of the more popular trade and professional publications are:

Air Cargo World
1270 National Press Building
Washington, DC 20045
(202) 661-3387, Fax (202) 783-2550
www.aircargoworld.com

American Shipper
300 West Adams Street, Suite #600
P.O. Box 4728
Jacksonville, FL 32201
(800) 874-6422
www.americanshipper.com

DC Velocity
Tower Square, Number 4
500 East Washington Street
North Attleboro, MA 02760
(800) 554-7470
www.dcvelocity.com

Food Logistics
445 Broad Hollow Road
Melville, NY 11747
(631) 845-2700, Fax (631) 845-2723
www.foodlogistics.com

Global Logistics & Supply Chain Strategies
150 Great Neck Road
Great Neck, NY 11021
(516) 829-9210, Fax (516) 829-4514
www.glscs.com

Inbound Logistics
5 Penn Plaza, 8th Floor
New York, NY 10001
(212) 629-1563, Fax (212) 629-1565
www.inboundlogistics.com

International Journal of Physical Distribution & Logistics Management
University of South Florida
Department of Marketing
Tampa, FL 33620-5500
(813) 974-6173, Fax (813) 974-6175

Journal of Commerce Group
33 Washington Street, 13th Floor
Newark, NJ 09102
(973) 848-7000, Fax (973) 848-7004
www.joc.com

Journal of Business Logistics
University of Oklahoma
307 West Brooks, Room 2
Norman, OK 73019-4001
(405) 325-5899, Fax (405) 325-7688

Logistics Management
275 Washington Street
Newton, MA 02458
(617) 558-4473, Fax (617) 558-4480
www.logisticsmgmt.com

Logistics Today
1300 East Ninth Street
Cleveland, OH 44114-1503
(216) 696-7000, Fax (216) 696-2737
www.logisticstoday.com

Material Handling Management
The Penton Media Building
1300 East Ninth Street
Cleveland, OH 44114-1503
(216) 696-7000, Fax (216) 696-7658
www.mhmonline.com

Modern Materials Handling
275 Washington Street
Newton, MA 02458
(617) 964-3030, Fax (617) 558-4327
www.manufacturing.net/mmh

Parcel Shipping & Distribution
2901 International Lane
Madison, WI 53704
(608) 241-8777, Fax (608) 241-8666
www.rbpub.com/parcelshipping.htm

Supply Chain Management Review
275 Washington Street
Newton, MA 02458
(888) 240-7324, Fax (617) 558-4480
www.scmr.com

Traffic World Magazine
1270 National Press Building
Washington, DC 20045
(202) 783-1101, Fax (202) 661-3383
www.trafficworld.com

Transport Topics
2200 Mill Road
Alexandria, VA 22314
(703) 838-1770, Fax (703) 548-3662
www.ttnews.com

Transportation Journal
509 Business Administration Building
University Park, PA 16802-3005
(814) 865-2872, Fax (814) 863-7067

Warehousing Forum
2041 Riverside Drive, Suite #204
Columbus, OH 43221
(614) 488-3165, Fax (614) 488-9243
www.warehousingforum.com

Warehousing Management Magazine
201 King of Prussia Road
Radnor, PA 19089
(610) 964-4385, Fax (610) 964-4381
www.warehousemag.com

Some of these publications, such as *Inbound Logistics* and *Logistics Management*, publish annual listings of the top logistics providers and the services they offer. *Logistics Today* publishes a directory of supply chain management software products. *Inbound Logistics* has an annual technology issue which lists the "Top 100 Logistics IT Companies." Copies of these are available upon request or can be found at the publication websites.

The Council of Logistics Management publishes on its website, www.clm1.org, a directory of logistics software. There is a brief description of packages from over 200 vendors organized into nine categories.

- Customer Relationship Management
- Forecasting
- Inventory Planning/Management
- Manufacturing
- Order Processing
- Other Advanced Planning
- Procurement
- Transportation Management
- Warehouse Management

There is no shortage of packages to choose from. There are over 100 Warehouse Management Systems and about the same number of Transportation Management Systems in the directory.

Trade Associations

Trade Associations are another good source of information. Most of the major logistics service providers will belong to one or more of these. Although membership does not necessarily guarantee excellence in performance, the association offices and directories are valuable resources.

The major groups are listed below:

Airforwarders Association, Inc.
1600 Duke Street, Suite #400
Alexandria, VA 22314
(703) 519-9846, Fax (703) 519-1716
www.airforwarders.org

Association of American Railroads
50 F Street, N.W.
Washington, DC 20001-1564
(202) 639-2400, Fax (202) 639-2286
www.aar.org

Express Carriers Association
P.O. Box 4307
Bethlehem, PA 18018
(866) 322-7447, Fax (866) 322-3299
www.expresscarriers.com

Healthcare Distribution Management Association
1821 Michael Faraday Drive, Suite #400
Reston, VA 20190
(703) 787-0219, Fax (703) 787-0275
www.healthcaredistribution.org

Intermodal Association of North America
7501 Greenbelt Center Drive, Suite #720
Greenbelt, MD 20770-3415
(301) 982-3400, Fax (301) 982-4815
www.intermodal.org

International Association of Refrigerated Warehouses
1500 King Street, Suite #201
Alexandria, VA 22314
(703) 373-4300, Fax (703) 373-4301
www.iarw.org

International Warehouse Logistics Association
2800 River Road
Des Plaines, IL 60018
(847) 813-4699, Fax (847) 813-0115
www.warehouselogistics.org

National Customs Brokers/Forwarders Association
1200 18th Street, N.W., Suite #901
Washington, DC 20036
(202) 466-0222, Fax (202) 466-0226
www.ncbfaa.org

Transportation Intermediaries Association
1625 North Prince Street, Suite #200
Alexandria, VA 22314
(703) 299-5700, Fax (703) 836-0123
www.tianet.org

Truckload Carriers Association
2200 Mill Road
Alexandria, VA 22314
(703) 838-1950, Fax (703) 836-6610
www.truckload.org

US Chamber of Commerce
1615 H Street, N.W.
Washington, DC 20062-2000
(202) 659-6000
www.uschamber.org

Industry Directories

In addition to the directories published by the above organizations, other useful listings are:

American Public Warehouse Register
Reed Business Information
275 Washington Street
Newton, MA 02158
(617) 558-4473, Fax (617) 558-4480
www.logistics-buyers-guide.com

Canadian Motor Carrier Directory
Transportation Technical Services
500 Lafayette Boulevard, Suite #230
Fredericksburg, VA 22401
(888) 665-9887
www.refrigeratedtrans.com

National Third Party Logistics Directory
Leonard's Guide
49 East Huntington Drive
Arcadia, CA 91006
(800) 574-5250
www.leonardsguide.com

National Warehouse and Distribution Directory
Leonard's Guide
49 East Huntington Drive
Arcadia, CA 91006
(800) 574-5250
www.leonardsguide.com

Warehouse/Distribution Directory
Primedia Information, Inc.
745 Fifth Avenue
New York, NY 10151
(212) 745-0100, Fax (212) 745-0121
www.primedia.com

*Who's Who In Logistics? Armstrong's Guide to Third
Party Logistics Service Providers*
Armstrong & Associates, Inc.
100 Business Park Circle, Suite #202
Stoughton, WI 53589
(800) 525-3915, Fax (608) 873-5509
www.3plogistics.com

Warehousing Directory
Reed Business Information
360 Park Avenue, South
New York, NY 10010
(646) 746-6400
www.reedbusiness.com

Local Information

When searching for providers in a particular city, besides personal contacts, the best sources are the Yellow Pages, local business newspapers and chamber of commerce directories.

Internet

A search of the Internet can yield a wealth of information. Web searches by provider association, or such key phrases as "logistics service providers" and "logistics third parties," will result in hundreds of sites to explore.

Websites

Most logistics service providers have informative websites which will outline the basic facts about the company, and the major ones also will provide case studies of solutions they have provided to clients with a particular need. These can be particularly helpful when seeking a provider with a certain kind of experience.

Other types of information are available, as well. For example, the "Top 100 3PLs" published annually by *Inbound Logistics* can be viewed at 3pl@inboundlogistics.com.

Professional Associations

Membership in one or both of the premier professional logistics organizations is a good indicator of the professionalism of the logistics service providers and their management.

The two associations are:

Council of Logistics Management*
2805 Butterfield Road, Suite #200
Oak Brook, IL 60523
(630) 574-0985, Fax (630) 574-0989
www.clm1.org

*This organization is scheduled to be renamed the Council of Supply Chain Management Professionals (CSCMP) effective January 1, 2005 (www.cscmp.org).

Warehousing Education and Research Council
1100 Jorie Boulevard, Suite #170
Oak Brook, IL 60521
(630) 990-0001, Fax (630) 990-0256
www.werc.org

While neither organization endorses providers and membership is open to all interested parties, their directories are excellent sources of information about the more progressive firms and their representatives.

Consultants

Finally, a less time- and resource-consuming approach would be to retain a logistics consultant to aid in the identification of appropriate providers. Some firms may choose to use a consulting firm throughout the outsourcing process; i.e., planning to implementation, while others may elect to use them only for the identification and qualification of potential service firms.

There are many excellent consulting firms in the logistics field, ranging from the independent to the large corporation. The individual consultants themselves often have extensive knowledge of the subject, and many have held positions with clients and/or providers.

Information on qualified consultants is available in much the same way as information on providers, but one quick and efficient way to identify qualified advisors is through the executive offices of the Council of Logistics Management or the Warehousing Education and Research Council.

Information Technology

There are hundreds of firms that offer supply chain execution software such as Warehouse Management Systems (WMS) and Transportation Management Systems (TMS). Identifying the right provider will be a complex and often tedious process. The eligible firms will range from major providers such as SAP to the smaller, more specialized firms. The best source of information will be from the actual clients of the providers. Talk to those who have had the experience, both successful and painful, before entering into discussions with the software companies.

Most important of all is a point that will be emphasized several times in this book. Involve knowledgeable and experienced client managers in the identification process and on through implementation.

Conclusion

As indicated earlier, there is no substitute for seeking out others who have outsourced, and paying close attention to their experiences, both good and bad. On the other hand, the various publications and associations will provide the hard information such as website, addresses, telephone numbers and in some cases, basic facts about the providers.

A few words of caution, however. Trade journals often will favor their advertisers in editorial exposure and/or identify a small percentage of available providers in their directories, often times at the expense of other qualified firms and experts.

Most published case studies are positive, with very little written about failures in outsourcing relationships.

Chambers of commerce more often than not will list only members in their directories, sometimes ignoring qualified providers.

Many logistics firms are privately held and do not divulge financial information. Even when it is listed, it may be an estimate and not a clear indicator of financial health.

A few of the directories, while very informative, tend to list only the larger logistics service providers; and there are a number of excellent regional or local firms that do not appear in some of them at all.

In summary, identification of providers is the point in the process where due diligence starts to become critical. Before a contact can be made or a Request for Proposal or Request for Information issued, it is absolutely vital to have a clear understanding of the available providers, the services they offer, and their suitability for your needs.

Chapter 6

Selecting a Provider

| WE'RE OUTSOURCING HALF OF OUR PRO-GRAMMING WORK TO ELBONIA TO TAKE ADVANTAGE OF THE TIME DIFFERENCE. | WE'LL HAND OFF OUR REQUIREMENTS AT THE END OF OUR WORK DAY AND GET BACK THE FINISHED CODE THE NEXT MORNING. | ONCE AGAIN, I HAVE NO IDEA WHAT THEY WANT. LET'S PRETEND WE DIED. |

DILBERT reprinted by permission of United Feature Syndicate, Inc.

Once the firm has established what functions it wishes to outsource, has developed a strategy for doing so, and has identified potential providers; it is time to begin the evaluation and selection process.

Whether you are going to engage in a simple transactional arrangement, work toward a partnership solution through a Request For Information, or move directly to a Request For Proposal, it is important to first establish the selection criteria.

These should encompass those strategic, tactical, and operational requirements that are critical to the company. While specific standards will vary with the outsourcing firm's unique needs, as well as the functions that are being outsourced, there are basic benchmarks that will be applicable to most arrangements.

Selection Criteria

Financial Stability

With the unprecedented bankruptcies and fiscal irresponsibility of several large U.S. firms, companies contemplating outsourcing have become more concerned about the financial health of logistics service providers. While not as widely publicized as the Enron, Tyco, and WorldCom problems, the third party industry has seen its share of financial difficulties. Many of today's outsourcing contracts are quite large, and firms are finding, sometimes the hard way, that some providers simply do not have adequate financial resources.

There have been several conspicuous failures within the logistics service provider industry; and while most LSP's are fiscally sound, well-managed businesses, these occurrences do demonstrate the importance of thorough financial diligence in selecting a provider.

This can be a relatively straightforward matter if you need to investigate a provider that is publicly held. Readily available financial statements will reveal any concerns. On the other hand, many providers are privately held and there is a reluctance, if not absolute refusal, on the part of many owners to reveal financial information.

The cost of an outsourcing start-up can be quite high, particularly in the information technology area. The value of many of the products being handled is quite high as well; and an undercapitalized provider can find itself in trouble very quickly.

It is absolutely critical that the outsourcing firm satisfy itself of the provider's financial stability before a contract is signed. Some providers will furnish serious prospects with audited financial statements before the final agreement, and every year thereafter. Others provide banking information which sometimes can be helpful, but not always an absolute indicator of financial health. Many times, the bank will reveal only vague details, none of which guarantee a sound financial base.

While there will always be *some* risk in outsourcing, there are a number of steps that can be taken to minimize an outsourcing firm's financial exposure.

(1) Insist on inspecting audited financial statements. Examine profit and loss statements and balance sheets for such things as net income, net worth, debt load, etc.

(2) Make sure the statements are examined by qualified financial personnel of the prospective client. Sometimes a well-meaning logistics manager will overlook important clues.

(3) Investigate the reputation of the auditing firm used by the provider.

(4) If funds are to be advanced, such as in the freight payment business, be sure that funds are not co-mingled. Also find out what types of investments are made (with your money) by the provider.

(5) Determine if bond coverage is available. If so, make sure that bonds adequately cover the risks. Some coverage, for instance, applies only in the event of theft or conversion.

(6) Explore the possibility of establishing minimum limits on financial assets. In other words, an outsourcing firm may decide it will not enter into a relationship with a provider that does not meet a certain net worth threshold.

(7) Consider the possibility of awarding contracts only if the total value of the contract is below a certain percentage of the provider's total revenue. An LSP should not be too reliant on one or two clients.

Some of this information will be provided reluctantly, but the prospective client must persist until satisfied. If a provider is financially healthy, responsible, and capable of handling the business, it will find a satisfactory method of demonstrating this to the outsourcing firm.

Whatever methods are used, thorough financial due diligence must be at the top of the list when qualifying potential providers. Financial stability must be confirmed and regular audits conducted. References should be checked carefully. Supply chain initiatives are complex and expensive and should be considered with the same care as any other large financial transaction of a firm.

Business Experience

Experience in providing logistics services in general, as well as in the client's industry, are extremely important. The provider must be well grounded in the services being provided (i.e., transportation, information technology, warehousing, order fulfillment, etc.) and ideally will have experience in the client's own industry.

While the latter is not absolutely essential, the provider must be able to demonstrate that the skills it does possess can be transferred with reasonable dispatch and efficiency.

If a start-up firm is selected, the client must be prepared to provide considerable resources during the start up and learning cycles. This can be particularly risky if the outsourcing company is contracting for services with which they themselves have had difficulty or lacked resources to manage efficiently.

Management Depth and Strength

When outsourcing it is important to remember that one of the products being purchased is expertise in providing the particular services. The logistics service provider must have a strong, skilled organization, as well as adequate, qualified management.

"Bench strength" is a problem for some providers, and it is critical that the client have a clear understanding of the management and labor force that will be devoted to the relationship. If at all possible, the potential client should be introduced to the manager with whom it will be working. If this person is not yet in the organization, the client should ask to be a part of the selection process.

One should be cautious of chief executive officers that indicate they will be *personally* responsible for the operation. That simply is not going to happen.

Reputation With Other Clients

The best substitute for personal experience is that of other customers and clients. The provider should be asked to provide a client list with contacts and telephone numbers.

A sufficient number of these – at least five – should be contacted to satisfy the outsourcing firm that it has a good cross section of performance. The potential client should choose the ones to be contacted, and should be wary of a limited number of references already pre-determined by the provider. The outsourcing firm also should request the names of former clients. Often, conversations with companies who have discontinued the use of the provider can be very revealing.

When talking with other clients, it is important to determine if the provider simply does well what they are told or if they are proactive and have a commitment to continuous improvements in performance and customer satisfaction.

Strategic Direction

Just as the outsourcer should have a strategy, so should the provider. Many do not, and still others seem to have a planning horizon of one afternoon. Granted, the logistics strategy of the client and the provider eventually should be one and the same, but the well-managed service firm is one that will have some sense of its own goals and objectives, as well. It should be well grounded in its current activities, but also have a strategy for expanding and improving on these. It should have commitment and direction.

Ackerman suggests that at a minimum, a provider should have asked itself five questions; i.e., [1]

(1) What business are we really in?

(2) Who is our preferred customer(s)?

(3) What do our customers think of us?

(4) What is our special magic?

(5) How will we survive?

Answering these basic questions will go a long way toward the provider's achieving the direction necessary to attract clients. In the selection process, the outsourcing firm should satisfy itself that the provider has the answers to most, if not all, of these questions.

Physical Facilities and Equipment

It goes without saying that the physical facilities must be sufficient to support the outsourced activity.

Warehouses should be clean and well lit with ceilings high enough to allow for extensive racking when required. Loading and unloading facilities should be adequate for the operation, and other unique operating characteristics should be provided for. For example, the ideal building for a cross-dock operation is quite different from the most efficient order fulfillment facility.

A food grade warehouse has still a different set of unique standards.

Warehouse and transportation equipment should be clean, painted, and well maintained. Regular preventive maintenance and replacement policies should be in place.

Operations

A careful evaluation of the provider's current operations will be required. Some of the necessary information will come out of discussions with other clients, but there will be no substitute for an in-depth operations and productivity assessment by a qualified individual or team.

This evaluation should include not only the basic physical operations, but also such things as safety, security, commitment to best practices, housekeeping, attention to detail, human resource practices, and quality of procedures manuals.

Information Technology

In any logistics operation, state-of-the-art systems are critical; and in such specialized areas as cross docking, order fulfillment, and freight bill payment they are an absolute necessity.

Any involvement with electronic commerce will require systems much more sophisticated than those usually available from most logistics service providers. State-of-the-art order processing systems, including such functions as the ability to verify credit cards, will be a must.

The evaluation of information technology assets will require knowledgeable experts in the field and should include such areas as hardware, software, operating systems, bar coding, imaging, handheld devices, sensor-based systems, satellite and other tracking systems, and internet access. Very important will be an understanding of, and compatibility with, various ERP systems.

To some outsourcing firms, Radio Frequency Identification (RFID) will be important. If so, the providers' capabilities in this technology should be explored carefully. As an increasing number of retailers are requiring RFID tags on cases and pallets, warehouse companies in particular will need the resources and capabilities to apply this technology efficiently.

The technology is not without controversy. Wal-Mart considers it to be the biggest supply chain breakthrough since the barcode.

Consumers Against Supermarket Privacy Invasion and Numbering (CASPIAN), on the other hand, sees the implementation of RFID as something far more ominous. The group and other privacy advocates view the practice of tagging pallets and cases as a step down the road toward the wholesale embedding of tiny RFID chips into individual consumer products – chips capable of transmitting information to anyone with a reader without your consent. They see endless possibilities for misuse of the technology in the future – whether it's a corporation snooping into your buying habits, a thief finding out what's in the trunk of your car (and its value), or a government tracking your whereabouts.

The fears, of course, are somewhat similar to the ones about the barcode when it was first introduced. Today, this technology saves the food industry alone $17 billion annually.

Since the use of RFID tags is sure to increase, it will be important to understand provider capabilities in this area.

Replacement and developmental budgets and schedules should be in place, and the entire IT function should be supported by sufficient, qualified staff.

Information technology requires substantial capital and expertise, and some logistics service providers have not been particularly strong in these areas. Just as with the financial analysis, investigation of these capabilities may be tedious, but it is absolutely necessary.

The procurement of warehouse and transportation management systems, as well as other supply chain management systems, will require a much more thorough analysis and process. This will be discussed later in the chapter.

Continuous Improvement Programs

The progressive logistics service provider usually will have a formal quality or continuous improvement program. Some may be ISO certified, while others may have lesser, but meaningful, programs in place.

It is absolutely critical that the provider selected must be one who is committed to ongoing performance enhancement, and has an identified procedure for accomplishing this. The RFI should require a detailed description of the programs in place.

Growth Potential

Most firms project ongoing growth through volume increases, new products, or new markets; and it is important for the logistics service provider to be in a position to support that growth.

While there probably will not be excess capacity immediately available, the selected provider should be in a position to provide that capacity or new services over a short or long term, depending on client requirements.

Security

While security is not a new issue in outsourcing, in the past it has not always received the attention it should have. Before September 11, 2001, and subsequent events, the prospects of terrorist attacks and workplace violence seemed so remote that very little thought was given to them. Now in addition to the risk of theft and pilferage we have a much greater need to secure our supply chain and products.

Most companies have adopted more stringent security standards; and when considering a logistics service provider, it is imperative that it be in a position to secure facilities, equipment, products and people as well or better than the outsourcing firm.

Information systems must be fully protected from outsiders, and information technology personnel should ensure that all necessary log-ins, passwords, and firewalls are in place.

The securing of a facility is a little more difficult to deal with. While no manager can eliminate the risks to a facility, its contents and its people, there are steps that a provider should take to minimize risk as much as possible.

Security begins at the property line. Ideally, a distribution center is a totally fenced environment with guard service to check all vehicles and persons entering of leaving the property. When this is not possible, there should be adequate lighting and a network of closed circuit television cameras that will provide a clear view of the perimeter of all buildings. Cameras should be monitored 24 hours a day, seven days a week. There should be no parking against the building except in the shipping and receiving areas: It does little good to have a clear line of sight around a building when it is blocked by cars and trucks.

When there is no guard, every vehicle or person entering the property should check in with a live person or video system. It is important to see the individuals – not just hear their voices.

Ideally, closed circuit television cameras will be used inside the facility, as well. Beyond that, all building doors, including those to the offices, should be locked. There are any number of key card and PIN number systems that will ensure that only those who are authorized to enter the buildings can do so. Truck drivers, of course, will not have the necessary identification and/or information and should be allowed entry through a limited number of doors that open into a confined area. Here they should be registered and given only limited access to the facility.

No receiving or shipping door should be left open at any time unless an appropriate distribution center employee is on hand.

If the facility handles unusually expensive or vulnerable products, these should be kept in caged areas within the building with access carefully monitored.

Securing a facility against outside intruders is relatively easy compared to protecting a facility from the enemy within, however. In many areas, distribution center labor is scarce; and companies are forced to hire personnel they might otherwise reject.

New employees should be screened carefully. A surprising number of companies do not perform background checks because of the expense involved. Yet this expense is negligible if it prevents even one problem; and this is quite likely, considering that 40 percent of all warehouse thefts are committed by employees.

Every prospective employee should have both a drug test and a background check; and in today's environment, integrity testing is strongly recommended, as well. These tests, administered by companies like Reid Psychological Systems and London House, screen for honesty, attitudes toward customer service, risk of drug and alcohol use, and more. The tests are in full compliance with all federal and state discrimination laws.

Finally, managers should be trained to recognize unusual or dangerous behavior. Deterioration in attendance, work habits and relationships all are warning signs and should be dealt with appropriately.

There is no fail-safe method for protection of property, products and personnel by a logistics service provider; but a well-implemented and -managed security program, thoughtful and careful hiring practices, management training, and good common sense will go a long way toward minimizing risks and increasing client confidence.

Chemistry and Compatibility

For over two thousand years, the Chinese have practiced the tradition of *Feng Shui*. Meaning literally wind and water, it is about being in harmony with one's surroundings and relationships. Although usually considered in more physical terms such as placement of structures and landscaping, its ultimate goal is to exist in a harmonious environment.

This is the same goal for which we should strive in outsourcing relationships. While business decisions should be made on the basis of hard facts and figures, decision-makers are human and should not ignore human instincts.

Just as marriage partners should be chosen with care, so should logistics partners. Instincts and impressions should be heeded; and if personal chemistry and compatibility are a concern at the outset, more often than not, the situation will not improve over time.

In ancient Chinese proverbial terms, "Raise the head and observe the sky above. Lower the head and observe the environment around us."

Ethics

It is an unfortunate sign of the times that we must check the moral fiber of the people and firms with which we deal. But when one looks at the actions of Enron, WorldCom, J.P. Morgan, Arthur Andersen, and other former pillars of American business, it is clear that firms must be extremely careful about the providers they deal with.

Some of the large providers will have formal ethics policies. Exel, for example, publishes its code of ethics right on its website. Other smaller providers may not have such formal written policies, but they should at least have some code of ethics for their employees. This does not necessarily have to be a written policy as much as a state of mind. In the words of Mason Cooley,

"Reading about ethics is about as likely to improve one's behavior as reading about sports is to make one into an athlete." [2]

An example of an ethical compliance audit is shown in Figure 6-a. The careful outsourcing firm will want to explore most, if not all, of these questions with the prospective providers.

Cost

While it should not necessarily be last in importance, neither should cost be the first and foremost consideration. While it must be considered in the selection process, it should be a factor only in deciding among firms that meet all the other criteria.

The manager who selects a provider solely on the basis of cost has committed to an outsourcing strategy that will have little chance of success.

Methodology

Once the criteria for selection have been agreed upon, they should be used by the outsourcing team in the evaluation of the various proposals. To facilitate this evaluation and conduct it in a more scientific and quantifiable way, the various factors should be weighted according to their importance.

By giving a numerical value to each, and rating them accordingly, a mathematical result can be determined for each provider being considered. Figure 6-b illustrates a form that may be used for the evaluation.

Request For Information

At this point, some firms will choose to move directly to a Request For Proposal which will be sent to prospective providers. As discussed in a previous chapter, however, a preferable approach is to develop a Request For Information which can be used to qualify firms for later receipt of the final RFP.

SUPPLIER ETHICAL COMPLIANCE AUDIT [3]

Yes	No		
☐	☐	1.	Does the company have a code of ethics that is reasonably capable of preventing misconduct?
☐	☐	2.	Is there a person with high managerial authority responsible for an ethical compliance program?
☐	☐	3.	Are there mechanisms in place to avoid delegating authority to individuals with a propensity for misconduct?
☐	☐	4.	Does the organization have effective communication of standards and procedures via ethics training programs for its employees?
☐	☐	5.	Does the organization communicate its ethical standards to suppliers, customers, and significant others that have a relationship with the organization?
☐	☐	6.	Do the company's manuals and written documents guiding operations contain ethics messages about appropriate behavior?
☐	☐	7.	Is there formal or informal communication within the organization about procedures and activities that are considered acceptable ethical behavior?
☐	☐	8.	Does top management have a mechanism to detect ethical issues relating to employees, customers, the community, and society?
☐	☐	9.	Is there a system for employees to report unethical behavior?
☐	☐	10.	Is there consistent enforcement of standards and punishments in the organization?
☐	☐	11.	Is there an ethics committee, department, team, or group that deals with ethical issues in the organization?
☐	☐	12.	Is there an attempt to provide continuous improvement of the ethical compliance program with the organization?

Figure 6-a: Ethical Compliance Audit

LOGISTICS SERVICE PROVIDER
EVALUATION SUMMARY

5 = Highest
I = Lowest

Criteria	Weight	Provider Scores		
		A	**B**	**C**
Financial Stability				
Business Experience				
Management Depth and Strength				
Reputation with Other Clients				
Strategic Direction				
Physical Facilities and Equipment				
Operations				
Information Technology				
Quality Initiatives				
Growth Potential				
Security				
Chemistry and Compatibility				
Cost				
Total	**100.0%**			

Figure 6-b: Evaluation of Potential Logistics Service Providers

The RFI also can be used to identify providers that can be helpful in the planning and design stages of the logistics arrangement, before making a final selection. The RFI will contain most of the information that would be sought in the RFP. It simply will not be as specific about the scope of work and will not request pricing.

The number of firms contacted will vary with the number of available companies identified; but generally speaking, RFI's should be sent to at least ten potential providers. Some may choose not to respond, and with others, it will be clear at the outset that they are not qualified. The goal of the RFI should be to identify at least three potential candidates.

Unfortunately, this RFI/RFP process is subject to a considerable amount of abuse within the industry. Often a firm will ask a provider to expend valuable time and resources in developing information for projects that are not being considered seriously. In some cases a firm may want to benchmark internal operations. In others, they will simply be going through an internally required competitive survey. In these instances, it is far more professional to simply ask a provider to assist you in whatever it is you are trying to accomplish. Deliberately misleading them may come back to haunt you later.

It is recommended that a "Notice of Intent to Respond" be included with the RFI. As shown in Figure 6-c, it simply asks the provider to indicate if it intends to respond. This will let the outsourcing firm know at the outset how many responses it will get, and from whom.

As with an RFP, the RFI should be clear and concise and provide for responses in a pre-determined format. The format should be designed in a manner that facilitates the evaluation of the criteria already identified.

At a minimum, it should contain the following.

Confidential
Request for Information (RFI)

INTENT TO RESPOND
to
Request for Information (RFI)
For

_____

RESPONDENTS ARE TO COMPLETE AND RETURN THIS FORM BY
NO LATER THAN ___(time)___, ON ___(date)___

If you intend to submit a proposal to this RFI, you must deliver a written notice of such intent to _(recipient)_ of _(company)_ by no later than _(time)_ _(date)_. _(company)_ may reject the proposal of any prospective provider who does not submit this form by the aforementioned date and time.

Please provide the following information:

Company Name:

_____

Authorized Representative (Name and Title):

_____

Circle One

Intent to Respond (Submit a Proposal): Yes No

| **If yes, you will submit a proposal for:** | a) ___ | ___ | ___ |
| **(itemize services: a, b, etc.)** | b) ___ | ___ | ___ |

Signature: _____

Telephone: _____

Return this completed form via fax or electronic mail to:

If you choose not to respond, please return the RFI in its entirety to the aforementioned name and address. Thank you in advance for your cooperation.

6-c: Notice of Intent to Respond to Request for Information

Background Information About Outsourcing Company

This section should describe the outsourcing firm and its basic businesses. It should include a general description of products manufactured or distributed, annual revenues, methods of distribution, and other helpful information, such as mission statements, numbers of facilities, and numbers of employees.

If publicly held, one effective method of providing such information is through the inclusion of the firm's most recent annual report with appropriate information highlighted.

Purpose of the Request For Information

This is simply the reason for the request. The objectives of the process should be described. This section should explain in detail what the outsourcing firm hopes to accomplish.

Scope of the Project

Here the specific activity or activities should be described, again in general terms. The overview should include enough detail for the providers to understand the magnitude of the project, but need not include a detailed scope of work; i.e., shipments by product line, line items per order, etc.

Project Schedule

The firm should set forth the timetable of the project, including due dates, as well as the schedules for notification and further decisions, including estimated start-up dates.

Too often, insufficient time is allowed to conduct the outsourcing process efficiently. A reasonable timeline for RFI's and their evaluation is:

Responses Due	4 weeks
Evaluation	3 weeks

Oral Presentations and Site Visits   3 weeks

From this point the times would vary depending on whether the outsourcing model is developed jointly or an RFP is issued. It is important, however, to allow ample time in the early stages of the process.

Evaluation Criteria

Evaluation criteria should be listed and explained clearly so the provider will know by what benchmarks it will be evaluated.

Response Guidelines

This section should describe the format for responses. Hard copies or electronic formats, or both may be requested.

Rules for making oral presentations, if required, should be presented here.

Respondent Qualifications

Keeping in mind the evaluation criteria, this next section should request specific information about the provider. Since every outsourcing arrangement will be different, as will its information needs, it is difficult to outline a precise list of the questions that should be asked; but the RFI should at least contain the following inquiries.

- What is your basic business?
- What services do you provide?
- When was the company founded?
- Is the company public or private? If public, please provide copy of latest annual report.
- If there is a parent organization, describe the relationship of businesses and strategies.

- Please provide the most recent three years' statements of profit and loss and cash flow, as well as balance sheets.
- Describe projected annual growth for the next three years. What will be the source?
- Describe strategies to be pursued in achieving this growth.
- Discuss your long- and short-term business visions.
- Provide resumes of key managers and charts for the remainder of the organization.
- Describe staffing policies for new account start-ups.
- What is your overall approach to the management of ongoing relationships?
- What is your annual employee turnover?
- Describe physical facilities and assets; i.e., square footage, tractors, trailers, etc.
- Describe your information technology platform, hardware, software, and operating systems. Recount your experience with ERP systems and clients utilizing SAP, etc.
- Describe your IT staff including development, integration, operation and support personnel.
- How would you organize your systems and staff to meet our needs?
- What percentage of your total revenue is accounted for by your largest client?
- Please provide names, contacts and telephone numbers for five largest clients.
- How do you measure performance of your operations and report it to clients?
- How do you handle client communications? How often?
- Have you had a contract terminated in the last three years? If so, why? May we contact the client for more detail?
- Describe in detail your approach to ethics, security, risk management and disaster recovery.
- Describe your quality and process improvement programs. Are you ISO certified?

- Provide an example where you have helped a client achieve benefits through your continuous improvement program.

As mentioned in Chapter 3, freight bill payment, while not the most important outsourced logistics function, can involve a considerable amount of a firm's funds, and it will be important to ask some additional questions. [4]

Financial Stability
- Is an audited financial statement available?
- What is the net worth (financial strength) of the firm?
- What is the net income of the firm?
- What types of external (independent) audits are performed on the outsourcing firm? What type of risk coverage is provided?
- Is the company public or private?
- Is it part of a financial institution?
- What type of fiduciary responsibility and protection are provided?
- Is a third party operations audit available?

Customer Support
- Are individual account representatives assigned to your company?
- Is there a planned customer calling program in place?
- Is a formal inquiry response system used to insure follow-up to all calls?
- Are all inquiries documented?
- Is there a dedicated EDI implementation group?
- Is there a dedicated support staff to handle vendor inquiries?
- Are there Internet and automated telephone inquiry capabilities available?

Quality Control
- Is there a formal, written quality control program in place?

- Is there a quality tracking program in place to ensure proactive processing?
- What types of employee training programs are in place?
- Does the firm conduct customer surveys and vendor surveys? How Often?
- Does this firm have a documented customer relations management process?

Technology
- Is the firm using the latest hardware and software technology?
- What are the future plans for handling data processing requirements?
- Can the firm handle all forms of electronic commerce?
- Does the firm handle all EDI standards as well as proprietary EDI formats?
- Does the firm have a separate EDI implementation staff?
- Can information be accessed via the Internet?
- Are Internet database applications available?
- What is the size of the information technology support staff?
- Is there a formal disaster recovery plan in place?

Other Considerations
- What is the depth of the management staff?
- Is there a dependence on key staff members?
- What is the experience of the staff?
- What is the stability and quality of the workforce?
- How many years has the company been in business?
- Who are the firm's client base?
- What is the outsourcing firm's vision for the future?

Figure 6-d is an example of a form that could be included in the RFI document. It is important to remember, however, that each client's needs are unique and information requests should be customized.

LOGISTICS SERVICE PROVIDER PROFILE

Company Name	
Address	
Phone	
Fax	
Parent Company	
Subsidiaries	

STAFF CONTACT(S)

Name	Title

ABOUT THE COMPANY

Years in Logistics Operations	
Last Full Year's Revenue	
Number of Employees	
Do You Hold ISO 9000 Certification?	
Do You Hold a Property Broker's License?	

Is your company Union _____ or Non-Union ___
Is your company Private ___ or Public _____

MARKETS SERVICED

Domestic		North America	
National		Other International	
Regional			

MAJOR CUSTOMERS

Customer	Location(s)

Figure 6-d: Example of Logistics Service Provider Profile Questionnaire

107

PRIMARY SERVICES PROVIDED
(Check All Services Your Company Provides)

Supply Chain Management Services

Analysis & Design Model		Process Reengineering	
Consolidation & Pool Distribution		Purchasing	
Consumer Response		Reverse Logistics/Returns Management	
Customized Store Displays		Shipment Consolidation	
Distribution Analysis		Supply Management	
Inventory Management		Telemarketing	
JIT		Other	
Market Research			
Private Fleet Conversion			

Warehousing Services

Cost Accounting		Pick & Pack	
Cross-Docking		Product Assembly/Sub-Assembly	
Distribution		Re-packaging	
Inventory Reporting		Sequencing	
Kitting		Shrink Wrapping	
Labeling		Storage	
Order Fulfillment/Processing		Warehouse Management	
Packaging		Other	
Pooling			
Number of Warehouses			
Total Square Footage			

Information Technology Services

Bar Coding		Route Optimization	
EDI		Satellite Communications	
Entire Supply Chain Management		Vehicle Tracking	
Internet		TMS	
WMS		Other	

Figure 6-d (continued)

Transportation Services

Air Freight Forwarder		Less-Than-Truckload Carrier	
Break Bulk		National Dispatch Service – Elec.	
Carrier Select'n & Perf'mnce Eval.		National Dispatch Service – Man.	
Courier		Ocean Freight Forwarder	
Dedicated Contract Carriage		Parcel Carrier	
Direct Store Delivery		Property Broker – Exempt	
Drayage		Property Broker – Non-Exempt	
Expedited Services		Rate Negotiation	
Fleet Management Operations		Rating & Routing	
Fleet Safety Compliance		Surface Freight Forwarder	
Freight Classification Services		Tracking & Tracing	
General Commodities		Traffic Management Services	
Household Goods		Transportation Quality Mgmt.	
Intermodal Marketing Company		Truckload Carrier (TL)	
International Freight Forwarder		Other	
Leasing			
Drivers			
Equipment			
Number of Tractor Units in Dedicated Contract Carriage			

Types of Trailers

Auto		Liquid	
Chemical		Refrigerated	
Dry Van		Tankers	
Flatbeds		Other	
Hazmat			

International Services

Billing Practices		NAFTA Consulting Services	
Booking		Security Policies	
Brokerage Transactions		Shipment Status	
Clearance Information		Track and Trace	
Compliance with Government Regulations		Trade Compliance	
Document Generation		VMI	
Import/Export Customs		Other	

Information Management Services

Claims Resolution		Inventory Controls	
Distribution Modeling		MRP (Matls. Requmnts. Planng.)	
DRP (Dist'n. Resource Planning)		Order Entry	
EDI Analysis/Implementation		Order Processing	
Freight Audit/Payment		Performance Measures	
Freight Consolidation		Sales Forecasting	
Inbound		Supporting Financial	
Outbound		Vehicle Routing/Scheduling	
Information Systems		Other	

Figure 6-d (continued)

Other Requirements

Any other special requirements that might influence the provider's response should be included. One example might be the inclusion of minority contractor or supplier information requirements. If there is such a requirement, the definitions should be clear to avoid misunderstandings.

One format for clarifying this is as follows.

Provider Profile – select the group that best defines your company.

(See Definitions Below)
_____ Woman Owned Business
_____ Minority Owned Business (Please indicate status
below)
_____ African American
_____ Asian/Pacific American
_____ Hispanic American

If you are a minority/woman owned business, are you certified as such by an independent third party?
_____ Yes _____ No
If yes, please name the certifying agency:

_____

Effective 7/1/99, if a company does business with the Federal Government, it must be certified by the Small Business Administration or a designated agency.

Definitions

Minority Owned Business:

A business enterprise that is at least 51% owned, controlled, and operated on a day-to-day basis by one or more minority individuals.

The term "minority" includes African Americans, Asian/Pacific Americans, Hispanic Americans, Native Americans, and other groups as identified by the United States Small Business Administration.

<u>Woman-Owned Business</u>:

A business enterprise that is at least 51% owned, controlled, and operated on a day-to-day basis by one or more <u>Caucasian</u> women.

(Note: A woman-owned firm where the woman is also a minority should be classified as a minority owned business above.)

Confidentiality

The RFI should contain language indicating that the information received will be held in confidence and not divulged without prior written consent.

It also should have attached to it a confidentiality agreement to be executed by the respondent. It should provide confidentiality protection for the outsourcing firm should the respondent be selected to receive a formal Request For Proposal.

Evaluation

Once the responses have been received, they should be evaluated according to the established criteria. Using the rating sheets, the top three should be identified, notified and scheduled for oral presentation, as well as personal visits by the selection team.

Oral presentations often will reveal weaknesses, strengths, and provide other impressions not readily identifiable in the written responses.

Site Visits

There is no substitute for an in-depth inspection of the physical facilities and operations of the finalist providers, regardless of the activity being outsourced. These should be conducted by qualified members of the selection team or other internal or external experts brought in for the purpose.

With ready access to computer software and sophisticated graphics, almost anyone can generate an attractive, convincing document; but a thorough site examination by knowledgeable personnel will quickly reveal whether the physical facts support the salesmanship.

During these inspections, facilities, operations, management, information technology and other aspects of the business can be examined closely; and the written responses can be compared to the visual conclusions.

A careful audit of six basic areas usually will either confirm or contradict the choice of the provider as a finalist. Some of the major points of interest will be consistent throughout various industries and projects. Others should be added or deleted where individual interests and requirements dictate.

Buildings and Equipment

- Office area
  - ° Cleanliness and condition of carpeting, walls, ceiling tiles, furniture.
- Restrooms
  - ° Cleanliness and adequacy of supplies; posted inspection logs.
  - ° Hand washing signs posted?
- Heating, ventilation and air conditioning equipment.
  - ° Condition, operations, and maintenance.
- Exterior

- ○ Condition of walls, doors, windows, and gutters. Is paint or repair needed?
- ○ Condition of exterior signage and landscaping.
- ○ Condition and size of driveways, aprons, and parking lots.
- ○ Cleanliness of dock leveler pits, condition of rubber bumpers and dock shelters.
- ○ Evidence of trash or standing water. Adequate trash receptacles?
- ○ Condition of exterior sprinkler equipment.
- ○ Are products, pallets, racks, etc. stored outside building?
- Interior
  - ○ Condition and cleanliness of walls and ceilings.
  - ○ Adequate lighting? All fixtures equipped with full complement of bulbs?
  - ○ Condition of dock levelers.
  - ○ Presence and condition of dock locks.
  - ○ Sprinklered? Any evidence of leakage?
  - ○ Ventilation fans working properly?
  - ○ Condition of racking.
  - ○ Quality and condition of pallets.
  - ○ Empty pallets neatly stacked?
  - ○ Condition of floor. Is it sealed? Are there cracks or chipping?
  - ○ Floor striped?
  - ○ Bay locations and aisles clearly marked? Any encroachments?
  - ○ Condition of products in storage. Storage practices.
  - ○ Condition of forklifts and attachments.
  - ○ Condition and cleanliness of maintenance shop. Proper preventive maintenance scheduling and record keeping.
  - ○ Condition and cleanliness of tractors and trailers. Outside appearance.

    º   General housekeeping. Adequacy of trash receptacles.
    º   Presence of floor scrubber.

Sanitation, Safety, and Security

- Sanitation
  - º Condition of bait stations and traps. Is there a layout map?
  - º Presence and/or condition of eighteen inch sanitary stripe around inside perimeter.
  - º Is there an outside pest control service? Condition of reports and records.
  - º Are signs in place restricting smoking, eating, or drinking?
- Safety
  - º Are locations of first aid stations posted? Properly equipped?
  - º Each shift covered by person with CPR and first aid training?
  - º Is there blanket and stretcher?
  - º What is emergency vehicle response time?
  - º Are trailers chocked? Signs for drivers?
  - º Equipment operators trained and licensed? How are new operators trained?
  - º Drivers trained and licensed?
  - º Frequency of fire inspections.
  - º Evacuation plan current and posted?
  - º Condition of fire extinguishers. Date of last inspection.
  - º Are there evacuation drills?
  - º Riser valves open and locked?
- Security
  - º Type of security alarm used. Problems with false alarms.
  - º Use of closed circuit cameras.

    º   Procedures for non-employee visitors, truck drivers, etc., on entering/leaving building.

    º   Are all truck, rail, and pedestrian doors checked periodically?

    º   Are alarm pass cards given to necessary personnel only?

    º   Key control.

    º   Are locks changed when keyed employee leaves the company?

    º   Lighting.

Inventory Control

- Review procedures for processing receipts, shipments, damages.
- Review procedures for controlling held inventory.
- Adequacy of inventory control system. Changes needed?
- Performance, physical vs. book accuracy.
- Is product properly rotated?
- Adequate procedures for handling customer returns?
- Blind tallies utilized?
- Satisfactory locator system?

Information Technology

- Systems utilized. Applicability and performance. Order processing, credit card verification, etc.
- Backup performed? How often?
- Off-site storage of backup files?
- Disaster recovery plan existence. Dated?
- Are all systems documented?
- All installed software licensed?
- Compatibility with client systems.
- Fixed asset register available? Match with inventory?

- Proper use of surge protectors? Equipment properly grounded?
- Hardware clean and dusted?

Data Entry

- Working areas clean and well lit?
- Accuracy.
- Speed.
- Distractions, radios, headsets, etc.
- Output.

Management and Administration

- Organization chart. Are positions filled? Chart current?
- Background of senior managers.
- General attitude of management.
- Relationships with employees.
- Management style.
- Knowledge of industry and company.
- Reporting relationships.
- Decisions made at right level?
- Employee turnover, including managers.
- Ratio of supervisors to employees.
- Intended staffing.
- Method of hiring and training.
- How does manager allocate personal time?
- Perceived strengths and weaknesses.
- Performance evaluation program? What levels? Actually used? Inspect records.
- Strategic plans.
- Plans for growth with client.
- Attendance policy? Enforced?
- Cross training?
- Incentive programs for employees?

- In compliance with all government requirements?
- Condition of personnel records.
- Employee appearance.
- Employee knowledge of company's goals.
- Background checks performed?
- Integrity checks performed?

Some may argue that this is too much detail or that some of the evaluations are unnecessary. Indeed for some projects, this may be the case, but the outsourcing client should always keep in mind that present attitudes about such things as housekeeping, maintenance, and employee relations are indicators of performance in other areas. In other words, what you see is what you will get.

Remember the selection criteria. If the on-site inspections contradict the written responses, any differences should be resolved; and of course, if the two are clearly in too much conflict, it may be necessary to eliminate the provider altogether.

When the inspections are concluded, previous evaluations should be confirmed or clarified.

Requests For Proposal

General

After the finalist providers have been identified and notified, and have demonstrated an excitement about forming a relationship, they should be provided with all the information necessary to develop a process, plan, and cost structure. Typically, this is done through the final Request For Proposal.

At this point, however, some outsourcing firms simply will choose a provider and work with its management in developing the blueprint for the relationship and negotiate the cost later. The advantage to this approach is obvious, in that the service provider becomes a partner in the process early on, and can lend valuable expertise and experience in developing the solution.

The assumption is made that mutually satisfactory pricing can be agreed upon. If this proves not to be the case, the by then almost fully developed program can be presented to another provider. As a practical matter, however, by this time, the two parties should have had enough discussion to have a reasonable expectation of reaching agreement on fees.

If, however, the potential client believes an RFP is necessary, additional disclosure will be required once the necessary confidentiality agreements have been executed.

Most, if not all, of the required provider information will have been provided in the responses to the RFI, but it will be necessary to provide a more detailed scope of work and specific pricing request.

Scope of Work

The scope of work should provide specific information about the services to be provided and as much underlying detail and data as possible.

In the case of freight bill payment for example, it would be necessary to provide such information as:

- Number of freight bills summarized by mode of transport.
- Approximate number of carriers utilized.
- Average amount per freight bill.
- Total annual freight charges.
- Accessorial charge detail.
- EDI vs. manual bill receipts.
- Coding requirements.
- Reporting requirements
- Internet access requirements.

In the more physical functions such as warehousing and transportation, considerably more detail would be required. This would include, but not necessarily be limited to:

- Product characteristics, dimensions, case weights, stacking heights, perishability, volume, and any unique requirements.
- Methods of shipment and receipt.
- Number of orders, daily, weekly, annually, number of line items, methods of receipt, seasonality.
- Summary of truckload, less-than-truckload and small package shipments.
- Data and reporting needs.
- Customer names and locations.
- Special services to be performed.
- Security required.
- Space requirements.
- Special equipment required.
- Special documentation required.
- Inventory values and tallying requirements.
- Information technology requirements.
- Information management service requirements.

Basically, the outsourcing firm must relate to the prospective provider everything it knows about its business, products, shipments, and logistics processes. Obviously, this is much more difficult than it sounds; but it is absolutely necessary if the outsourcing arrangement is to be successful.

Before submitting its response, the provider should arrange for a visit to other locations where similar operations are conducted, either in-house or in the facility of another provider. Without this visual perspective it will be extremely difficult to digest the data and relate it to day-to-day operations.

Pricing

Finally, the RFP should contain a request for pricing. It should indicate how the fee structure is to be developed. Methods of pricing vary from industry to industry and firm to firm, and it is important that the provider understand exactly how pricing is to be submitted.

To a great extent, it will be determined by the type of contract into which the outsourcing firm wishes to enter; but whatever structure is desired, it is critical that the prospective provider have enough information to price the services intelligently.

In later chapters both costs and contracts will be discussed in considerable detail. At this point, it is sufficient to say that responses must be in consistent formats to facilitate comparisons of the costs of the various providers.

It should be noted here that if the outsourcing firm desires to conduct a formal Request For Proposal process without a Request For Information, the document should include all the information outlined herein for both documents.

Information Technology

Purchasing supply chain technology such as Warehouse and Transportation Management Systems will require a different and much more detailed process. The requirements will be much more technical and such factors as functionality and adaptability must be evaluated by IT personnel. The technology vendors usually will provide a template for the information they will need, but the average logistics manager must turn to more qualified colleagues for research, evaluation, and selection.

One well-known technology vendor, High Jump Software, provides an online RFP template for warehouse management systems. (See Appendix 6-1.) Vendor templates are available for other systems; i.e., TMS, etc., as well. These will serve as an informed blueprint for effective and successful technology outsourcing.

The two most important considerations in selecting an IT provider will be their stability and pricing structure. There have been a number of business failures in the software industry, and it will be critical to select a stable provider that will be around ten years from implementation.

Secondly, beware of low system sales prices and high maintenance fees. "The license price of an application is a onetime price. Maintenance you'll have to live with forever." [6]

Final Selection

When all proposals have been received, they should be re-evaluated using the same criteria, but adding the final variable of cost. Assuming nothing has changed with the other benchmarks, and all providers in the short list would be satisfactory choices, pricing may be the determining factor.

There may be times when there are only one or two clear choices of provider for the logistics problem at hand. If it is common knowledge that the service firm can offer a satisfactory solution, there really is no need to look further for the logistics system design. Price negotiation can come later.

A case in point involved Fender International, the international operation of Fender Musical Instruments. [5] Fender went directly to UPS Worldwide Logistics for assistance in revamping its supply chain operations in Africa, Europe, and the Middle East.

Before contacting UPS, Fender shipped to distributors in those countries via ocean container, with three to five months' lead time. This presented both demand forecasting and economic order quantity difficulties, and resulted in a generally unsatisfactory system.

Now UPS Worldwide Logistics manages inbound shipments to a distribution center in Roermond, The Netherlands, where products are inspected for quality, and distributor and dealer orders are filled.

Results have been dramatic with lead times reduced to three days rather than three months. In addition, customers can order exactly what they want. UPS WWL is even continuing the service of tuning and setting up guitars before shipment, an offering that has been a Fender hallmark.

Another example involved a division of Mercedes-Benz USA that provides high-end accessories. In 1999, the division was experiencing a variety of fulfillment issues; i.e.,

- Orders were not shipping on time and/or correctly.
- The backorder rate was extremely high.
- There was no good business intelligence on the movement of products.

MBUSA went to Connextions, a technology company providing web-based fulfillment and related supply chain management services; and together they developed a technology infrastructure that not only resolved the problems, but also enhanced performance significantly while reducing costs dramatically. [7]

Whether the ultimate selection is made through direct contact, an RFI/partnership approach or the formal RFP process, before a final decision is made, more presentations, visits, and negotiations may be necessary. Once this has been accomplished, however, the successful provider should be notified as quickly as possible.

While unforeseen delays can occur, the submission of proposals is expensive and time consuming; and all respondent providers should be treated with respect and sensitivity. If a provider is not the successful bidder, it should be communicated with promptly with an explanation of why it was not selected.

Conclusion

The selection process will require an inordinate amount of time and resources. Countless hours will be spent by the evaluation team in reading proposals, listening to presentations, visiting provider facilities, and meeting with other team members. On a number of occasions team members no doubt will want to skip a step or somehow shortcut the decision-making process.

The logistics manager or project champion must ensure that this does not happen. Absolute and total due diligence is imperative. The rewards for a successful outsourcing relationship can be great, but the price of failure can be high.

Chapter 7

Understanding and Evaluating the Cost of Outsourcing

It's better to do nothing with your money than something you don't understand.

- Suze Orman

While it has been suggested that cost should not be the primary consideration in selecting a logistics service provider, no one will argue that it is not an important factor in most decisions.

After the outsourcing firm has developed its own costs, it then must compare these with the projections of the providers submitting proposals, or at least those in which it has some interest. It is important, therefore, to understand the various methods of costing and pricing utilized by the providers and how they will impact on the contracting decision.

Warehousing Costs

While various warehouse-based providers use different techniques in pricing their services, generally they will separate their costs into three basic categories when developing proposals; i.e., *handling*, *storage*, and *customer service* or *administrative*.

Handling

Handling costs are those costs associated with the handling of the product from the time it arrives at the warehouse dock until it leaves the dock again for its final destination. Basically, they include labor, equipment, and miscellaneous expenses.

Labor expenses will include wages (straight time and overtime), fringe benefits (including such things as pensions, vacations, and sick leave), taxes, and any costs for training and education.

Equipment costs will consist of lift trucks, attachments, order pickers, pallet jacks, batteries, fuel, maintenance, and rental, if appropriate. If the equipment is owned by the provider, there will be factors for depreciation and interest charges.

The miscellaneous category can be a little more difficult to define, but should include only those non-labor or equipment costs that are associated with handling the product. For example, pallets would be included. Racks would not. Other miscellaneous costs might include supplies, warehouse and carrier damage recouping, waste disposal and demurrage and detention.

Obviously, if the provider is quoting on a new operation, all the cost projections will be based on estimates. Both labor and equipment costs will be impacted by such things as how product is received and/or shipped; i.e., truck, rail car, unitized or loose, the number of stock keeping units to be stored, and the number of line items per order. Inventory turnover rates of the various items or groups of items will have a direct relationship to travel time within the warehouse.

It will be important to both parties that the projected account profile be as accurate as possible to prevent errors in handling cost projections and subsequent disagreements over fees.

Storage

Storage costs will include all costs associated with the housing of the product. The space may be a portion of a building or an entire facility. Obviously, if a dedicated facility is involved, costs are easier to project since there will be no allocations, but the basic components will be the same. These expenses generally are categorized as facility, grounds, utilities, equipment, and service.

Facility costs include the lease or ownership expenses (rent or depreciation and interest), real estate taxes, insurance, and maintenance. Usually, maintenance costs will be separated by interior and exterior, but in both cases will include supplies, materials, equipment, labor, and repair. If a contract maintenance service is utilized, the cost will be charged to the building account, as will the cost of full-time building maintenance employees.

Grounds expenses will consist of landscaping maintenance, parking lot cleaning and repairs and such related services as snow removal and tree trimming. Where a building is shared by various tenants, they are charged a monthly fee for what is referred to as "common area maintenance," or "cam charges."

Utility costs such as gas and electric are considered to be storage expenses. Telephone costs are not.

Storage equipment would include such things as racks and bins; and costs for this category would be comprised of rent (or depreciation and interest) and maintenance, including parts and labor. Often, the maintenance costs will be combined with those for the building itself.

Service costs are comprised of those for sanitation and pest control, security and guard services, or any other expenses solely related to the building.

127

Administrative or Customer Service

The final broad category of costs for the provider covers the administrative expense. These are the expenses of the provider that are not included in the handling and storage accounts. Some providers refer to this entire category as customer service expenses; but while this has a pleasant connotation, it is not totally accurate.

Expenses in this group often are allocated to a number of clients and should be scrutinized carefully. The most important of these are salaries, office, and data processing costs.

Salaries include those for executives, marketing and sales personnel, and others not included in the direct labor category.

Office expenses will consist of rent or ownership costs for space and equipment, as well as expenditures for utilities, telephone, janitorial service, printing, postage, supplies, messenger services, and numerous other office related categories.

Data processing costs cover those for hardware, software, maintenance, lines, licenses, and other ancillary activities. These can be quite significant for the provider and the client; and some outsourcing firms may wish to install their own data processing systems either to achieve economies or ensure compatibility with in-house systems.

Warehouse management systems often are included in this category, but legitimately, could be included in storage costs, as well.

Other administrative costs include those for automobiles and such activities such as legal, consulting, marketing, advertising, dues, subscriptions, training, and travel. While these are legitimate costs of operating a logistics service business, the client should take care that it is not burdened with an inordinate share of these.

Once the logistics service provider has developed all its costs, it will include a desired margin of profit and prepare the fee proposal.

Fee Structures

While there are a number of fee structures the provider might suggest, the prospective client should indicate how it prefers to have the charges stated. As indicated in Chapter 6, to avoid misunderstanding, this should be made clear in the RFP. The outsourcing firm must be able to compare current and projected costs accurately and should specify the structure that will facilitate that.

The most common types of fee structures are *unit rates, cost plus percentage,* and *cost plus management fee.*

Unit Rates

Unit rates are quoted as a fixed amount of money per unit, such as cases, eaches, hundredweight, or unit loads.

The rate quoted usually is paid when the product is received, but covers the cost of moving the product in and out of storage and reshipping. Since this gives the provider the advantage of receiving the total revenue at the outset, the outsourcing firm may want to insist that handling costs be divided between inbound and outbound movements.

Storage may be included in the rate as well, but for most contract warehousing arrangements, it is recommended that these charges be handled separately. If a large portion of a building or an entire facility is utilized, it is recommended that the parties execute a separate lease agreement. This is discussed in more detail in Chapter 9.

In any event, the rate per unit structure is easy to use and understand, and the cost is easy to estimate since it is unaffected by volume.

As mentioned earlier, however, the projected profile is critical since significantly lower or higher volume than anticipated can have a major impact on both parties.

Cost Plus Percentage

This type of arrangement provides for reimbursement to the provider of all costs associated with the account, plus a margin calculated as a percentage of those costs. Sometimes referred to as an "open book contract," the disadvantage to the client is immediately obvious. There is no financial incentive for the provider to reduce costs or improve productivity.

While there are some advantages to the outsourcing firm such as the ability to scrutinize the provider's costs and efficiencies, this type of arrangement could be heavily biased in favor of the provider.

Cost Plus Management Fee

A much more desirable form of open book arrangement is the cost plus management fee arrangement. It is identical to the cost plus percentage agreement with the exception of one important factor. The management fee is stated as a flat charge per month or year and does not vary with cost.

This structure, of course, can encourage the provider to be more productive; but there is no method for sharing in the improvement, since the lower costs are simply passed on to the client, along with the set management fee.

The most effective use of a cost plus management fee arrangement is in conjunction with gain sharing provisions or incentive programs. Either method provides a stimulus to the provider to reduce costs and improve service and productivity, since there is a sharing of the benefits. Figure 7-a contains a comparison of the three structures, and they are discussed further in Chapters 9, 10, and 15.

Cost Comparison

The most difficult quantitative activity in the outsourcing process will be comparing the costs of current, in-house

	Unit Rate	Cost-Plus	Management Fee
ADVANTAGES	• Easy to use • Understood and familiar to most • Client's costs vary with volume • May be coupled with other approaches • May include volume guarantees • May be supplemented with incentives • Inherent incentive for vendor to be productive • May be adjusted to the volume level actually achieved	• Vendor profit is known and capped • No need to inflate rates for contingencies • Effective in start-up, when cost structure is uncertain • May be used in combination with other approaches • If vendor enhances productivity, benefits accrue to the client • Less risk to all parties vs. unit rate • Vendor does not suffer if volume, shipping/receiving patter, etc. are inaccurately estimated	• Reduces disagreements over separate charges, tasks and service levels • Provides incentives to enhance management productivity • Useful when "units" are difficult to define and when volume and shipping patterns are uncertain • Places a cap on vendor profits, and the level of profit and overhead is fixed and known
DISADVANTAGES	• Risks accrue to either client or vendor if volume and other factors are not as predicted • No inherent incentive to share productivity gains with client • Hard to use if the "unit" is difficult to define • Inflated to include risks of contingencies • May create disagreements over tasks, services and costs	• No built-in incentive to reduce costs and enhance productivity • Need some type of mechanism to monitor cost levels and establish reasonable cost benchmarks	• No built-in device for passing along productivity gains • May be difficult to determine the appropriate level of the fee • No incentive for the vendor to expand needed management/supervisory efforts • No build-in incentives to improve effectiveness (service level)

Figure 7-a: Comparison of Contract Warehousing Fee Structures. Reprinted with permission from "Contract Warehousing," prepared by the Warehousing Research Center for the Warehousing Education and Research Council, Oak Brook, Illinois; 1993

operations with those of a logistics service provider. Not all firms will have the luxury of activity-based costing, and the identification of all relevant costs will be difficult. Fixed, variable, direct or indirect, they must be included in the analysis as precisely as possible. Some allocations will be difficult to quantify, but they must not be ignored.

While each firm's chart of accounts will be different, Appendix 7-1 contains a suggested format for comparing the variable costs of an in-house warehousing operation with those of a logistics service provider. It can be modified to include or exclude accounts that are not applicable to individual situations.

Transportation Costs

Transportation rates are considerably more straightforward and almost always are quoted in cost per mile or per hundredweight. Unless a firm operates a private fleet, the cost comparisons for the most part will consist of comparing the charges of one carrier to those of another.

Most of the expenses associated with motor carriage are variable and vary directly with miles traveled. When developing rates, the carrier will consider its fixed costs such as general, administrative, and depreciation; its variable fuel, maintenance, insurance, and labor expenses; and the desired profit.

It must also consider the volume commitment by the shipper, the value of the commodities to be shipped, susceptibility to loss and damage, and its own traffic lanes.

If a firm is comparing the cost of operating its own fleet with that of a contract carrier, a more detailed analysis will be required. Usually, however, private trucking operations tend to be "free standing;" and costs are less difficult to capture.

Appendix 7-2 is a pro forma cost structure one firm uses to manage transportation expenses. This form, when completed, can be used to compare in-house and outside carrier costs.

Freight Bill Audit and Payment

The fee structures for freight bill auditing and payment are not as complicated as those for either warehousing or transportation. Separate charges are established for freight bills received manually and those received through electronic data interchange (EDI) since the level of processing labor required is different; and fees are levied for certain reports, as well as Internet access to data.

There is one unique aspect, however, that does not appear in the pricing for other logistics services. As discussed earlier, a portion of the provider's profit is derived from the use of client funds between the time they are received and the deposit of the check by the carrier. This "opportunity value" of funds, commonly called the float, can be significant to the provider particularly during periods of high interest rates. While this is a perfectly acceptable and common practice in the industry, it is important that the client understand the concept and its value.

Conclusion

Only the major costing concepts have been discussed here; and in practice, there will be different structures introduced for these and other services. Two important principles will apply, however, regardless of the services being outsourced or the charges therefore.

First of all, the RFI or RFP and subsequent profiles must be as accurate as possible. The quality of the fee structure established will be as good as the accuracy of the information provided.

The scope of work must be reviewed by both parties and each must have a reasonable level of confidence in the facts and figures it contains. Over the long term, everyone loses if key input is made incorrectly or is misunderstood. It goes without saying that the input should be honest, as well.

Secondly, in spite of everyone's best efforts, there will be inaccuracies. Information may not be available or may be

133

incomplete or vague. Assumptions may change, as can market conditions and trade characteristics. The outsourcing firm and the provider should be prepared for this, make allowances for such contingencies, and discuss them openly.

Contracts should provide for these adjustments; but most important, the client must be objective and realistic. Too often the provider hears the words, "I can't do anything about it now. We already are locked into our budget."

The mistake many outsourcing firms make is in trying to negotiate rates and charges to a level that inhibits the provider's ability to prove satisfactory service at a reasonable profit. These firms would do well to remember the adage, *Who pays well is served well*.

Outsourcing relationships must be based on mutual trust and respect. In no aspect of the arrangement is this truer than in the rate structure.

Chapter 8

Defining Expectations

The expectations of life depend upon diligence; the mechanic that would perfect his work must first sharpen his tools.

- Confucius

Once the costs associated with the outsourcing arrangement and the corresponding cost reductions or increases of the user firm have been clearly identified and understood, it is time to move to the next step in implementing the program. While at this point, the client may get pressure from the provider to enter into a contract, this is premature.

It is critical to have a clear understanding of expectations before an agreement is signed. Any number of outsourcing relationships have failed because of a client's unrealistic or misunderstood expectations. The fourth paragraph of this book stated that "lack of understanding on the part of both user and provider, more often than not, is the major cause of difficulty and failure in logistics outsourcing relationships."

This point cannot be emphasized too much. All too often, providers are asked to submit bids based on inadequate information regarding volumes, size of shipments, modes of transportation, seasonal variations, etc. Unfortunately, some firms do not have a clear understanding of what they are trying to outsource or have had difficulties providing the service in-house. In other instances, they have not been through the processes discussed in the earlier chapters, and are poorly prepared to even discuss an outsourcing relationship, let alone enter into one.

Finally, the cost of providing the service, especially in the area of information technology, often is underestimated or misunderstood.

In some instances, the logistics service provider, on the other hand, caught up in the enthusiasm surrounding a possible new client, even with inaccurate or incomplete information, will develop a cost structure for, and commit to, arrangements that do not reflect the reality of the situation. Once it develops greater knowledge and experience with the operation, the provider often finds it has made a decision it simply cannot live with.

To avoid this later confrontation, to the extent possible, expectations should be spelled out and defined precisely. At this juncture it is not necessary to develop all the policies and procedures that will apply to the operation. This is important and should be done, but only after the contract has been negotiated and the start-up is being planned. Expectations are not the "rules." They are the basis for the rules.

Expectations

Even if all policies and procedures are not in place, the expectations should not be defined in general terms, but within precise limits. Since failure to meet these can sometimes form a basis for terminating an agreement, many, if not all, of them should be incorporated by reference into the contract. It is therefore very important to have them agreed upon prior to negotiation of the final agreement. Examples of such expectations follow.

Productivity or Gain Sharing

If the client expects the provider to pass on savings through such things as productivity improvements, the concept and method of measurement must be clearly understood to avoid later disagreements. It will be important to include this in the contract or service agreement.

Service Requirements

While the outsourcing arrangement must remain fluid and dynamic, there will be certain "going in" service requirements. These can range from hours of operation such as 24/7 to percentage of orders shipped complete. They will vary by industry and activity, and could include the following or other similar measurements:

- Days and hours of operation.
- Percentage of orders shipped on time.
- Percentage of orders shipped complete.
- Total order cycle time.
- Emergency order handling.
- Customer communications.
- Invoicing.

Again, the requirements should be realistic, and allow some flexibility. If for example, the client controls inventory levels, it would be inappropriate to hold the provider responsible for out-of-stocks, unless it was due to failure to unload product or some other issue of non-performance.

Operations

Usually there will be certain basic operating requirements in such areas as:

- Productivity
- Warehouse damage
- Inventory variations
- Radio frequency scanning
- Proof of delivery
- Defining Expectations
- EDI
- Product recall systems
- Consolidation
- Claim handling
- Housekeeping and sanitation
- Security

These and other expectations should have established percentages or limits, but ones that allow a reasonable margin for error. While we should all strive for perfection, we must recognize that it still is beyond our mortal grasp.

Financial

When outsourcing an activity such as freight bill payment, financial issues become much more significant. The client will want to be very strict in such areas as

- Proper coding
- Correct auditing
- Payment according to client direction
- Accurate payment
- Reporting

While some margin of error should be provided for, measurements should be more restrictive than some of the other non-financial stipulations.

Defining expectations is a difficult part of the outsourcing process; and more often than not, the logistics provider will disagree with some of the required performance parameters. It would be very easy to move into a relationship based on vague requirements, but a responsible provider should not accept anything less than precise expectations. A responsible client will not ask them to do so.

Possible Points of Friction

Both the client and the provider will have some idea of friction points that may arise during the course of the relationship. There will be some surprises due to the uniqueness of the activity and other unforeseen circumstances, but there also will be some more or less predictable events.

Obviously, the first course of action is to identify and remove as many potential friction points as possible. Agree that certain things simply will not happen. This will eliminate some of the later disagreements, but certainly not all.

As elementary as it may sound, one excellent method of preparing for the inevitable is to play a "What If?" game. The involved firms should sit down together, ask the questions and jointly formulate the answers. It no doubt will be appropriate to include provisions in the contract for some of the more critical possibilities. For example, what if:

- the information provided to the provider turns out to be inaccurate or incomplete?
- either firm files for bankruptcy?
- either firm is acquired by another?
- there are major changes in the provider management structure?
- performance deteriorates?

- customer complaints exceed acceptable limits?
- expectations change or become unclear?
- severe personality, management, or cultural conflicts develop?
- the client falls behind in payment for services?
- the lead provider loses control over subcontractors?
- the provider lets its physical assets deteriorate?
- the provider begins to run an unsafe or unsanitary operation?
- the provider decides it must have an immediate rate increase?
- the arrangement simply does not work anymore?

This discussion is not intended to provide all the possible questions and, most assuredly, not all the possible answers. It is intended, however, to stimulate open thinking prior to the execution of the contract. A simple paragraph or two in the written agreement can save hours of disagreement at a later date.

For example, the client and provider may want to agree at the outset that if the account profile turns out to be significantly different than that on which the contract is based, parts of the agreement can be re-opened at the end of a pre-determined period.

Or, if service deteriorates to an unacceptable level, the contract can provide for the assumption of operational responsibility by the client or another provider.

Conclusion

Whether dealing with expectations or possible conflicts, clarity and honesty are the basic ingredients of a successful outsourcing relationship.

Expectations must be clearly defined and agreed upon. Potential friction points should be recognized where possible and steps taken to minimize their impact on the arrangement.

The ultimate objective should be to conduct the relationship on a business-like basis without the complicating factor of human emotion. When difficulties arise, emotions run high. A pre-determined course of action will go a long way toward keeping both business and personal relationships intact.

Chapter 9

Developing the Contract

He is a benefactor of mankind who contracts the great rules of life into short sentences that may be easily impressed on the memory, and so recur habitually to the mind.

- Samuel Johnson

By its very nature, a logistics outsourcing contract conflicts with the flexibility that is so necessary in the ever-changing marketplace. One popular logistics scholar defined a contract as a binding, legally enforceable agreement between two parties, but went on to say that if honorable people entered into a business agreement, they should not require a written contract. If, however, one of the parties is less than honorable, there could exist no written contract that would prevent abuse. [1]

Notwithstanding this, our society has become more litigious; and it is increasingly important to reduce our agreements to a written document. This is particularly true in logistics outsourcing where lack of clarification and understanding often cause difficulties.

It is therefore strongly recommended that any logistics outsourcing relationship be covered by a well-defined, legally sound contract, and that it be executed *before* the operation starts up. Surprisingly, there are clients that will ask a provider to begin operations before the agreement has been signed; and even more surprising is the fact that there are providers who will do it.

While in the past verbal representations and commitments often were reliable, the "my word is my bond" approach has become less dependable. There are a number of sobering anecdotes about both clients and providers that did not live up to their promises. Although to the maximum extent possible, flexibility and ability to change should be protected, a written contract is critical.

(Please note the author is not an attorney, and no legal advice, either implicit or explicit is intended. Logistics service contracts should be developed by qualified legal experts, but hopefully with input from a qualified logistics expert.)

Several types of contracts will be discussed, and sample agreements have been incorporated as appendices.

Public Warehousing Agreement

Perhaps the most basic type of logistics outsourcing contract is the standard public warehouse agreement. Traditionally, public warehouses have been used for fairly short periods of time to store excess inventories such as production overruns or promotional items. Some manufacturers, for example, might use public warehouses to store and distribute test market items. Whatever the purpose, in most instances, the agreements are for thirty days, renewable if necessary at the end of each month. This is in contrast to a contract warehouse arrangement which usually is for one or more years.

There are instances where the public warehouse contracts stay in place for years, usually when the client does not wish to make a long-term commitment or the project continues for longer than expected. However, this is not the typical usage.

A public warehouse contract is consummated when the warehouseman issues a rate proposal, and it is accepted and signed by the client. An example of such a contract is shown in Appendix 9-1. Some documents will not contain this much detail; but when in doubt, it is a good practice to err on the side of more information rather than less.

Storage and handling charges usually are quoted in cents per hundredweight or other units, with accessorial charges shown separately.

The standard terms and conditions approved and promulgated by the International Warehouse Logistics Association are incorporated by virtually all public warehousemen in the country. When entering into the public warehouse contract, the user firm should pay particular attention to Section 11 of the standard terms and conditions. The language is as follows:

Liability and Limitation of Damages – Sec. 11

(a) *The Warehouseman shall not be liable for any loss or injury to goods stored however caused unless such loss or injury resulted from the failure by the warehouseman to exercise such care in regard to them as a reasonable careful man would exercise under like circumstances and warehouseman is not liable for damages which could not have been avoided by the exercise of such care.*

(b) *Goods are not insured by the warehouseman against loss or injury however caused.*

(c) *The Depositor declares that damages are limited to _____, provided, however, that such liability may at the time of acceptance of this contract as provided in Section 1 be increased upon Depositor's written request on part or all of the goods hereunder in which event an additional monthly charge will be made based upon such increased valuation.*

145

(d) Where loss or injury occurs to stored goods, for which the warehouseman is not liable, the Depositor shall be responsible for the cost of removing and disposing of such goods and the cost of any environmental clean up and site remediation resulting from the loss or injury to the goods.

Often there is a misunderstanding about the liability of the warehouseman for the goods on deposit. Under the Uniform Commercial Code he is bound only by the prudent man rule outlined in Section 11(a). He can neither reduce nor increase his level of responsibility. The UCC prohibits a reduction in liability, and the warehouseman that commits to increased responsibility jeopardizes his own warehouse legal liability protection.

The outsourcing firm also should be sure it is in agreement with the damage limitation shown in Section 11(c) in the event there is some liability on the part of the warehouse.

The safest course of action is to make certain that products are adequately covered by the client's own insurance.

Contract Warehousing

If the outsourcing firm intends to enter into a longer-term arrangement which requires allocated space in a facility or even an entire building, it usually executes what is commonly called a contract warehouse agreement. Speh has defined contract warehousing as "a long-term, mutually beneficial arrangement which provides unique and specially tailored warehousing and logistics services exclusively to one client, where the vendor and client share the risks associated with the operation." [2]

The four basic ingredients of contract warehousing are *exclusivity, shared risk, extended time frame*, and *tailored services*.

The *exclusivity* usually involves an assigned block of space or building, an exclusive work force and management, assigned materials handling equipment, or more often than not, all of the above.

Shared risk provisions guarantee client use of the dedicated space for a specific period of time, assistance in providing or paying off equipment, or other commitments. With such guarantees, the provider, in turn, can afford to invest more intellectual and financial resources than he might otherwise. Reduced risk for the provider usually means a more economical arrangement for the client.

The *extended time frame* may be as little as one year or as much as five or more years. This extended period reduces risk and allows time for development, operating proficiency, and other efficiencies.

In contract warehousing arrangements, the provider usually offers a number of more complex, exclusive, or *tailored services*. These can range from hours of service to assembly or packaging.

There is no one contract that will apply to arrangements of this type. Since the outsourced services are customized according to client requirements and operations, each one will be different. The outsourced activities usually do not conform to the provider's standards of operation as much as they do the client's.

Regardless of what it covers, the contract should be as brief as possible. Obviously, certain legal requirements must be met; but it is desirable to express these in as few words as possible. Some logistics service contracts are so long and complicated, they defy understanding, not to mention interpretation.

It is important to remember that most relationships eventually end for one reason or another. Just as death or divorce will terminate a marriage, at some point, there will be reasons to conclude the outsourcing relationship. Over time, conditions and requirements change, and what might once have been a good arrangement can become unsatisfactory or obsolete. It is critical that the contract contain a fair and equitable method of dissolving the relationship, when and if the necessity arises. Indeed, many, if not most, outsourcing legal disputes involve contract terminations, either voluntary or involuntary. It is absolutely essential that the outsourcing firm have protection from business disruptions as relationships are ending. Often when a provider is notified of a contract termination, it will provide only a minimum of services, if that.

Brad L. Peterson of the legal firm of Mayer, Brown, Rowe & Maw suggests that the secret of getting adequate exit provisions is to ask yourself seven questions. [3]

1. Why will you want to terminate? (For cause, convenience, etc.) He uses an excellent example in suggesting a provider may meet its contractual obligations, yet fail in a larger way; i.e., Enron, Tyco, WorldCom, etc.

2. What termination rights will you give your service provider? From a client perspective, provider termination rights should be as few as possible.

3. What will you do when the contract terminates?

4. What will you need from your service provider to make a smooth transition?

5. How will you give the service provider incentives to provide termination assistance?

6. Can you "build for exit"? (This would involve requiring the provider to use client resources that would be left in place in the event of termination.)

7. Could you use early termination assistance to reduce risk? (Right to obtain key termination services such as a procedures manual, etc. before giving notice.)

While the parties should not begin the relationship on a negative note, the ultimate goal should be to protect both provider and client and avoid expensive, disruptive litigation.

Judge Learned Hand once said, "As a litigant, I should dread a lawsuit above all else, other than sickness and death." [4]

One method of minimizing dispute issues is through Alternative Dispute Resolution (ADR). Many firms are finding mediation and arbitration to be more effective and less expensive vehicles for resolving contractual issues.

Mediation is a process whereby an impartial third party (mediator) intervenes in a dispute with the consent of both parties and assists them in reaching agreement. The final decision is made by the parties with the mediator in effect facilitating the process.

Arbitration, on the other hand, involves the submission of disputes to a neutral third party or panel who renders the final decision. Parties are entitled to the same remedies they would receive in court, but arbitration usually is a much more civilized method of accomplishing this.

The benefits of arbitration were recognized by the U.S. Supreme Court in Allied-Bruce Terminix in 1995, stating [5]

- Arbitration is less expensive than litigation;
- Arbitration has simpler rules;
- Arbitration does not disrupt business dealings among the parties; and
- Arbitration is more flexible in scheduling.

The outsourcing firm should not let the excitement of the new program cloud its practical judgment; but at the same time, it should remember the most important point of all. *This is not an adversarial relationship!* While contract negotiations may be difficult at times, the contract drafters should view the arrangement as an alliance, not a grudging agreement between opposing forces.

Unpleasant contract negotiations can taint the corporate relationship and often carry over into the day-to-day operations and personal relationships, as well.

The Warehousing Agreement

As indicated earlier, it is impossible to offer an agreement that would apply to all situations, but the following suggested provisions hopefully will aid in the drafting of the contract.

While this information is believed to be informed and accurate, it is not intended to be legal advice. Before execution of the agreement, the services of a competent legal professional should be sought.

A sample contract based on this discussion is reproduced in Appendix 9-2.

Preamble

THIS AGREEMENT is made and entered into this _____ day of _____, 20___, by and between _____, a _____ corporation ("Client"), and _____, a _____ corporation ("LSP").

Whereas Clause

WHEREAS, Client is in the business of _____ and desires to engage LSP to provide _____;

WHEREAS, LSP can provide _____.

NOW, THEREFORE, in consideration of the mutual agreements, covenants and conditions contained herein, the parties agree as follows:

The Whereas Clause basically outlines the services to be performed and the provider's ability and willingness to provide them.

Facilities

LSP agrees to provide _____ square feet of warehouse space located in the building at _____. These facilities will be used exclusively for the storage and handling of Client goods and operation of Client account.

This section defines the specific amount and location of the space assigned to the client. This may be an entire building or a portion of a larger building.

It is recommended that when an entire building is utilized, a separate lease agreement be executed. This will facilitate the user's assumption of the operation or the engaging of a different provider if for some reason it is necessary to do so.

If this option is pursued, the above language would read as follows:

LSP agrees to provide the services covered by this agreement in the building Client is leasing from LSP located at _____. This facility will be used exclusively for the storage and handling of Client goods and operation of Client's account in accordance with the terms and conditions of this Agreement and the corresponding Warehouse Lease Agreement attached hereto as Exhibit _____.

Products

The products that will be stored and handled pursuant to this Agreement are listed in Exhibit _____. Client represents and warrants that he has the right and authority to store them with LSP.

Client represents and warrants that there are no known potential health, safety, and/or environmental hazards

151

associated with its products or the storage and handling thereof.

This language simply provides a listing of the products covered under the agreement. A responsible provider should require the representations and warranties regarding ownership and hazards.

Logistics Service Provider Responsibilities

Here, the services to be performed by the provider are outlined. They can be included in the body of the contract, but usually are included in appendices to the agreement. If the client has a standard operating procedures manual, it should be incorporated by reference into this section.

This section should include all the rules and requirements of the operation. For example, if the outsourcing firm is a food company, this section should contain a provision stating that in the case of a multi-tenant building, the LSP will not store or permit to be stored any product that, by reason of odor or otherwise, would be harmful to the client's products.

In the case of order fulfillment operations, the precise requirements of the client must be defined clearly, including the remedies for non-performance.

Any documentation and paperwork requirements should be included here as well.

Client Responsibilities

The section will spell out the responsibilities of the client, as well as the reports, materials, etc. it is expected to provide. Examples are guaranteed condition of products when they are received, reasonable inbound delivery schedules, proper marking and packaging, order entry responsibilities, etc.

Other operational responsibilities might include the provision of supplies, forms and materials for both warehouse and office use.

Rates and Charges

Client agrees to pay LSP the rates and charges set forth in Exhibit _____, attached to this agreement and made a part hereof. Invoices will be prepared _____ and will be payable within _____ ( ) days of their receipt by Client. Rates and charges for handling will be subject to review annually on the anniversary of the contract, subject to the provisions of Section _____.

The exhibit should contain all the rates and charges applicable to the operation, basic or special. They should be spelled out clearly, particularly the charges for special or extra services such as extra labor or additional inventories.

The timing for issuing and payment of invoices should be included in this section, as well.

Finally, the Rates and Charges language should provide for at least an annual review of the handling rates. As labor and other costs increase, it is appropriate to provide the service firm with reasonable increases in rates.

Rates for warehouse space usually are protected for the term of the agreement with the exception of escalators for taxes and insurance on the building.

This concept is very important. If a firm is entering into a true partnership, it will want the logistics service provider to make a reasonable profit. An unprofitable service firm is never an efficient one, and it is foolhardy to expect otherwise. If the client feels that requested rates are too high for the value it receives, or if the operation has service or operational deficiencies, it should exercise its termination options. One should never attempt to improve operations by withholding funds. It simply does not work.

Term

The term of this Agreement shall commence on _____, and shall continue in full force and effect through _____ *unless terminated earlier as hereinafter provided.*

This Agreement may be terminated by the parties as follows:

(a) LSP may terminate this Agreement during the aforesaid term, if it shall have previously given at least ninety (90) days written notice that the then existing handling rates as set forth above are reasonably deemed by LSP to be inadequate and no agreement concerning a substituted handling charge shall have been reached and put into effect by the parties within the ninety (90) day period. LSP may not render such notice during the first 12-month period that this Agreement is in effect and render such notice only once during any calendar year thereafter.

(b) Client may terminate this Agreement during the aforesaid term should LSP fail to perform satisfactorily the services required hereunder. However, prior to terminating for unsatisfactory performance, Client shall give written notice to LSP at least ninety (90) days prior to its exercising said right, and shall in said notice set forth the reasons for said termination. If LSP corrects the conditions giving rise to the unsatisfactory performance within said ninety (90) days to Client's satisfaction, the Agreement shall not terminate provided, however, that Client's satisfaction with LSP's corrective efforts shall not be unreasonably withheld.

(c) Notwithstanding the prior provisions of this Section 4, if LSP does not maintain the premises so that they reasonably comply with all applicable laws, rules, and regulations pertaining to the warehousing of _____ products, including those of the _____ and of Client, Client may terminate this Agreement on ninety (90) days written notice. However, Client shall notify LSP of such failure to comply and shall allow thirty

(30) days for LSP to correct such inadequacies specified in such notice.

(d) If, during the term of this Agreement, the warehouse in which space is leased or assigned to Client located at _____ is damaged by fire or other cause so as to interfere substantially with the storage of Client's products therein, then, if the warehouse shall not be repaired within one hundred and eighty (180) days thereafter, unless failure to make such repairs is due to causes beyond LSP's control, such as strikes, work stoppages, weather conditions, inability to obtain materials, etc., this Agreement may be terminated at the option of either party by written notice to the other.

This section outlines the term of the agreement, but also provides termination options in the event of certain circumstances.

For the provider, the ability to terminate the agreement if requested rate increases are refused will be very important. Such requests should be allowed only once per year, but the provider should be afforded some protection against the user's unreasonable refusal.

These paragraphs also provide valuable options for the outsourcing firm. The client may terminate the agreement in the event of unsatisfactory, uncorrected performance. This cannot be done unilaterally since the provider should have the right to at least attempt corrective action; but such a provision does afford a client a necessary option to continued poor performance.

Paragraph (c) will be particularly important to the firm distributing food products. If the provider does not maintain the facilities according to the specifications of the client, the Food and Drug Administration and other appropriate governmental bodies, the outsourcing firm must have the right to terminate the agreement. A similar provision would be necessary in the case of chemicals or any other products requiring unique care.

Paragraph (d) simply provides a method of terminating the agreement in case of damage to the property.

If a building lease is in effect, cancellation of the handling agreement does not affect the lease agreement. The outsourcing firm will have the option of providing its own labor and equipment or contracting with another provider.

Liabilities and Indemnities

It is agreed that LSP's services hereunder shall be rendered as a merchandise warehouseman in the State of _____ and as an independent contractor and in no wise partner or agent of Client.

LSP agrees to hold Client harmless from any and all claims asserted by any parties whomsoever insofar as the same shall arise because of the fault or negligence, actual or alleged, of LSP, its agents, servants, or employees occurring on the premises described in the Agreement.

In no event shall LSP's duties to Client under this Agreement exceed that of a reasonable prudent warehouseman under _____ state law. LSP shall not be liable for any loss or injury to goods stored, however caused, unless such loss or injury resulted from the failure of LSP to exercise such care in regard to the goods as a reasonably careful man, owning similar goods, would exercise under like circumstances.

LSP does not insure Client's goods against loss or injury however caused.

Client agrees to hold LSP harmless from any and all claims asserted by any parties whomsoever, insofar as the same shall arise because of the fault or negligence, actual or alleged, of Client, its agents, servants, or employees.

Except as otherwise stated herein, if requested, each of the parties hereto shall advise the other of all applicable insurance coverage.

LSP shall maintain at its expense such insurance as will fully protect it from claims under Workers' Compensation and Occupation Disease Acts and from claims for damage for bodily injury, including death, and for property damage, which may arise from operations under this Agreement, whether such operations by LSP or by any subcontractor or anyone directly or indirectly employed by either of them.

LSP also agrees that such insurance shall include the following:

(a) Workers' Compensation Insurance in compliance with the Workers' Compensation Act of _____ if such act requires part of all of liability to employees for occupational accidents or diseases to be satisfied by such insurance, or insurance in a State Fund, for liability to employees for occupational accidents or diseases and pay all premiums and taxes required by the Workers' Compensation Act of _____ if such Act requires insurance of part or all of LSP's liability with the State Fund.

(b) Employer's Liability Insurance on all employees not covered by a Workers' Compensation Act, for occupational accidents or disease with limits of liability of not less than _____ for any one accident or disease.

(c) Comprehensive General Liability Insurance with limits not less than _____ combined single limit bodily injury and property damage per occurrence.

Certificates of Insurance showing compliance with the foregoing requirements shall be furnished by LSP when it returns the signed Agreement to Client. Certificates shall state the policy or policies will not be cancelled nor altered without at least ten (10) days prior written notice to Client.

If Client shall so request, LSP shall furnish Client for its inspection and approval such policies of insurance with all endorsement, or confirmed specimens of proof thereof, certified by the insurance company to be true and correct copies.

Maintenance of such insurance and the performance by LSP of its obligations under the foregoing paragraph shall not relieve LSP of liability under its indemnity agreement set forth in this Agreement.

Just as with the public warehouse contract, it is very important to recognize and compensate for the provider's limited liability. The outsourcing firm should maintain its own product insurance, but should make certain that the provider carries the necessary workmen's compensation and liability insurance. The applicable state law should be scrutinized carefully.

Inventories

Physical inventories will be taken and reconciliation made once each _____. LSP shall also conduct weekly cycle count inventories at Client's request.

Once each year, after the end of the fourth quarter, if there are inventory losses and warehouse damages in excess of inventory overages which exceed _____ of _____ percent of *the total case volume handled by LSP during such year, LSP shall pay Client upon presentation of an invoice therefor an amount equal to such amount in excess of _____ of _____ percent times Client's production and inbound transportation costs.*

Inventory policies will vary by firm. Some will require monthly or quarterly physical inventories, while others will be satisfied with an annual count. Still others will rely primarily on cycle counts.

Whatever the frequency, it is important to define the requirements and the allowable shrinkage. A manufacturer of expensive electronic components may allow none, while food distributors often provide for damage and shrinkage of one eighth of one percent, or slightly more in some circumstances. Another method of handling shrinkage could be as follows:

Client agrees to a shrinkage allowance each year during the term of this Agreement of ___% of cases shipped. Based on the 20__ projected shipped case volume of _____, the maximum allowance would be ____ cases, this figure to be updated annually. As well, Client agrees to a damage allowance of ___%. Based upon the 20__ projected shipped volume of _____, the allowance would be _____ cases, this figure to be updated annually. These allowances will apply in the case of loss or damage to goods or mysterious disappearance, however caused.

There is no hard and fast rule, but the outsourcing firm can rest assured that the provider will attempt to negotiate for such an allowance.

Force Majeure

Neither party shall be responsible for delays, failure, or omissions due to any cause beyond its reasonable control, wheresoever arising and not due to its own negligence or intentional misconduct and which cannot be overcome by the exercise of due diligence, including, but not limited to labor disturbances, riots, fires, earthquakes, floods, storms, lightning, epidemics, war, disorders, hostilities, expropriation of, confiscation of properties, interference by civil or military authorities or acts of God.

Confidentiality

LSP acknowledges that in the course of rendering warehousing services under this Agreement, Client may disclose to LSP, or LSP may come into the possession of information as a result of its relationship with Client under this Agreement, respecting the business and affairs of Client, including data pertaining to Client's products and customers. LSP acknowledges that such information is confidential and proprietary to client, and covenants and agrees to keep such information in the strictest confidence, and to take all necessary steps to assure that its employees will keep in the strictest confidence all information and not disclose any such information to any third party without the prior written consent of client. This covenant shall survive the termination or expiration of this Agreement.

Conflict of Interest

Often parties will want to include conflict of interest provisions in the body of the contract to cover such matters as solicitation of employees and the receipt of gifts.

Client and LSP acknowledge and agree that the personnel employed by each company in the performance of or in connection with the activities of the parties contemplated by this are important assets of their respective companies. Therefore, without the prior written consent of the other, neither Client nor LSP shall solicit for employment the employees or the officers of the other (or any of their subsidiaries or their affiliates) for employment by them or any affiliate or subsidiary of either of them. Such non-solicitation shall be for a period of this Agreement and for a period of six (6) months after the termination of this Agreement.

Client and LSP further agree and acknowledge that a monetary remedy for a breach of this provision would be inadequate and may be impractical and extremely difficult to prove, and such a breach would cause each of the companies irrevocable harm. In the event of a breach of the provisions hereof, each of the parties will be entitled, in addition to any monetary damage it may subsequently prove, to temporary and permanent injunction relief, including temporary restraining orders, preliminary injunctions and permanent injunctions. This provision of the paragraph shall survive the termination of this Agreement.

LSP shall not pay any salaries, commissions, fees, or make any payments or rebates, to any employee or officer of Client or to any designee of any such employee or officer, or favor any employee or officer of Client or any designee of any such employee or officer, with gifts or entertainment or significant cost or value with service of goods sold at less than full market value.

Assignment

This Agreement shall inure to the benefit of and be binding upon the successors and assigns of the parties hereto, provided, however, neither party to this Agreement shall assign or sublet its interest or obligations herein, including, but not limited to, the assignment of any monies due and payable, without the prior written consent of the other party, which consent shall not be unreasonably withheld. Notwithstanding the aforesaid, Client shall not need the prior consent of LSP in the event Client *assigns this Agreement to a parent, subsidiary, affiliate or a company into which Client is merged or with which Client is consolidated.*

This provision outlines the limited circumstances under which the agreement may be assigned to others.

Applicable Law

This Agreement shall be governed by, construed and enforced in accordance with the laws of the State of

_____.

Notices

Any notice or demand required or permitted hereunder shall be given in writing and shall be considered as having been given by either party to the other party upon the facsimile transmission confirmed by the mailing thereof to such other party at the following addresses or to such other address as such other party may from time to time specify in writing:

If to LSP:

_____

_____

_____

If to Client:

_____

_____

_____

Arbitration

If the parties wish to submit disputes to arbitration, the contract should include appropriate language.

The parties to this Agreement agree to arbitrate all disputes, controversies, or differences that may arise between the parties with respect to any of the provisions of this Agreement. Either party may give written notice to the other of its decision to arbitrate any dispute. The notice shall specify the issue(s) to be arbitrated. The parties may agree on one arbitrator but if agreement cannot be reached then each party shall select one (1) arbitrator and the third arbitrator shall be appointed by mutual consent of the parties. In the event the parties cannot agree upon such third arbitrator, the two arbitrators shall jointly select a third arbitrator. The parties agree to arbitrate in accordance with arbitration rules and procedures. The decision of the arbitrator or majority of such three arbitrators, including but not limited to assessment of the cost of the arbitration, shall be final and binding.

In some cases the parties will want to attempt a mediation before proceeding to arbitration. If so, the following or a similar clause should be inserted prior to the arbitration provision.

The parties agree that any claim or dispute relating to this Agreement, or any other matters, disputes or claims between us, shall be subject to non-binding mediation if agreed to by the parties within 30 days of either party making a request to the other by letter. Any such mediation will be held in _____ and shall be conducted according to the mediation rules of the National Arbitration Forum.

(For more information on mediation and arbitration, contact the National Arbitration Forum, www.arbitration-forum.com.)

Entire Agreement

This Agreement, together with all exhibits and attachments, constitutes the entire agreement between the parties, and there are no other terms and conditions.

Amendment and Waiver

This Agreement may not be amended or varied except by the written agreement of the parties hereto, and all waivers of any rights must be in writing to be effective.

Execution

IN WITNESS WHEREOF, the parties have caused this Agreement to be executed by their authorized representatives as of the day and year first above written.

LOGISTICS SERVICE PROVIDER

By _____
Title _____

CLIENT

By _____
Title _____

Warehouse Lease Agreement

If the outsourcing firm elects to combine the Warehousing Agreement with a lease of the facility being utilized, it will be necessary to execute a Warehouse Lease Agreement to run concurrently with the Warehousing Agreement.

While the Warehousing Agreement can be terminated for specific causes, such termination does not automatically cancel the lease. The lease can only be terminated according to its own terms and provisions.

Often, the client firm will want to continue the operation either with its own labor force or with another provider; and the major advantage to the two-part agreement is that it allows that flexibility.

The Warehouse Lease Agreement is nothing more than a standard real estate lease and does not have to be lengthy. It should, however, at a minimum, contain the following provisions.

Preamble

The preamble identifies the parties to the lease agreement.

Description of Premises

This section describes the premises subject to the lease and identifies all parking lots, rail sidings, etc. included in the leased premises.

Terms and Rental

The beginning and end date should be shown, along with the rental and how it is to be paid. The start date of the lease should be the same as that of the Warehousing Agreement.

This section also should include the charges and method of adjustment for additional items of expense such as taxes, insurance, common area maintenance, and other items not included in the base lease cost.

Partial Cancellation Privileges

In some instances, when a large facility is involved and future needs are uncertain, the lessee may be able to negotiate a method of canceling some portion of the lease.

The following language outlines one way this might be specified in the agreement:

Lessee shall have the right to cancel up to _____ percent (%) of the square footage covered by this lease (in _____ square foot increments) after the _____ and _____ years of the Agreement, providing _____ days notice is given. The earliest such notice may be given is at the beginning of the _____ year. If such notice is given, Lessee agrees to pay a one-time penalty cost per square foot to be determined as follows:

$_____ per square foot times the square footage cancelled in year _____.

$_____ per square foot times the square footage cancelled in year _____.

The penalty will be paid in _____ monthly installments, commencing _____ months prior to the date of termination.

Such a provision has the practical effect of increasing provider revenue on the shorter term of the cancelled space. Take for example, a seven-year lease with cancellation privileges for up to 25 percent of the total space. This option might be available after year five with 365 days' notice. A penalty would be established for space cancelled after years five and/or six. This methodology simply increases the rate on the cancelled space to that which would have applied on a five- or six-year lease rather than the total seven years.

It is also possible to add a formula for restoring previously cancelled space.

Unique Maintenance of Facility

As with the Warehousing Agreement, it is important to include a provision requiring the provider to maintain the space in a manner suitable for the products stored such as food, chemicals, and other goods requiring special attention.

Renewal Options

The outsourcing firm will want a renewal option, assuming the facility is intended to be a long-term part of its distribution system.

Permitted Uses

This section outlines what activities may be conducted in the building and what may not be. This would be particularly important to the provider if the client assumed control of the building or leased space.

General Maintenance Requirements

In this section, the client or lessee agrees to maintain the space and at the end of the lease, surrender it in as good condition as it was at the beginning of the term.

Signage

If the lessee wants to place its own signage on the property, a provision should be included in the lease.

Repair Obligations

This section will require fire and other damage repair within a reasonable period of time, or the lease may be cancelled.

Assignment Restrictions

Here, the provisions for sub-letting all or part of the leased space will be spelled out.

Hold Harmless Clause

This section provides for mutual indemnification for negligence of employees, agents, and others.

Applicable Insurance and Subrogation

Language should be included to ensure that both parties have appropriate insurance.

Bankruptcy Provisions

This portion of the lease will spell out the remedies in the event of the bankruptcy of either party.

Notices

Appropriate parties for any notices under the lease should be listed here.

Right to Quiet Enjoyment

This language simply provides that if the lessee pays the rent and abides by the terms of the lease, he is entitled to utilize the premises without interference.

Option to Purchase

If a provider builds a new facility exclusively for the client, the client may at some time want to purchase the building. If there is even a remote possibility of this, an option to buy should be included in the lease.

One way this might be accomplished is through the following language which would be added to the lease.

_____ ("Lessor" or "Seller") agrees that _____ ("Lessee" or "Buyer") shall have an option to purchase the LEASED PREMISES on the _____, _____, and _____ anniversary date of this Agreement. The purchase price for the LEASED PREMISES, which are the subject of this Option Agreement, shall be determined by the following procedures. Upon proper exercise of said option by Buyer within a period no later than ninety (90) days prior to the option exercise dates specified above, the Seller shall select a disinterested qualified commercial real estate appraiser who shall be "MAI" certified and licensed in the State of _____ as a commercial real estate appraiser ("Seller's Appraiser"). Seller's Appraiser shall appraise the premises at the full cash fair market value as of the date of the exercise of said option by Buyer. The cost of said appraisal shall be shared equally by Buyer and Seller. In the event Buyer objects to the valuation of Seller's Appraiser, Buyer may, within ten (10) days after receipt of Seller's appraisal and at its own cost, hire a disinterested qualified commercial real estate appraiser, who shall be "MAI" certified and licensed in the State of _____ as a commercial real estate appraiser ("Buyer's Appraiser"). Buyer's Appraiser shall appraise the LEASED PREMISES at the full cash fair market value as of the date of the exercise of said option by Buyer. In the event Seller objects to Buyer's appraisal within ten (10) days after receipt thereof, Seller and Buyer agree that Seller's Appraiser and Buyer's Appraiser shall, by mutual agreement, and with the cost of said appraisal to be shared equally by Buyer and Seller, choose a third disinterested appraiser with the same qualifications as outlined above for Buyer's and Sellers' appraisers, who shall appraise the LEASED PREMISES at the full cash fair market value as of the date of the exercise of said option by Buyer. The valuation of the LEASED PREMISES as determined by said third appraiser shall be binding on both Buyer and Seller. The purchase price for the LEASED PREMISES shall be the full cash fair market value as finally determined by the appraisal, but in no case less than the *outstanding debt on the building and will not include any amount for commissions or other costs that would be incurred in selling through brokers or agents. Any transfer or transaction tax imposed in connection with sale of the LEASED PREMISES pursuant to this paragraph shall be equally shared by the Seller and Buyer. Upon such purchase by Buyer, this Lease Agreement shall be terminated and all responsibilities of each party herein.*

The remainder of the warehouse lease will cover other routine requirements.

Appendix 9-3 provides a complete sample Warehouse Lease Agreement suitable for execution in concert with a Warehousing Agreement.

Alternative Fee Schedules

In some instances, the outsourcing firm will choose to enter into a *Cost Plus Percentage* or a *Management Fee* type of arrangement, rather than pay on a per-unit basis. In either case, the Warehousing Agreement must contain all cost projections. These estimates are extremely important to the client regardless of the approach used.

If the contract reflects a cost plus percentage fee schedule, the provider will project the various costs associated with the account, and each week or month will bill either those costs plus a percentage for its profit, or actual costs plus the percentage, depending on the agreement.

If a flat management fee is levied, the billing will be for projected or actual costs, plus the management fee.

Either way, the client must have some estimate of the charges that will be billed on a month-to-month basis. If at all possible, the firm should negotiate to reimburse the provider for the projections in the agreement plus the applicable percentage or management fee, barring some mitigating circumstances.

There is no "typical" method for calculating the percentage of reimbursement. Contracts may provide for a calculation on handling costs only, handling and equipment costs only, or total costs.

Usually, some charges will be billed on a weekly basis, and some invoiced monthly. Figure 9-a is an example of a weekly billing schedule. A similar schedule should be made a part of the contract.

Figure 9-b illustrates categories of cost that typically are billed on a monthly basis. Such a schedule should be incorporated along with the weekly billing attachment.

Figure 9-c is a suggested billing summary, summarizing the first two schedules.

In most cases, the remainder of the terms of the warehousing Agreement or Warehouse Lease Agreement, if utilized, will remain unchanged.

Transportation

Although most products shipped by truck in the United States are done so on a transactional basis, contract motor carriage is the preferred method for the firm contemplating a serious outsourcing relationship. As is the case with the Warehousing Agreement, there is no one best form of document, but contract motor carriage agreements tend to be more straightforward.

Often the carrier will be able to provide a contract form that requires little modification.

Here again, while flexibility should be maintained, the agreement should be as brief as possible.

A contract may be entered into for either truckload or less-than-truckload services. These will be slightly different due to the differences in services required, but general provisions will be very similar. Provisions of a representative truckload agreement will be discussed and a sample contract is contained in Appendix 9-4. Please remember that the terms and conditions may not apply in all jurisdictions or to all situations. Professional legal advice should be sought before any such document is executed.

SCHEDULE _____
WEEKLY BILLING RATES

Supervision

___ Warehouse Manager   Salary & Benefits $_____
___ Warehouse Supervisor's Salary & Benefits   _____

Clerical Labor

___ Straight Time Hours @ $_____ per hour $_____
___ Overtime Hours   @ _____ per hour   _____
___ Hours of Contract Labor @_____ per hour   _____

Warehouse Labor

___ Straight Time Hours @ $_____ per hour $_____
___ Overtime Hours   @ _____ per hour   _____
___ Hours of Contract Labor @_____ per hour   _____

Recouping and Sanitation Labor

___ Straight Time Hours @ $_____ per hour $_____
___ Overtime Hours   @ _____ per hour   _____

Total Weekly Billing $_____

Figure 9-a: Typical Weekly Billing Schedule – Cost Plus Contract

SCHEDULE _____
MONTHLY BILLING RATES

Warehouse Lease Cost or Rental
_____ Square feet at $_____ per month $_____

Additional Space
_____ Square feet at $_____ per month $_____

Equipment
_____ Forklifts at $_____ per month $_____
Maintenance at   _____ per month   _____

_____ Order Pickers at   _____ per month   _____
Maintenance at   _____ per month   _____

_____ Pallet Jacks at   _____ per month   _____
Maintenance at   _____ per month   _____

_____ Scrubbers at   _____ per month   _____
Maintenance at   _____ per month   _____

_____ Attachments at   _____ per month   _____
Maintenance at   _____ per month   _____

_____ Tanks of Fuel at   _____ per month   _____

_____ Miscellaneous at   _____ per month   _____
Pallet Maintenance   _____
General Maintenance   _____

Accessorial

_____ Bills of Lading @   _____ each   _____

Total Monthly Billing $_____

Figure 9-b: Typical Monthly Billing Schedule – Cost Plus Contract

SCHEDULE _____

**CALCULATION OF MANAGEMENT FEE
TO BE BILLED MONTHLY**

Total Weekly Billings $_____

Monthly Billing   _____

Total $_____

Times _____% Fee Equals $_____

- or -

Monthly Management Fee $_____

Figure 9-c: Calculation of Management Fees

174

Preamble

> THIS CONTRACT is made and entered into this _____ day of
> _____, 20__, by and between _____,
> hereinafter referred to as Company and _____,
> hereinafter referred to as Carrier.

Whereas Clause

> WHEREAS, Carrier is engaged in the business of transporting
> property for hire by motor vehicle, is duly authorized by the
> appropriate state and federal regulatory authorities to operate
> as a motor carrier transporting the property hereinafter
> described, within the territories hereinafter described, and
> desires to serve Company as a contract carrier by motor
> vehicle; and

> WHEREAS, Company, having authority to choose the Carrier
> for transportation of freight to be tendered under this
> Agreement, desires to enter into an Agreement with Carrier
> providing for transportation of such quantities of Company's
> property as it, its suppliers and consignors may tender to
> Carrier for shipment, between designated origins and
> destinations;

> NOW THEREFORE, in consideration of the mutual promises
> herein contained, the parties hereto agree as follows:

The Whereas Clause establishes that the carrier is ready, willing, and able to perform the services being contracted for and has the appropriate legal authority.

It is a good idea to incorporate a copy of the authority into the contract as an appendix, as well.

Scope of Agreement

Carrier shall transport between origins and destinations designated by Company, products named in Schedule A attached hereto, under such terms and conditions and at such rates and charges as set forth in Schedule B attached hereto, as the same may be supplemented or amended pursuant to Sections ___ and ___ hereof.

Shipments made under this Contract shall be subject to the rules and regulations attached as Schedule C. This Contract shall supersede any conflicting bill of lading or tariff provision. Amendments to rules must be made in the manner described in Sections ___ and ___ hereof to be effective as to transportation provided under this Contract.

This section identifies, through attached schedules, the origins, destinations, products, terms and conditions applicable to the contract.

Schedule A should designate all the products of the Company that will be covered by the contract.

Schedule B should outline all the terms and conditions of the transportation, including rates, accessorial charges, discounts, if any, and special waivers. (Examples shown in the appendix are just that, and should be modified according to individual situations.)

Schedule C will cover any unusual arrangements such as fuel surcharges.

Payment of Freight Charges

Payment of freight charges shall be the responsibility of the Company, consignee, or other party as set forth by the bill of lading. Payments shall be due within ____ days following receipt of invoice by Company. However, a late payment will not alter the application of discounts, rates and charges. Shipments must be invoiced as soon as practicable after delivery, but in no event more than _____ days thereafter; failure to bill charges to Company within the said _____ days shall waive forever any right of Carrier to bill to or collect from Company charges for any shipment not billed, regardless of any rule, regulation or understanding to the contrary.

Since the sunset of the Interstate Commerce Act, there are no regulatory requirements for the payment of freight charges, so the agreement for responsibility and timing must be included in the contract.

Minimum Volume Commitment

Company agrees to tender to Carrier and Carrier agrees to transport for Company a minimum of ___ shipments of Company's freight during the initial term of this Contract, and during each subsequent renewal hereof. Should this Contract be terminated at any time other than the conclusion of the initial term hereof or the end of any subsequent renewal period, the minimum quantity of freight provided in this section as applying to the final partial term hereof shall be reduced by the proportion the unexpired portion of the term bears to one year.

Should Shipper fail to tender or to have tendered to Carrier the minimum volume set forth in this Section, such failure shall not change in any respect the rates or charges due Carrier for shipments which Shipper did tender or have tendered for movement.

Contractual rates almost always are, or should be, lower than transactional rates, but require a minimum commitment by the shipper. The agreed-upon minimum number of shipments is incorporated into this section.

Rate and Rule Changes

Rates and charges in the Contract shall not be increased during the term of this Contract, and rules shall not be changed, except by mutual written agreement of Company and Carrier.

Unless otherwise agreed in writing, no rate increase by Carrier shall take effect on less than ____ days' notice to Company.

Rate reductions (including cancellation of a proposed increase) may be made on ____ days' notice to Company.

These paragraphs outline the terms and conditions under which rates and charges may be increased or decreased. Rate increases usually require fifteen days' notice, but reductions only one. While this may seem somewhat biased in favor of the shipper, the shipper can adjust to a reduction much more readily than to an increase which may affect its own prices, relationships with customers, etc.

This section also should specify exactly how billing should be submitted and in what format. This will be particularly important if the shipper has a TMS or other automated process.

Loss and Damage

Carrier will be liable for loss or damage to the Goods only while in the care and control of the Carrier, and when it results from the negligence or intentional acts of the Carrier, its employees, subcontractors, or agents. In no event will the Carrier be liable for concealed damage or where the loss or damage is caused by an act of God, the public enemy, and act of Company or its employees or agents, a public authority or the inherent nature of the Goods. Carrier's liability to Company for any loss or damage to the Goods shall not exceed the direct cost to the Company of the Goods involved, including transportation to the point of loss or damage, less its salvage value, if any.

A claim under this contract for loss, damage, injury or delay to a shipment shall be made in writing or electronically within ____ days after delivery or tender of delivery of the shipment, or, if it is not delivered or tendered for delivery, within _____ months after a reasonable time for delivery has elapsed. If shipment is made at a released value, it will be declared on the Bill of Lading.

Any action at law or suit in equity pertaining to a shipment transported by Carrier shall be commenced within ____ years from the date Company receives written notice from Carrier that Company's claim or any part thereof has been disallowed.

This section spells out liability and terms of settlement. Provision for released values, if any, should be included in this section. Also, if the company is successful in negotiating "offsets," the provisions will appear here; i.e.,

Company shall have the immediate right to offset freight or other charges owed to Carrier against claims for loss, damage or delay, or for overcharge and duplicate payment claims, unless Carrier disputes such claims.

Undercharges and Overcharges

Any action or proceeding by the Carrier to recover charges alleged to be due hereunder, and any action or proceeding by Company to recover overcharges alleged to be due hereunder, shall be commenced no more than _____ (___) days after delivery or tender of delivery of the shipment with respect to which such charges or overcharges are claimed. To the extent permitted by applicable law, the expiration of the said _____- day period shall be a complete and absolute defense to any such action or proceeding, without regard to any mitigating or extenuating circumstance or excuse whatever. Undercharge claims may not be collected unless notice is received by *company within ____ days of the original freight bill date.*

The terms and conditions of collection of overcharges and/or undercharges by either party must be indicated.

For both loss and damage and undercharge and overcharge claims, the applicable law within the contractual jurisdiction should be reviewed before executing the Contract.

Distinct Needs of Shipper

A company may want to ensure that the carrier meets the continuing needs and requirements of the company. In the ever-changing environment of the twenty-first century this could be a very important provision. Examples of important considerations are shown in Schedule D of the contract in Appendix 9-4.

Carrier agrees that it will provide service to Company as a contract carrier by motor vehicle, which is and will be designed to meet the distinct needs of Company. Carrier shall tailor its service to meet those needs more particularly set forth in Schedule D attached hereto, as well as those indicated elsewhere in this Agreement. There shall be a review on an ongoing basis on the requirement to alter or amend the service standards from those initially needed by Company, so as to make certain that the distinct needs of Company continue to be met. Carrier agrees to train its personnel who provide and will provide service to Company to ensure that Company receives that service which meets and will continue to meet Company's distinct needs.

Insurance

Carrier, at its own expense, agrees to carry and keep in force at all times public liability, property damage, cargo, and workmen's compensation insurance with such reliable insurance companies and in such amounts as Company may from time to time approve and such as will meet the requirements of federal and state regulatory bodies having jurisdiction of Carrier's operations under this Contract. Certificates of insurance showing Carrier's compliance with the provisions of this section shall be furnished to Company prior to any transportation under this Contract and whenever Carrier changes or renews its insurance coverage.

This paragraph covers the carrier's insurance obligations. The company should make sure that the carrier has the necessary insurance coverage in adequate amounts.

Independent Contractor

It is the specific intention of the parties that this Contract not be construed to make Carrier or any of its agents or employees in any sense a servant, employee, agent, partner or joint-venture participant of or with Company, and Carrier is not authorized or empowered by this Contract to obligate or bind Company in any manner whatsoever. Carrier shall conduct operations hereunder as an independent contractor, and as such shall have control over its employees and shall retain responsibility for complying with all federal, state and local laws pertaining in any way to this Contract. Said responsibilities include, but are not limited to, provision of safe equipment appropriate to haul Company's property tendered under this Contract, assumption of full responsibility for payment of all state and federal taxes for unemployment insurance, old age pensions, or any other social security law or laws as to all employees or agents of Carrier engaged in the performance of this Contract. Carrier shall not display Company's name on any motor vehicle equipment it provides under this Contract without specific authorization to do so from Company.

The Carrier must be identified as an independent contractor and in no manner affiliated with the Company.

Indemnification

Carrier agrees to indemnify and hold Company harmless from any and all claims for death or injury to persons, and loss or damage to property of any nature arising from Carrier's transportation of property for Company. Carrier further agrees to comply with all applicable federal and state statures, rules and regulations, including judicial interpretations thereof, and to also indemnify and hold Company harmless from any and all claims or fines arising from Carrier" transportation of property of Company in violation of any such statute, rule or regulation.

Force Majeure

Neither Company nor Carrier shall be liable for failure to perform caused by acts of God, public authority, revolutions or other disorders, wars, strikes, fires or floods.

Notices

All notices required or permitted to be given under this Contract shall be in writing and shall be deemed to have been sufficiently given when received if delivered in person, when deposited at the telegraph office if transmitted by telegraph, or when deposited in the mails of the United States Postal Service, certified, return receipt requested, postage and other charges prepaid, and addressed to the respective parties at the following addresses:

CARRIER:

_____

_____

_____

COMPANY:

_____

_____

_____

Confidentiality

Neither party shall disclose the terms of this Contract to any third party except: (1) to a parent, affiliate or subsidiary corporation; (2) as may be required by law; (3) to any attorney, auditor or consultant who has a need for the Contract in the performance of professional services for a party.

Term

_This Contract shall remain in full force and effect for ____ (__) year(s) from the date hereof (herein referred to as the initial term of this Contract), (and from year-to-year thereafter,) subject to the right of termination by either party at any time on _____ (__) days' notice to the other party sent by certified mail, return receipt requested._

The term may be any length desired, but usually is one year. Regardless of the length, most contracts can be terminated by either party on thirty days' notice.

Amendment

This Contract shall not be amended or altered except in writing and signed by authorized representatives of both parties.

Assignment

Without the prior written approval of Company, Carrier shall not assign this Contract, and shall not assign any rights under *this Contract to a third party. Any unapproved attempted assignment shall be null, void, and of no force or effect; should it be attempted, Carrier agrees to pay to Company any expenses including reasonable attorneys' fees that Company may incur in defending against any action or conduct related thereto. This Contract shall be binding upon each party's heirs, successors and assigns, if any, including any successor or assign by operation of law.*

Execution

IN WITNESS WHEREOF, the parties have executed this Contract on the day and year first herein written.

CARRIER:
By: _____
Title: _____

COMPANY:
By: _____
Title: _____

Hours of Service

In January, 2004, the Federal Motor Carrier Safety Administration implemented new rules for drivers' hours of service.

Drivers will be allowed to drive up to 11 hours followed by a 10-hour break versus the current 10 hours followed by an eight-hour break; remain on duty for 14 consecutive hours versus the current 15; and be required to go off duty for 10 hours versus the current eight. The new rules eliminate the current ability to log "on duty, not driving" for rest periods and waiting time; and regardless of what the driver is doing at the time, when the 14 hours are up, he or she cannot move the truck. The driver must log "off duty" for the required down time. This, of course, has many implications for distribution center operations, and many are developing new systems and procedures that will help drivers get the most out of their time.

But if a company goes to the trouble, it should make sure it gets credit for its efforts. When contracting with carriers, negotiate incentives that will provide rewards for enhancing carrier productivity. There's no reason why the distribution center manager shouldn't share in the savings.

Combination Agreement

When a firm contracts with a provider for a full line of services such as warehousing, transportation, and order processing, it will want to execute one agreement for the entire operation.

The general terms and conditions of such a contract will be very similar to those for warehousing and/or transportation with the major difference being in the scope of services or responsibility sections.

Usually due to their length or complexity, the description of goods and services will be in separate schedules or attachments. At a minimum, these schedules should include the following.

Description of Goods

A complete description of the products to be handled should be included. Just as in the Warehousing Agreement, the Client should warrant that there are no known potential health, safety, and/or environmental hazards associated with its products or the storage and handling thereof.

Services

A complete list of the services to be performed should be included. This list should be specific and itemize each function such as receipt, storage, unpacking, packing, assembly, disassembly, order preparation, shipment, and transportation.

Service Area

Especially if transportation is to be provided, the geographic scope of the activity should be specified.

Other Provisions

Other terms and conditions such as rates and charges, claims, insurance, allocated space and confidentiality can be developed using language similar to that in the other agreements.

Freight Bill Payment

The last type of contract to be discussed is the agreement to outsource freight bill audit and payment services.

These contracts usually are fairly brief and vary with the provider. They range from a one page outline of services from a small provider to the more sophisticated agreements used by the larger firms.

While the agreement need not be lengthy, it should be very clear on the services to be performed and the compensation therefor. Appendix 9-5 provides a sample Freight Bill Payment Service Agreement similar to the one discussed here.

Preamble

> THIS SERVICE AGREEMENT ("Agreement") is made and entered into as of the ____ day of _____ 20__, by and between _____ ("Client"), a _____ corporation, and Freight Bill Payment Company ("FBPC"), a _____ corporation.

Whereas Clause

WHEREAS FBPC is in the business of handling pre-audit and payment of freight bills. _____ desires to hire FBPC to perform pre-audit, data capture, freight payment and management information services for carriers used by _____ (the "Carriers"). The parties desire to enter into this Agreement and to fully set forth their understanding of the terms, commitments and conditions of their relationship.

NOW THEREFORE, in consideration of the promises hereof and the mutual commitments and conditions hereinafter set forth and other good and valuable consideration, the receipt and sufficiency of which is hereby acknowledged, the parties hereto, intending to be legally bound, hereby agree as follows:

As with the other agreements, this section of the agreement sets forth the desires and commitment of both parties regarding the services to be rendered.

Engagement

_____ hereby engages FBPC and FBPC hereby agrees to perform pre-audit, data capture, freight payment and management information services for _____.

Services to Be Provided

FBPC will provide the following services:

Pre-Audit. FBPC will audit freight bills, including but not limited to, duplicate payments, rates, classifications, discounts, extensions and verification. However, _____ will be responsible for providing FBPC with updated material regarding any changes in rate agreements with certain Carriers.

187

Data Capture. FBPC will capture data from all freight invoices and accompanying documentation as required by _____.

Freight Payment. Payment will be performed on a weekly basis, with checks being issued to each Carrier on _____'s behalf. _____ will transfer funds to FBPC each __(day)__ and Carrier checks will be mailed the following __(day)__.

EDI Payment. FBPC shall have, and hereby confirms that it does have, the capability to receive electronic billings from such of the Carriers as may be so designated by _____.

Reports. FBPC will compile and submit to _____ those standard weekly reports and customized monthly reports listed in Exhibit A, attached hereto.

Internet Access

Internet Access. FBPC will provide _____ with secure access to its data through the Internet and will provide _____ with training in the use of such system at no charge to _____.

This section of the contract is very important and should be specific as to exactly what services will be provided. For example, the client reports that have been agreed to should be listed in a separate exhibit to avoid future disagreement about charges for producing reports.

If Internet access to data is available (and the client should insist that it is), the procedures for accessing the data should be defined and client personnel trained.

The FBPC may provide the client with proprietary software ("SW"). If so the service agreement will contain some additional language.

__Software and other web services received__. FBPC will provide Client with SW and web system maintenance and upgrades for the entire term of this Agreement. Upon termination of this Agreement, Client hereby agrees to return all software and materials and copies thereof, relating to SW. In addition, Client acknowledges that it has no ownership rights in SW.

FBPC represents and warrants that it is the owner of SW and that it has the right and authority to license SW to Client and that there exist no outstanding claims, allegations or requests for license that SW infringes any copyright, patent, trade secret, trademark, service mark or any other intellectual property right of any third party.

FBPC will defend, indemnify and hold harmless Client, its affiliates and subsidiaries and their officers, directors, employees, representatives, agents and subcontractors from and against any and all claims, allegations and requests for a license that SW or its use infringes any US or foreign copyright, trademark, patent or any other intellectual property right of any third party. In the event FBPC or Client is enjoined from using SW, FBPC , at its expense, shall procure for Client the right to use SW or modify SW so it is non-infringing. If it is not commercially reasonable for FBPC to procure such right or to modify SW so it is non-infringing, either party may terminate this Agreement upon 30 days' prior written notice to the other.

Errors

In the event of errors by FBPC, FBPC shall file claims to recover incorrect payments at their own expense.

Pay careful attention to this provision in the contract. Some freight bill payment companies will attempt to insert language that indicates they will not be liable for overpayments, but simply agree to process the claim for incorrect payments.

Renewal and Termination

The term of this Agreement will be for _____ (__) months from the date first entered above. Except as provided in Paragraph(s) _____, this Agreement will renew on an annual basis until cancelled. Cancellation without cause requires a minimum ____-day prior written notice by either party.

The term of the agreement can be whatever the parties desire, although most freight bill payment service agreements provide for a ninety-day cancellation without cause.

Fee Schedule

The fees to be paid to FBPC for the services set forth in Section ____ herein, are listed on Exhibit B attached hereto and are based on the profile by _____ and summarized in Exhibit C. Fees shall be billed and paid weekly. In the event fees are not paid as agreed, FBPC reserves the right to terminate this Agreement upon 30 days' written notice.

If after six (6) months of experience, the profile varies significantly from the profile projected in Exhibit C (+ or − 15%), FBPC reserves the right to reopen the fees for negotiation. This applies not only to total transactions, but also transactions within each category.

If no agreement is reached within 30 days of a request for a modified fee schedule, either party may terminate this Agreement upon 30 days' written notice.

The fee schedules for freight bill auditing and payment are more precise than those for most other logistics services. In addition, the profile of the account is more important since different types of bills require different levels of effort by the provider.

Separate charges should be established for rail, motor, and air bills and for manually received bills versus those received through Electronic Data Interchange.

Coding and accounting requirements should be indicated and priced, as well as the number and types of reports that will be required.

The profile also will provide the freight bill payment company with some idea of the amount of "float" it can expect from the client's account. As discussed earlier, this can be an integral part of the pricing structure; and if the number and dollar amount of bills by mode contained in the profile is inaccurate, it will impact on the profitability of the account, either positively or negatively. Consequently, it is in the best interest of both parties to re-examine the profile after about six months' experience. If the transaction base is significantly different from that initially projected, a re-negotiation of the fees may be appropriate.

On-Site Audit

_____ has the right to perform on-site audits at FBPC on those processes relating to the _____ account.

This provision simply gives the client the right to review the processes used in paying its bills for accuracy and efficiency.

Miscellaneous Provisions

Severability. _If one or more of the provisions contained in the Agreement shall for any reason be held invalid, illegal or unenforceable for any reason, such invalidity, illegality or unen-_

forceability shall not affect any other provision of this Agreement, which shall be construed as if such invalid, illegal or enforceable provision had never been contained herein.

Counterparts. This Agreement may be executed in counterparts, each of which shall be deemed an original, but all of which together shall constitute one and the same instrument. This Agreement and all other documents to be executed in connection herewith are hereby authorized to be executed and accepted by facsimile signatures and such facsimile signatures shall be considered valid and binding as original signatures and may be relied upon by the parties hereto.

Entire Agreement. This Agreement supersedes all prior understandings, representations, negotiations and correspondence between the parties, constitutes the entire agreement between them with respect to the matters described, and shall not be modified or affected by any course of dealing, course of performance or usage of trade. It may not be changed orally but only by an agreement in writing executed by the parties hereto.

Governing Law: Enforcement. This Agreement shall be construed in accordance with the laws of the State of _____, and the rights and liabilities of the parties hereto, including any assignees, shall be determined in accordance with the laws of the State of _____. In any litigation the prevailing party shall be entitled to recover from the losing party reasonable attorneys' fees and other costs and expenses of the litigation.

Default. FBPC agrees that institution of, or consent to, any insolvency proceedings constitutes default and may result in cancellation of entire Agreement.

Execution

IN WITNESS WHEREOF, the parties have hereunto affixed their names or caused their names to be hereunto affixed by the undersigned officers who are thereunto duly authorized as of the date first above written.

By: _____

Its: _____

FBPC

By: _____

Its: _____

Conclusion

While the contracts discussed here will cover most outsourcing instances, there are other types of agreements for these and other services. Air and package carriers such as FedEx and United Parcel Service will have unique agreements, as will a variety of other providers such as software vendors.

Whatever agreement is executed, the terms should be clear, flexible, and mutually satisfactory. Both parties must remember that while they are working toward common goals, these goals may change, or each party's interests may differ from time to time. The contract must allow for these dynamics through reasonable, non-adversarial language.

Chapter 10

Gain Sharing

The inherent vice of capitalism is the unequal sharing of blessings.

- Sir Winston Churchill

The most common criticism of the typical contract warehousing agreement is that it affords no incentives for productivity improvement. The provider will receive the same revenue per unit, the same percentage reimbursement, or the same management fee, regardless of how efficient the operation becomes.

Often the client, over time, will make changes in procedures, product lines, packaging, materials handling techniques, or other factors affecting productivity in the warehouse, but realize nothing in the way of economic return.

The provider, on the other hand, as the operation matures, also may improve operating efficiencies, or conversely, since the rate structure is fixed, may do nothing to achieve improvements in productivity.

One answer to this dilemma is gain sharing, or the sharing in savings generated through productivity improvements.

As with any program of this type, the difficulty is in the measurement. How do the parties establish a benchmark which they can agree to, that can be used as the base case? What do they do in the event product mix changes? In a consumer goods warehouse, for example, a forklift operator can handle considerably more cases of spices in an hour than he can thirty-pound bales of sugar or flour.

The outsourcing firm could suggest a productivity level based on its own experience or that of other providers; but the sophisticated provider probably would not agree to such an approach. The most reliable and agreeable method is to let the provider gain experience with the account for six months or even a year, then establish a benchmark applying to the total operation.

The contract then could be amended to provide for a reduced rate per unit or a reduced fee, if productivity reached certain levels above the benchmark. The fees should be constructed so that both the client and the provider share in the savings.

Since, if this method is chosen, a contract amendment is required, the original agreement should reflect this intention.

If the benchmark is established carefully, based on valid data, it should always be exceeded. If it is not, it is a good indicator that the client should take a hard look at the operation.

Another less cumbersome method of rewarding superior performance is through the use of incentive payments to the provider. In programs of this type, performance targets are set for various categories, and if these goals are exceeded for a predetermined length of time, cash incentives are paid to the provider.

The following pages contain examples of programs and contract provisions that have worked well for some outsourcing companies. However, there is no "cookie cutter" approach to these agreements. Each company must decide what is best for its own operations.

The following is an example of a relationship utilizing a cost plus management fee contract with gain sharing.

Cost Plus Management Fee with Gain Sharing

The compensation is comprised of four basic components.

- Monthly space cost
- Weekly fixed handling costs
- Weekly variable handling costs
  - ° Warehouse
  - ° Clerical
- Weekly contribution to G&A plus margin

Monthly Rates and Charges

Base Rent

Cost of leased space (square footage X monthly rate = monthly charge)

Base rent can be increased annually to cover proportionate amount of increases in taxes, insurance, and maintenance.

Space may be reduced with 90 days' notice, but not below certain minimum.

Weekly Rates and Charges

Fixed Handling $_____ per week

Fixed Handling Charges are comprised of

Indirect Payroll
Building Manager
Benefits
Warehouse Supervisors
Benefits
Customer Service Supervisor
Benefits
Sub-Total
Material Handling Equipment
Cherry Pickers (man-aloft)
Chargers for above
Stand-up (Reach) Lift Trucks
Sit-Down Lift Trucks
Powered Pallet Jacks
Manual Pallet Jacks
Sub-Total
Regional Support (BUM + Admin/Financial Analyst)
Benefits
Other Administrative Costs
Furniture & Fixtures
Office Equipment (computers, facsimile, copy machine, etc)
Data Processing Software & Equipment
Janitorial Expense
Travel & Entertainment + Dues & Subscriptions
Insurance (Warehousemen's Legal Liability + General + Umbrella Liability)
Communications Expense (telephone, T-1 Line, Facsimile, etc)
Supplies (Office + Cafeteria)
Total Other Administrative Costs
Sub-Total

If a mutually agreed-upon reduction in these components is made resulting in reduced costs to LSP, the weekly charges to Client will be reduced by the amount of the cost reduction.

Variable Handling

Warehouse $_____ per line item

Clerical $_____ per line item

The costs per line item are based upon agreed-upon productivity benchmarks and hourly wage/benefit costs.

Example:

Standard line items per hour	5
Hourly wage/benefit rate	$15.00
Cost per line item	$ 3.00

Both warehousing and clerical components are calculated in the same manner.

If the actual line items processed exceed the standard, LSP will credit client with 85% of the resultant savings, or $10,000 per month, whichever is greater for the first three months agreement is in effect. Thereafter the sharing is reduced to 60%.

Example:

Confirmed processed line items per hour	=	7
Divided into hourly rate of $15.00	=	$2.14
Assumed benchmark cost	=	$3.00
Less actual experience	=	2.14
Actual savings	=	$ .86

Multiply total line items processed in month

(100,000) X .86   = $86,000

85% of $86,000   = $73,100

to be credited against next month's invoice

New benchmarks will be set at the end of each calendar year.

If the profile provided by the client changes, causing the line items processed per hour to decrease, LSP will increase the line item charge with 30 days' notice. LSP will not be allowed to adjust the rates for any other reason.

Fixed Contribution to Corporate G&A + Margin

$_____ per week

The Weekly Fixed Contribution to Corporate G&A + Margin is comprised of

Corporate Executive Salaries (CEO, COO, CFO, CAO, CIO, etc)
Benefits
Key Account Management Salaries
Benefits
Human Resources and Payroll Salaries
Benefits
Other Corporate Staff Wages
Benefits
Sub-Total

Data Processing, Software and Equipment
Hardware Equipment
Software Licensing Fees
Hardware Maintenance and Repair
Systems Development (Consulting, System Modifications, and Conversions)
Sub-Total
Other Corporate General & Administrative Costs
Furniture & Fixtures
Office Equipment (facsimiles, copy machines, etc)
Maintenance & Repairs
Personal Property Taxes
Consulting Fees (Audit, Legal, Operational, etc)
Travel & Entertainment + Dues & Subscriptions
Insurance (Employee Dishonesty + General Liability + Umbrella Liability)
Communications Expense (telephone, T-1 Lines, Postage, Express, etc)
Supplies (Office, I.T. and Cafeteria)
Training Expenses
Sub-Total

The above provision covers only productivity improvements. Other arrangements base incentives on performance in other areas, as well; i.e.,

Cost Plus Management Fee with Incentives

1. All actual costs of the operation are passed through to client.

2. Add to this a Management Fee consisting of:

   ° Corporate Allocations

° Profit

3. Profit varies by performance in four areas, each worth 25% in the calculations; i.e.,

° Shipping Accuracy
° Inventory Accuracy
° Variable Cost Management
° Fixed Cost Management

Targets are agreed upon by both parties, and profit varies upward or downward depending on performance, and according to a pre-determined scale.

Although every company will have its own measurement criteria, most will fall into these four categories plus on-time shipments or deliveries. These are discussed in more detail in Chapter 13.

Some firms will establish programs based on guaranteed throughputs. One leading provider has an arrangement with a client which pays incentives when standard productivity levels are exceeded.

For example:

Productivity Guarantee

Location 1	3000 pounds per man-hour
Location 2	3400 pounds per man-hour

Wage Rates (including benefits)

Location 1 $12.95 per hour
Location 2   15.10 per hour

The language in the contract is straightforward. It states simply, "*Cost reductions resulting from actual productivity improvement when compared to the Productivity Guarantee will be equally shared on a monthly basis between the parties; e.g., fifty percent (50%) of the monthly cost reduction will be credited against the amount to be invoiced by (LSP) for the month.*"

A typical variable labor charge billing would look something like this.

Month _____

Location	Throughput/Prod. Guar.	Billable Hours	Actual Hours	Difference
1	20,000,000/3000	6666.6	5602.1	1064.5
2	30,000,000/3400	8823.5	8097.2	726.3
Total		15490.1	13699.3	1790.8

Billing

Variable Labor	6666.6 X 12.95 = $86332.47
	8823.5 X 15.10 = 133234.85
	$219,567.32

Gain Share Credit	1064.5 X 12.95 X .50 = 6892.64
	726.3 X 15.10 X .50 = 5483.56
	12,376.20
Variable Labor Billed	$207,191.02

It is interesting to note that in this particular arrangement there is no penalty to the provider if they fall below the guarantee. In that case, they bill the billable hours times the wage rate.

Some programs are based solely on savings against budget with a graduated savings scale. One such arrangement provides the following:

	Shared By	
Savings as % of Budget	Client %	Provider %
0 – 3.0	100	0
3.1 – 6.9	50	50
7.0 – 9.9	25	75
10+	0	100

This schedule provides an excellent incentive for the provider since the more they save, the more they get. However, this is in a contract environment that also measures performance in productivity, space utilization, sanitation, damage, order accuracy, and inventory accuracy.

Although most programs provide for an equal sharing of productivity gains, some firms prefer to allocate credits on a time schedule such as that in the first example in this chapter. One company combined a time schedule with idea origination and developed the following schedule of sharing.

Cost Improvements	Months	Client	Provider
LSP Initiated	1 – 9	50%	50%
	10 -	100%	0
Client Initiated	1 -	100%	0
Jointly Initiated	1 – 3	50	50
	4 -	100	0

There are a few programs that are purely incentive-based; i.e., they provide for cash payouts rather than shared savings. For example, one leading U.S. firm will pay out to its providers amounts of up to 6% of the provider revenue from the account, for outstanding performance in customer satisfaction, inventory management, and order fulfillment, as well as other unusual operational accomplishments. The provision that makes this program particularly interesting is that 100% of these bonus payments must be paid out to provider employees serving that client.

This is but a sampling of the provisions that may be in effect. Some are more complicated, more comprehensive or more punitive; but whatever program is developed, it is important that all contracts have some provision for gain sharing. It is difficult to believe that improvements in any operation cannot be made over time; and resulting cost benefits should be shared.

With any program, two points must be kept in mind. First of all, allow time for the operation to get up and running before attempting to establish benchmarks against which to measure performance – a minimum of six months. Jan L. A. van de Shepscheut of California Institute of Technology summarized it well when he said, "*In theory there is no difference between theory and practice. In practice, there is.*"

Secondly, be sure that the contract provides for the program even though the details are not yet defined. Language such as the following should be included in the initial agreement.

Gain Sharing

It is the intent of the parties to create a program, (the "Gain Sharing Program"), designed to save costs and fees associated with the provision of Services hereunder. Any cost saving efforts or processes initiated or created by Client shall not be included in the GS Program. The GS Program shall commence no sooner than one hundred eighty (180) days after the date that LSP's proprietary warehouse management system goes into production in support of Client's business, and no later than two hundred seventy (270) days thereafter, unless agreed to in writing by Client and LSP. Prior to the GS Program beginning, Client and LSP shall agree in writing on baseline operational requirements including, but not limited to, staffing, facilities, and operational processes utilizing LSP's proprietary warehouse management system capabilities, and minimum operational metrics and the related improvements required to be in place. In order for LSP to be eligible to earn any percentage of shared savings realized within a quarter, LSP must consistently perform at or above all the baseline operational requirements for that quarter.

Conclusion

As suggested earlier, there can be almost as many different gain sharing arrangements as there are outsourcing relationships. Regardless of the plan and its components, it is extremely important that some type of scheme be incorporated into the operation. A well planned and managed gain sharing program can provide enormous benefits for both clients and providers.

Chapter 11

Establishing Policies and Procedures

When everything else fails, read the instructions.
- Source Unknown

As discussed in the previous chapter, it is virtually impossible to include all the necessary policies and procedures in the contract; and most firms will incorporate a standard policy and procedure document into the contract by reference. By doing so, the parties agree that this manual is the official blueprint for the operation. Ideally, the procedures will have been seriously considered by both parties as they have moved through the negotiation and contractual processes.

Most user firms embarking on an outsourcing relationship fall into one of three categories:

- *Those who already have logistics policies and procedures that can be adapted easily to the outsourced operation;*

- *Those who do not understand their own processes well enough to reduce them to a comprehensive manual;*
- *Those who depend on the provider to learn and develop them for itself.*

Obviously, the first category is the most desirable, but a surprising number of firms fall into the latter groups. Too often, functions are outsourced because they are not understood or managed well by the outsourcing firm; and no reliable procedures are in place. Here, it will be critical to involve the provider in the development of the processes. If the provider selection was made properly, its management will be able to manage the compilation of a workable set of procedures.

On the other hand, the firm that allows the provider to develop the procedures unilaterally is destined for trouble. It must be a joint effort; and while a provider may be experienced in the client's industry or type of operation, each relationship is unique and has its own set of requirements and challenges.

It brings to mind a personal experience of some years ago when a major food manufacturer was searching for a provider in a particular city. One of the candidates had some experience in the food industry, and the owner obviously considered himself an expert in the field. During preliminary discussions, each time a point was made, he would respond that he was quite familiar with it, and in fact, became somewhat agitated by the entire conversation. Finally, he blurted out, "We know all about that stuff. We used to handle..." (another food company).

Of course, about the only similarity between the two companies' logistics operations and those of the other firm was that they both distributed food products.

Policies and procedures are the road map to a successful outsourcing experience. Just as one should not embark on a journey in a strange country without a map, neither should a firm or a provider start the outsourcing journey without a clear understanding of the processes and expectations.

More importantly, mutually agreed-upon procedures will help to establish accountability. It is absolutely critical that all parties understand what they and their companies are accountable for. This is particularly true when the client has an onsite manager in place at an outsourced facility.

A case in point: One large national firm contracted with a provider to operate a distribution center, with one of the client's employees assigned to that location to act as a liaison between the two parties. Unfortunately, a disagreement over the distribution center's layout arose even before the first shipment was made.

The client's representative decided to retain a consultant friend to design the facility's layout. Though the recommended configuration was flawed, the client's representative insisted, over the provider's protests, that the consultant's layout be used. The result was nothing short of a warehousing disaster. Both travel times and operating costs far exceeded the standard. As a result, the provider lost money from the first day of the relationship.

The line in the sand had been drawn. The client blamed the provider for poor operating procedures and practices. The provider insisted that it was hamstrung by the inefficient layout. If there had been a clear delineation of responsibilities, this wouldn't have happened.

It should come as not great surprise that this relationship was a failure. It would not have been, however, had there been a written definition of responsibility and accountability. Conflicts inevitably arise in relationships, but if there is a clear understanding of each party's accountability, it's possible to resolve most of these.

Developing the Manual

Chapter 8 is a discussion of the definition of expectations for the outsourcing relationship. The expectations, which should have been made clear and agreed upon prior to the development of a contract, will form the basis for the "rules of engagement" that will be included in the procedures manual. While each operation will be unique, and user and provider requirements will differ, there are a number of subjects that should be covered in any manual. Some of the major ones will be discussed here, but both parties should be very diligent in developing their own set of procedures. If done properly, the manual will be voluminous, but it will be essential to a successful operation.

Logistics Strategy or Policy

By now, the outsourcing firm should have developed its outsourcing strategy and overall policy; and ideally, the provider participated in its development. A statement of this policy should be included as the first entry into the manual. It is the very foundation of the operations and expectations and should service as a constant reminder to both parties of the goals and objectives of the relationship.

It need not be lengthy, but should describe in simple terms the strategic positioning of the operation in the overall logistics strategy of the client.

Inbound Receipts

After the policy statement, perhaps the best place to begin the procedures discussion is when the inbound shipments arrive at the provider's dock. This section will contain procedures for receiving products and will cover such things as:

Customer Returns. Is authorization required? What documentation should be prepared? (Include necessary forms.) What if products are damaged or infested?

Inbound Damage. How should inbound damaged products be handled and/or disposed of? Should they be reconditioned, returned, or destroyed?

Overages and shortages. How will they be handled and/or accounted for?

Infestation/Contamination. Procedures should describe ways to identify, as well as the method of handling the product when it is unacceptable. What constitutes contamination; i.e., rodents, odor, insects, etc.?

Equipment Inspection. Transportation equipment should be inspected to ensure that no conditions exist that could have contaminated or harmed the product.

Freight Claims. Requirements for documentation of loss and damage and inventory reconciliations. Claim filing procedures.

Physical Unloading. Description of unloading procedures, starting with chocking or locking of trailers. Inspection of product, segregation of damage, putting away and tagging of product, rotating in bays where necessary. Replenishment of pick lines.

Documentation. What information is to be included on unloading manifest? Will checker unload from shipper loading document or make an independent count?

Production Code Reconciliation. In the handling of food and other sensitive products, it will be important to make sure that code dates on products and documents match.

Before moving to the next section, the parties should be sure that they have covered and included the necessary forms for all warehouse receiving activities.

Warehouse Operations

This portion of the manual should include procedures for maintaining the warehouse space and the handling of the product within the building. Representative subjects to be covered will be:

Building Maintenance. Requirements for maintenance and housekeeping, including sanitation.

Regulatory Compliance. Outlines agencies and legislation with which provider must be in compliance.

Warehouse Damage. Sets forth the allowances and rules therefor.

Product Reconditioning. What product should be reconditioned and how should it be done? Code date constraints?

Stock Rotation. Defines guidelines for rotating stock; i.e., oldest product first, first in – first out, etc.

Stock Locator Systems. The system for putting away and locating of stock should be described.

Product Recall. If a product recall system is necessary, all procedures should be spelled out clearly. This should include code date reconciliations, product traceability requirements, and a provision for test recalls.

Product Hold. All guidelines for products placed on hold should be clearly defined.

Warehouse Layout. If there are warehouse layout requirements, they should be included to avoid misunderstandings.

Safety and Security. It is in the interest of both parties to ensure a safe and secure workplace.

Employee Training. Provisions should be made for a continuous program for the training of new and existing employees.

Inventory Management

Many firms prefer to manage their own inventories and retain responsibility for the scheduling and replenishment of the provider's facility. This, of course, removes responsibility for out-of-stocks and other inventory related problems from the provider; but even when such a system is in place, there can be disagreements about the presence of certain items in the warehouse, inbound shipment scheduling, or proper handling of critical items.

In other cases, the provider will be solely responsible for inventory levels and the related activities such as replenishment.

Whichever method is used, the procedures and responsibilities of each party should be delineated quite clearly. Product availability and on-time shipping are two of the most critical performance measurements of a distribution operation; and not surprisingly, the most frequent source of conflict between the parties.

Order Processing

Order entry and handling procedures should be included in the manual, as well. Included in this section will be:

213

Order Entry. How will orders be received and transmitted to the shipping facility? (Sample forms should be included.)

Order Handling. The procedure for moving the order through the system should be described. Who will come in contact with it? For what purpose? What are time requirements for shipment?

Emergency Orders. How should orders be handled that do not conform to the routine guidelines?

Back Orders. What is the policy for handling out-of-stocks and back orders?

Depending on the type of operation being outsourced, order entry and handling requirements may vary significantly between firms. With customer service being so critical in most transactions, order-handling guidelines must leave no margin for error or misinterpretation.

Outbound Shipments

Procedures for loading or assembling outbound shipments, whether they be by truck, rail, air, or package carrier should be included here.

Removing Product From Stock. Rotation requirements should be re-emphasized, as well as directions for moving the product to the dock or order assembly area.

Vehicle Inspection. In the case of truck or rail shipments, vehicles should be inspected for suitability for loading. If forms are required, they should be included.

Damage Prevention. If dunnage or other product protection is required, it should be specified.

Loading. Loading procedures and diagrams should spell out product placement, and the handling of pallets and/or slipsheets should be explained. If stretch wrapping is utilized, its application must be described.

Documentation. Samples of loading sheets should be included, and necessary notations prescribed; i.e., production code dates, location in vehicle, etc.

Transportation

If the provider is responsible for transportation, these procedures should be included in the manual also. Whether the provider provides the transportation or utilizes other carriers, certain requirements must be met.

Carrier Selection. If another carrier is utilized, the rules for carrier selection must be spelled out. Who selects the carrier? Is there a preferred list or a precise requirement?

Routing Guide. If there is a prescribed routing guide, it should be included as part of the procedures manual. This will eliminate any controversy or misunderstanding about which carriers are to be used. These guides usually will include not only the specific carriers to be used between certain points, but the applicable rates, as well.

There is no one correct format for a routing guide, but Figure 10-a illustrates one that is clear and concise. Notice that it provides not only the name of the carrier to be used to specific destinations, but it includes the rate as well as the desired allocation for each carrier stated as a percentage. It also shows at a glance, the penalty incurred when other than first choice carriers are used.

TRUCKLOAD ROUTING GUIDE

FROM   CHICAGO

TO POINTS IN   ILLINOIS

Preferred Carrier	A	B	C
$ Per Mile	1.50	1.50	1.43
Desired %	40	35	25
Maximum Loads/Week	15	10	5

Preferred carrier assignment by city. Every effort should be made to conform to above percentage allocations.

To	(1) Preferred Carrier	(2) Second	Penalty Over (1)	(3) Third	Penalty Over (2)
Aurora	A	C	$_____	B	$_____
Belleville	A	C		B	
Bloomington	A	C		B	
Carbondale	A	C		B	
Des Plaines	C	B		A	
Effingham	A	C		B	
Galesburg	A	C		B	
Kankakee	A	C		B	
Moline	A	C		B	
Peoria	C	B		A	
Rockford	C	B		A	
Springfield	C	B		A	
Vandalia	C	B		A	

Figure 10-a: Example of Routing Guide Applicable From a Chicago Distribution Facility to Points in Illinois.

216

This, or a similar guide, should be developed for each state served by the facility. While this particular example applies to motor carriers, such a format would be equally applicable to rail, air, or package shipments.

Transportation Contract. If contracts with carriers are in place, copies should be included in the manual. Even though the provider may not be directly responsible for transportation, it should be familiar with the obligations and provisions of the agreement.

Administrative

In addition to the basic product handling, storage, and shipping requirements, there will be any number of other subjects to be covered in the procedures. For the sake of discussion, these have been grouped under one heading; but in many cases, it will be appropriate, because of their importance, to incorporate them as independent sections. Some of the more important of these are:

Accessorial Charges. This language should elaborate on that of the contract. What extra services will be compensated for? At what rate? Is prior approval needed? These include such categories as extra labor for physical inventories or other overtime.

Billing for Services. How often will provider bill for services? What documentation is required?

Bills of Lading. Who will provide the bill of lading forms? (Include sample.)

Consolidation Programs. If the provider maintains a consolidation program, it is critical that the rules for inclusion be clear. What orders may be consolidated? Can orders be held for consolidation? How long? While

217

consolidation programs can reduce transportation costs, procedures must be in place to ensure that customer service is not adversely affected.

Contacts. The names, telephone numbers, e-mail addresses, and fax numbers of responsible parties on both sides should be identified and kept current.

Customer Communications. In some instances, the provider will have direct communications with the client's customers. Procedures for these must be carefully explained. There is little margin for error in these sensitive relationships.

Performance Measurement. In a subsequent chapter, measuring performance will be discussed at some length; but suffice it to say, the provider must clearly understand what is going to be measured, what standards will be used, and the methods of measurement. These performance standards may include sanitation, warehouse operations, productivity, on-time shipping, product availability, product rotation, or any number of other requirements. Whatever they may be, they must be clearly defined. If forms are going to be used for inspections and evaluations, samples should be included so the provider will know the precise nature of the measurements.

Physical Inventories. While the contract usually spells out the number of physical inventories that will be included in the service fees, the methods of taking the inventories are not. The requirements, techniques, and reporting of both full and cycle inventories should be stated; and sample reports included where appropriate.

Proof of Delivery. If proof of delivery on any or all shipments is required, it should be indicated, along with the reporting requirements.

Quality. When the maintenance of specific quality or ISO programs is mandatory, the specific obligations should be included.

Systems. This section of the manual very well could be as lengthy as those for the remainder of the procedures combined, but it will be very important. The agreed-upon systems and their output should be precisely defined. These will include, but by no means be limited to, such things as order entry systems, EDI, warehouse management systems, radio frequency scanning, automated rating systems, or even the systems for running conveyors and pick lines. Depending on the level of computerization or mechanization in the operation, the performance of the various systems very well could be the foundation of the entire operation.

Dispute Resolution

Finally, a good procedures manual will contain provisions for resolving disputes or softening points of friction. In spite of everyone's best efforts, there will be disputes and disagreements. A procedure should be in place for dealing with these; so when they do arise, they can be resolved with a minimum of disruption and emotion.

Conclusion

The policies and procedures discussed in this chapter obviously apply primarily to a basic distribution operation. All would not be applicable to other types of arrangements; and to some, none would be. An order fulfillment facility, for example, would be more concerned with picking lines, conveyors, UPS, or FedEx. A freight bill payment operation would require a totally different set of procedures.

Hopefully, however, these suggestions will be helpful to many and stimulate *all* to develop a thorough and manageable set of guidelines and methods for the outsourcing relationship, whatever it may be.

Drafting such a manual will be time consuming and frustrating; but in the long run, it can be the glue that holds the operation together.

Chapter 12

Implementation

*There's nothing remarkable about it. All one has to do is to hit
the right key at the right time and the instrument plays itself.*
                                    - Johann Sebastian Bach

Other than the ongoing management of the outsourced
application, the most important operational aspect of the entire
process will be the implementation or startup of the new facilities
or services. As Mr. Bach suggested, if you live in a perfect world,
there is nothing to it. If not, the process must be extremely well
planned and executed.

The Transition Team

Once the contract is signed and the policies and procedures
have been developed and agreed upon, the responsibility for
implementation should be transferred to an implementation or

transition team. This group should be comprised of individuals other than those who were a part of the project team. While the same functions or disciplines may be represented, presumably the project team was comprised of more senior managers; and it is now time to pass the mantle to those who will be responsible for implementing and managing the relationship on a continuing basis.

The project champion, usually the senior logistics executive, still should maintain overall responsibility; but the actual implementation will be managed by others. The entire project team should act as a steering committee, with its members providing guidance to their individual representatives, as well as the group as a whole.

The composition of the transition team will depend on the activity being outsourced; but for the purposes of this discussion, a full-line distribution center or integrated logistics operation will be assumed. Less complex efforts may require smaller teams.

Since the senior logistics executive will still have other responsibilities, another team leader should be appointed from the logistics area. Ideally, this will be the individual who will have continuing responsibility for the outsourced function.

Other team members should represent:

- Human Resources
- Sales
- Management Information Systems
- Transportation
- Warehouse Operations
- Customer Service
- Inventory Management
- Risk Management (Insurance and Security)

and any other function that will be impacted by, or have an influence on, the new facility or activity. Team members should be those that will be involved after the implementation phase, and it is important that they remain a part of the process. Too often, start-up teams move in quickly, perform their tasks, and disappear. While individuals and responsibilities may change from time to time, there should be a representative from all the appropriate functions and disciplines available throughout the term of the contract. In other words, the transition team transcends into a relationship team.

Finally, the logistics service provider must be represented on the team by the individual who will have direct responsibility for the account. He or she should have the strong support and involvement of the senior executive; but just as with the client, the chief executive officer cannot be expected to manage the outsourced operation on a day-to-day basis, unless, of course, it is a single-client arrangement.

While care must be taken to ensure that teams do not become too large and unwieldy, they must be large enough to encompass all the appropriate functions. It will not be unusual to have as many as ten members of the group.

A sophisticated provider will insist on access to certain client representatives and information. Schneider Logistics, for example, requires

- A single point of contact to act as a liaison between themselves and the customer;
- Access to client facilities and briefings from client associates on current business processes;
- Access to information required to populate the provider's database;
- IT resources to evaluate, design and implement connectivity solutions in conjunction with Schneider;
- A cross-functional customer team to review Schneider's plans and processes to ensure positive, value-added effects on customer operations. [1]

The Transition Plan

The first and most important task of the transition team will be to develop the implementation plan, starting with the schedule or timetable.

Timetable

As with the membership of the transition team, the timetable will vary with the type and complexity of the operation. Warehousing, transportation, freight bill payment, software installation, and other activities all will be different. Likewise, schedules will vary between the transfer of existing operations and the start up of new ones.

The important thing to remember is that a realistic timetable should be established and adhered to. Often, there is a tendency to take as long as a year to make a decision to outsource, then expect the provider to be up and running efficiently in thirty days. These hurried, poorly planned startups almost always create difficulties that in some cases are never overcome.

A timetable of ninety to one hundred and twenty days should be reasonable for most outsourcing arrangements, assuming all the planning and policy development have been completed. Obviously, if the startup can be accomplished more quickly, it should be; but in matters of implementation, conservatism is the preferred policy.

If at all possible, startups should be scheduled for those times when volume is projected to be lowest. Also, if startup dates can coincide with accounting periods, such as the beginning of a quarter or fiscal year, financial reporting will be easier.

If another outsourced operation is being discontinued simultaneously, the transfer should be made at the end of the agreement period if practical. While at times they may be necessary, early terminations often can result in considerable expense.

Task List

The list of tasks to be accomplished should be developed by the entire team and reviewed frequently as implementation progresses.

The tasks should be organized by weeks, and the list should show precisely what needs to be done, when it will be done, and who is responsible. Figure 12-a is an example of a format that can be used for this purpose. One individual should be assigned responsibility for receiving input and issuing updated reports. This person should be cautioned, however, not to get so involved in the format and graphics of the report that the work plan becomes subordinate to the publication.

The task list may contain literally hundreds of entries, depending on the complexity of the project; but in all plans, there will be certain basic areas that it will be necessary to cover.

Communications

At this point in the process, if the recommendations up until now have been followed, the project team will have agreed with the provider on expectations, policies, and procedures; and a contract will have been executed. These documents should be shared with the transition team. They will be the foundation for each step in the implementation process.

Appropriate information also should be shared with others in the company who will be directly affected by the new operation. For example, the sales and marketing departments should be informed of the new distribution plans and how they will impact on such things as order processing and customer service. Although it will be the responsibility of their representatives on the transition team to keep them informed, at the outset, a higher level briefing should be conducted. They, in turn, should decide how and when customers are to be notified.

START-UP PLAN
_____Distribution Center

Week	Activity	Resp Ind	Sched Comp	Actually Comp	Remarks
1.					
2.					
3.					
4.					
5.					

Figure 12-a: Example of Implementation Task List

If labor unions are involved, the contracts usually contain provisions for notification of such changes, and an early understanding with the union is critical. Although less of a problem now than in the early 1980's, the elimination of a unionized trucking operation can be particularly difficult. Such things as unfunded pension liabilities can increase the cost of a shutdown enormously. Although these issues should have been considered much earlier in the process, continuing communications are very important.

In the for-hire transportation area, new and existing carriers should be notified of the changes and provided information about their impact on individual shipment volumes.

If the activity is being transferred from one logistics service provider to another, the current provider should be notified as soon as the decision is made. Ending relationships will be discussed in more detail in a later chapter, but nothing is to be gained by trying to keep the move confidential at this point. While there is a risk of service deterioration once such a decision is announced, the risk of not informing the provider is much greater. More often than not, if treated fairly, they will pride themselves on assisting in a smooth transition.

Notwithstanding the above, be prepared for the worst. The transition plan must contain a course of action to be taken if a provider simply refuses to maintain a reasonable level of service or cooperation. One way to do this is to develop a contingency plan that provides for other existing facilities to assume additional volume on a short notice. While this may be expensive because of such things as overtime, equipment rentals, and other unplanned activities, customer service can be protected.

Human Resource Issues

Affected employees should be notified as early in the process as possible. If they are to be adversely impacted by the outsourcing, every effort should be made to assist them in any way that is practical. Reasonable severance packages should be provided, as well as assistance in locating other employment.

Special attention should be paid to The Worker Adjustment and Retraining Notification Act (WARN), which became effective February 4, 1989. This legislation offers protection to hourly, salaried, and management employees, as well as their families, by requiring employees to give sixty-day written notice of any mass layoffs or plant closings.

WARN is applicable to employers...

- employing 100 or more full time workers, or

- employing 100 or more full and part-time employees who in the aggregate, work at least 4,000 or more hours per week.

Violations of the act can result in liability for the affected employees' loss of pay and benefits, including medical expenses, for a period of up to 60 days, including attorney fees and costs.

Often the new provider will be able to hire some of the employees; and assuming they are reliable and have a good work ethic, everyone benefits.

Employees who will not be provided for should be informed of that. They should not be left in a state of limbo, wondering what the final outcome might be. If they are necessary over the short term, offer them bonuses to remain with the company during the transition period.

In communicating with the employees, the overriding principles should be speed, honesty, and sensitivity.

As the outsourcing firm is planning to decrease its work force, the provider most likely is planning to add new employees. While for the most part, this will be the provider's responsibility, there should be discussions and general agreement about the necessary skills involved.

Changeover Method

Another extremely important and early decision that must be made is exactly how the new operation will be phased in. Obviously, there are a number of ways to proceed. When moving to a dedicated truck fleet, for example, it is possible to shut down an operation one day and begin the new one the next. The same is true with freight bill payment services. All carriers can be given a date after which all bills should be mailed to the new provider.

Almost everyone who has ever been through an outsourcing transition, however, will agree that regardless of the activity, a phased-in approach is much more desirable. This is especially true for broader programs.

There are several advantages to the phased implementation. First of all, such an approach facilitates the training of employees and the testing of new systems and procedures on a gradual basis. By transferring small amounts of volume at a time, there is ample opportunity to learn right at the outset. There is nothing worse than a group of untrained warehouse and office employees inundated with orders they do not know how to handle. One well-respected warehouse literally was "brought to its knees" by taking on more than it could accomplish at one time. It did not insist on a reasonably phased implementation, and within days, the entire operation was hopelessly behind schedule. Errors and late shipments were the rule, and customer service of the new client quickly dropped to an all time low. As a result it was necessary to relocate the operation before it ever had an opportunity to succeed. The warehouse company never quite got over the ill will and tarnished reputation it acquired; and within a short time, it was sold to another firm.

The client manager in charge of the transition no longer is employed there.

Secondly, a phased-in approach minimizes the total inventory requirement. As shipments are transferred gradually from the old location to the new, inventories at the first facility are decreased as they are increased at the new one. Otherwise, it would be necessary to carry duplicate inventories for some period of time. When the inventories at the closing facility are at a minimum, the remainder of the stock can be transferred to the new location.

The type of phase-in will vary by firm. It can be by division, geographic or sales territory, or particular groups or classes of customer. The team should be sure, however, that each segment of the phase-in is representative of the total operation. In other words, do not transfer only unit loads of easy to handle items, followed by volume made up of small orders, or difficult to pick items. It would be somewhat analogous to teaching a teenager to drive an automobile with an automatic transmission, only to give him one with a five-speed straight transmission for his birthday.

Training

Although the selected provider may already handle similar products, or use similar distribution techniques, it will be necessary to train all personnel in the policies and procedures of the new client. This can best be done onsite as the operation begins; and it is at this point that most, if not all, of the transition team should begin spending a large portion of their time at the new location. Each member of the group should train provider personnel in their respective areas and be available to answer questions and assist in problem resolution.

It is at this time, also, that any necessary cross training by client employees, particularly those that may be leaving, should be accomplished.

While it is helpful to send the service provider's employees to an existing location for indoctrination prior to startup, this only supplements the training. It is not a substitute for onsite, hands-on education.

Members of the transition team should reside at the new facility until they are comfortable that the provider is able to operate on its own. When this is accomplished, although they should remain on call and continue to serve as resources, ongoing management will be the primary responsibility of the logistics manager that has chaired the group.

Other Issues

Someone once said, "The devil is in the details;" and this is particularly true with an outsourcing implementation. The task list must include everything from laying out the warehouse and striping the floor to ordering bill of lading forms, stationery, and order pickers. One good way to ensure that nothing is omitted is to review the operations and requirements at similar existing facilities. Do not leave anything out or assume it will take care of itself. Put it on the list.

Conclusion

While this chapter has considered a fairly broad logistics application, whatever the outsourced activity is, large or small, a detailed plan must be developed and the same basic principles adhered to. They should differ only in quantity and not quality.

Above all, listen to the logistics service provider. The firm was selected because it was perceived to be the best choice for the task at hand. Its core competency is logistics, and in this regard, can offer valuable and meaningful advice.

A well planned, documented, and managed implementation can be an enormous source of pride for those who worked so hard to make it happen.

Chapter 13

Managing the Relationship

You don't manage people; you manage things. You lead people.
- Admiral Grace Hopper

Managing an outsourced relationship is not an easy assignment. Prior to implementation, contracts, procedures, and personnel all should be in place, as well as expectations and possible friction points identified; but from time to time, interests and goals will differ. Inevitably, conflicts will arise, and must be dealt with. Even when differences are minimal, managing the provider will be a full time job.

Obstacles

Everest Group, Inc., an outsourcing consultant, has assisted many clients in developing the causes of dysfunctional outsourcing relationships; and their experience has shown that the most common contributing factors to these are:

- Pricing and service levels are established at the start of the contract and usually contain no meaningful mechanism for continuous improvement.

- Differences in buyer and supplier cultures often cause misunderstanding and distrust. Even if the cultures are compatible, the two parties still have fundamentally different goals and objectives that are frequently difficult to harmonize.

- All outsourcing contracts are based on key assumptions regarding technologies, business conditions, personnel, and other relevant issues. As soon as the contract is signed, these assumptions begin to change. However detailed the contract or favorable the terms, most contracts cannot anticipate the changes in an evolving environment. This phenomenon tends to ensure that one, if not both, of the parties will become disenchanted with the relationship. Longer-term contracts that lack flexibility tend to increase the likelihood of dissatisfaction.

- Once the contract is in force, there is a great temptation for both parties to sub-optimize the relationship and attempt to better their lot at the expense of the other. The inflexible nature of the contract usually favors the supplier.

- Buyers frequently underestimate the time and attention required to manage an outsourcing relationship, or worse, they hand over management responsibility to the supplier. The supplier begins to operate in a priority vacuum, and service levels tend to deteriorate because the supplier's agenda is not in sync with the buyer's business objectives.

- Lack of management oversight is usually the result of two factors: The team that negotiated the contract often does not stay engaged in contract management. A new team that may or may not understand the contract's intentions is given responsibility for managing the relationship.

- Employees that understood the pre-outsourced environment have been transferred to the supplier's team. This disruption in continuity can have significant adverse effects on the outsourcing relationship.[1]

In discussing outsourcing relationships, Peter Bendor – Samuel, Editor of *Outsourcing Journal*, has made an interesting distinction between partnerships and alliances. In suggesting that most contemporary outsourcing arrangements are alliances rather than partnerships, he said,

"A partnership is an association with another entity in a joint endeavor, where both parties have joint interests, joint risks and rewards. In a partnership, the interests are undivided. In an alliance, there is a pact or agreement between the parties to cooperate for a specific purpose and to merge their separate interests and efforts for that common purpose. The two work together for each other's good. Their pact (or the contract) establishing their alliance and agreement to perform a specified function together provides for flexibility. It also recognizes that their interests will differ at times." [2]

Such an arrangement by its very nature will produce cultural differences, and this is particularly true with logistics outsourcing. While the objective of the two parties may be the same, their methods of achieving those goals may be quite different.

For example, the client more often than not will be more bureaucratic, and employ an elaborate approval process before significant (or sometimes insignificant) change can be made. A logistics service provider, on the other hand, tends to be more entrepreneurial and able to make decisions quicker. (It has been suggested, however, that as logistics service providers become larger, they too are becoming more structured and averse to rapid change.)

In-house logistics managers often may see the provider as a threat to their control or job security, and never totally embrace the relationship. While they may give it lip service and do what has to be done, they are not completely committed to the success of the operation.

As the Everest Group suggested, another common source of difficulty is the leaving of the supplier to its own management devices. Too often, either through lack of interest or lack of expertise on the client's part, the logistics service provider will be expected to operate on its own, with little or no direction.

While certainly this is desirable, and indeed one of the primary reasons for outsourcing, advice and counsel must be *available* even though it is not utilized every day.

Effective Management

In Chapter 8, it was suggested that as many potential friction points as possible be identified in advance; and even though this may have been accomplished, they will not resolve themselves when they do arise. The client must have in place an effective management structure and process for the relationship, not only to resolve conflict but to manage the ongoing activity.

The Relationship Manager

Ideally, the logistics manager that has chaired the transition team during the implementation of the outsourcing arrangement will be the relationship manager, but this may not be the right choice. The client must be sensitive to the principle that managing relationships requires quite a different skill set than managing logistics activities. While managers may be good logistics problem solvers, they simply may lack the necessary managerial and leadership capability.

Robert E. Sabath, a veteran supply chain consultant, put it very succinctly when he said, "Successful managers of [outsourced] relationships need to be problem solvers, innovators, facilitators, and negotiators who have exceptional people skills and the ability to get things done. Most managers who take the traditional logistics career path never have a chance to learn the skills required to be a good relationship manager. Nor do they have an interest in them." [3]

The relationship manager then must strike a fine balance between being a logistics problem solver and a leader that can motivate and facilitate superior performance by the provider. He or she must be accessible, willing to listen, a good communicator, and have a high sense of integrity. The manager must be available to the provider when assistance is needed. As our society becomes more technical, it is easy to lose sight of what good communications really consist of. When a provider has a problem that requires client attention, messages in voice mail and e-mail communications simply are not good enough. The manager must be available for a two-way voice dialogue either by telephone, or if necessary, in person. Unfortunately, too many business people have become more enamored with the various message devices than they have with the messages themselves.

Once contact is made, the manager must be willing to listen carefully to the issue and its impact on the task at hand. Since the selected provider is an expert in his field, the defined problem may be one that will require some research and thought. A hasty, uninformed response will do more harm than good, and while proper care must be taken to make sure that resolution is prompt, it must also be appropriate.

Finally, the relationship manager must have a high sense of integrity. Many times, problems with the outsourced operation are the fault of the client; and in too many cases, client representatives are unwilling to accept responsibility for their own actions or lack thereof. The manager must be honest and forthright in dealing with these issues and be willing to place responsibility exactly where it should be.

Frequently, the major relationship challenges will not be with the provider, but within the client organization itself. The manager then must be able to negotiate and influence internally as well as externally. As pointed out earlier, some personnel will be quick to criticize and even undermine; and the outsourcing manager must have the position and standing within the organization to combat these negative forces.

He or she must have the respect and influence necessary to resolve cross-functional issues quickly and non-politically.

At the risk of digression, the necessity for relationship management expertise will not be limited to outsourcing. In 2003, the Council of Logistics Management published an "official" definition of the term supply chain management. The second part of the definition states, "Importantly it also includes coordination and collaboration with channel partners, which can be suppliers, intermediaries, third-party service providers, and customers."

As suggested earlier, in many cases logistics managers have not been conspicuous by their relationship skills. Many good logisticians simply haven't mastered the skills required for effective supply chain management – human relations skills, negotiating expertise, and a knack for fostering collaboration and integration among them. If they expect to succeed at the next level, they must find a way to acquire them.

Integration

Users of logistics service providers should treat them as extensions of their own business. In a logistics relationship, the provider will be the last contact with the product before it is shipped to the customer, and as such, is one of the most important representatives of the client.

The provider should be considered as much a part of the logistics process as an in-house operation and treated accordingly. While ensuring this is the primary responsibility of the transition team, the relationship manager must assume the responsibility for making sure that the necessary steps have been taken.

Each function that is impacted by, or has any impact on, the outsourced operation must make certain that any process changes are reviewed by the providers prior to implementation. Not only might they receive some good suggestions, but the impact of such changes must be understood and communicated. For example, if a new order entry system is being contemplated, the logistics service provider must be consulted early in the process since their requirements may be quite different from in-house needs. To install such a system without this input could be disastrous.

Outsourced operations should be treated in precisely the same manner as in-house operations. They are an integral part of the company, and it is absolutely critical that this not be forgotten or overlooked.

Communications

Poor communication is second only to poor planning as a major cause of outsourcing relationship failure.

Communications on all aspects of the logistics arrangement must be frequent and two-way. This applies not only to the relationship management communications discussed earlier. If the provider is truly integrated into the client organization, it must be kept fully informed of every aspect of the business that will affect it or influence its operations. For example, advance notification of such things as deals, promotions, or possible labor disputes can be critical to the scheduling activity.

Often, the logistics service provider is expected to operate in an information vacuum; and if this becomes the rule rather than the exception, the entire operation will become reactionary. This is the first step toward failure.

Similarly, the provider must be encouraged to keep the client fully informed about its operations and plans. Unanticipated scheduling or shipping problems, work stoppages, or equipment shortages are just a few of the unpleasant surprises that can send shock waves throughout the system. The client relationship manager must be sure that the relationship is such that two-way, open, honest and prompt communication is encouraged, expected, and accepted. There is no quicker way to sabotage a relationship than to allow unpleasant surprises.

The Dalai Lama has said that

"...to act altruistically, concerned only for the welfare of others, with no selfish or ulterior motives, is to affirm a sense of universal responsibility." [4]

While this is a goal for which we all should strive, it is not one we are likely to ever reach in totality. However, in dealing with any issues, whether they be client- or provider-provoked, there are some basic rules which, if followed, can make even unpleasant communications somewhat more tolerable.

1. These are business, not personal, issues.

2. Approach all problems openly with the responsible party. Do not operate with a hidden agenda.

3. Treat the other party as you would like to be treated were the roles reversed.

4. Do not become emotional.

5. Do your homework. Make sure you have all the facts before confronting.

6. Do not act impulsively.

7. Do not exaggerate or embellish. While the addition of a few details can make a problem seem even more entertaining and embarrassing, this only complicates the

resolution and certainly does little to cement a relationship.

8. Give the other party time to respond. To demand an answer "in fifteen minutes" allows no time for research and only adds to the dilemma.

9. As part of the solution, develop a plan for preventing a recurrence.

10. Share the problem and its method of resolution with others. This will enhance everyone's understanding.

The most important rule of all, however, is to maintain open communication at all levels at all times. Do not communicate only when there is a problem.

There is no one best schedule for, or frequency of, communications between client and provider, but an example of a program that was effective for one relationship was that of the Professional Health Care Sector of Kimberly-Clark Corporation and the InterAmerican Group, now a part of USF Logistics, Inc. [5]

These two companies utilized a number of different types of communication at a number of different levels; i.e.,

- Daily telephone conversations between operations personnel.
- Monthly conference calls between customer service personnel of the two companies.
- Client visits to the InterAmerican facility several times a year.
- Annual meeting of all logistics service providers, where client outlined its plans and providers exchanged information and solutions.
- Performance evaluations using a monthly report card.

- Open, frequent communication between senior managements of both firms.
- Provider participation in planning with client customers.
- Provider visits to client customers to discuss operational issues.

A number of companies utilize the annual meeting concept quite effectively. Experience has proven that the provider representatives attending feel more involved in the client's operations, and of course use the sessions as forums to exchange ideas with the other providers.

Customer visits by provider personnel also can be quite effective as long as they are made by qualified, informed representatives.

The appropriate methods of communication will depend on the nature of the specific relationship, but whatever means are utilized, both parties should err on the side of over-communication.

Measuring Performance

In 1610, Galileo Galilei said, "We must measure what can be measured, and make measurable what cannot be measured." Over the years, this statement has evolved to the more direct, often-quoted axiom, "You cannot manage what you cannot measure." But today, some 400 years later, logistics managers still struggle with the premise.

Much has been written about measuring the performance of logistics service providers, and different firms have different standards and levels of measurement. For example, a pharmaceutical client would be much more concerned about batch controls and error rates than would an appliance manufacturer. Some firms have developed meaningful performance and productivity standards and metrics, but a surprising number have not. There is no valid reason for not having a well-thought-out and meaningful measurement program in any outsourced operation. Although literally hundreds of rules and suggestions for establishing metrics exist, the following four basic axioms will apply across all industries and providers. These are:

A. The first axiom is the tried and true, "*You can't manage what you can't measure.*"

B. "*Make measurable what cannot be measured.*"

C. *Measure only what is important and actionable.*

D. *Performance measurement must be balanced.*

The first axiom is particularly applicable to logistics operations. If the client does not know how the provider is performing against agreed upon standards and benchmarks, it will be impossible to evaluate not only the provider's efficiency, but the client's own customer service performance, as well.

Not mentioned nearly as often is the second part of Galileo's admonition, "Make measurable what cannot be measured." In other words, the task is to identify activities within the warehouse in discrete segments against which you can establish measurable and achievable standards. As the relationship evolved, standards should have been identified and agreed upon; but as the operation comes on line, it is important to initiate and conform to a regular measurement program. Realistic, measurable standards should be set, and performance accurately evaluated against these. A common mistake is to establish standards that are so vague they are absolutely meaningless. This creates unnecessary work for both parties.

Examples of sound, measurable criteria are:

- Productivity
- Order Fill Rate
- On-Time Performance
- Inventory Variations
- Order Cycle Time
- Line Item Accuracy
- Number of Orders Handled
- Space Utilization

Measure only what is important. This is another area that often leads to "report abuse." Some managers will become so fascinated by the reports themselves that they will insist on measuring meaningless trivia. If it does not have an impact on the operation, its cost, or customer service, forget it.

As indicated in the fourth axiom, the measurement must be balanced. Too many measurements can bury the operation in details and lead to friction between the parties. Too few or too general evaluations make the performance difficult to manage. Timing should be balanced as well. Don't measure everything every day.

What Should Be Measured?

As indicated earlier, there are several areas that lend themselves to accurate and meaningful measurement; but every firm will rank the importance of these differently. The most common areas of measurement are *warehouse operations, sanitation, productivity, order cycle time, on-time performance (shipping and/or delivery), order fill, and inventory variations.*

Warehouse operations usually are evaluated by personal visits and evaluation can be quite detailed. Ordinarily, there will be a monthly inspection with a more thorough audit conducted annually.

Sanitation will be very important to clients in the food and related industries, and detailed monthly evaluations of each facility should be made.

Productivity can be measured in different ways, but most firms will want to measure some form of productivity per person-hour. This can be orders, line items, cases, unit loads, or any other unit of measurement that is important to the user firm.

Order cycle time is simply the time elapsed between the time an order is received and the time it leaves the dock. In a highly sophisticated order fulfillment operation, this time will be measured in hours; in other more relaxed environments, in days.

On-time performance will be a measurement of either on-time shipping or delivery, or both.

Order fill, or orders shipped complete, determines the number of orders that were shipped complete as ordered, without any back order.

Inventory variations can be determined by calculating the differences between physical and book counts. In many situations, physical count is required to match both client and provider book inventories.

As indicated at the outset of this discussion, there are literally hundreds of measurement techniques. For example, *DC Velocity* in its metrics research divided the measurements into four basic segments; i.e.,

1. *Cost* such as various costs as a percentage of sales, costs per unit, and operating ratios.

2. *Quality* metrics such as order fill, line fill, damage percentage, and backorders.

3. *Time* of order cycle, pieces per man-hour, overtime hours, etc.

4. *Other* measurements such as miles per gallon, workforce turnover, and equipment utilization.

Whatever metrics are installed, Kate Vitasek and Steve Geary suggest that there are "Twelve Commandments of Successful Performance Management" that separate a great company's efforts from those of a good company. [6]

1. Lead: Practice what you preach.
2. Focus: Know your goals.
3. Balance: Use a balanced approach.
4. Beware: Know the point of your metrics.
5. Involve: Get employees engaged.
6. Apply: Be metrics users and *not* just "collectors" or "posters."
7. Anticipate: Use metrics as your headlights.
8. Integrate: Layer your metrics like an onion.
9. Listen: The voice of the customer.
10. Benchmark!
11. Be Flexible: There is no holly grail of metrics.
12. Patience: Crawl before you walk.

Methods of Measurement

Warehouse Operations and Sanitation

Warehouse operations and sanitation usually are evaluated on a monthly basis with more comprehensive inspections performed annually. For a food manufacturer, the sanitation performance will be the most serious evaluation of the two, and harsher penalties should be enforced for non-compliance.

For years, the Nabisco Foods Group (now a part of Kraft) conducted a "1000 Point Audit" at each of its outsourced warehouse operations. The audit is tactical in nature and focuses on compliance with operating and sanitation policies.

In the operations area, the evaluation is concentrated on:

General Appearance
Receiving Dock
Stock Locator System
Shipping/Order Selecting
Sanitation
Stock Rotation
Security
Reconditioning Area
Temperature/Humidity Control

Administratively, compliance with procedure is measured in the following categories:

Customer Returns
Held Product
Case Control
Receiving Records
Shipping Records
Reporting

Each item evaluated is given a point value ranging from five to fifteen, for a total of one thousand; and at the conclusion of the evaluation, each operation is given a numerical score. Scores of fewer than nine hundred points are considered to be unsatisfactory.

One of the most comprehensive in the industry, this audit was a valuable tool for measuring and managing Nabisco logistics service providers.

Appendix 13-1 is an example of another warehouse operations audit, suitable for use during an annual inspection. It can be scaled back for less thorough monthly or quarterly reviews, and a variation of such a form also can be used for the initial evaluation of potential providers.

Sanitation audits can be conducted by client quality assurance personnel or by outside agencies. There are several good firms that specialize in sanitation audits, and often a user firm will utilize a combination of retained and in-house inspectors to manage the sanitation program.

It is very important in the sanitation area that the provider know exactly what is required; i.e., storage practices, baits or traps required, inspection procedures, etc. Once the provider understands the requirements, compliance must be consistently acceptable. Little room for error should be allowed.

Appendix 13-2 illustrates a typical inspection form for evaluating sanitation practices in a food warehouse.

Ratings should depend on the severity and number of deficiencies observed, and deficiencies usually are divided into three categories; i.e.,

- *Critical* – A condition that *would* result in a regulatory criticism if observed, such as actual infestation or contamination.

- *Major* – A condition that *could* result in such criticism, such as imminent potential for contamination.

- *Minor* – A deficiency, but one that is unlikely to cause product adulteration.

Productivity

Whatever productivity items are measured, they should be evaluated against realistic and mutually agreed-upon standards. These can be derived from either historical data developed from experience or through pre-engineered handling standards. (For a good discussion of this subject, see *Warehousing Profitably – An Update*, by Kenneth B. Ackerman.) [7]

Some of the most common measurements are cases or unit loads per person-hour, orders per person-hour, or order lines per person-hour. The calculations are all similar. For example, simply take the total cases shipped during a month and divide it by the total person-hours worked; i.e.,

Assume shipments of 760,000 cases per month.

Assume 20 employees working 173.2 hours per month each, or a total of 3,464 person-hours.

$760,000 \div 3,464 = 219$ cases per person-hour.

If this represented 6,000 orders, the calculation would be $6,000 \div 3,464 = 1.73$ orders per person-hour, and so on.

This sample calculation was based on an average 4.33-week month and 40 hours per week per employee. In actual practice, one would simply use the exact hours worked during the period being measured.

Order Performance

Calculations for the other performance criteria also are fairly straightforward. For example:

Order Cycle Time = Date Shipped – Date Received

(If measured in hours, simply measure the number of hours between order receipt and shipment.)

On-Time Shipment = Orders Shipped on Time/Total Orders; i.e., **98** orders shipped on time/100 total orders = 98% on-time performance.

On-Time Delivery = Orders Delivered on Time/Total Orders.

Order Fill = Orders Shipped Complete/Total Orders.

Overall product availability can be measured by simply dividing the total number of cases shipped by the total cases ordered.

Costs can be calculated as well, by multiplying the number of hours worked by the fully allocated cost per hour of the operation.

Most outsourcing firms will give providers a monthly rating or "report card." Figure 13-a illustrates how such a summary might be constructed.

Figure 13-b is an actual example of a "report card" used by Kimberly-Clark Corporation.

Inventory Variations

Inventory performance usually is determined by balancing the physical inventory, whether it be cycle or total, against the book inventory of the provider, as well as that of the client. The contract contains provisions outlining how the discrepancies will be dealt with, but consistent unfavorable variations can be an indicator of other problems, such as orders shipped incorrectly or receipts not counted accurately. Often these errors will manifest themselves in other measurement calculations; but whether they do or not, the underlying causes should be investigated thoroughly.

In addition to measuring compliance with standards, the performance of each logistics service provider can be compared

PERFORMANCE REPORT FOR
MONTH OF _____ 20___
PROVIDER_____

Measurement	Calculation	Target	Actual	B/(W) Target	Last Month
Cases/Person-hour	Cases Shipped Total Hours				
Orders/Person-hour	Orders Shipped Total Hours				
Order Lines/Person-hour	Order Lines Shipped Total Hours				
Order Cycle Time	Time Shipped Minus Time Received				
On-Time Shipments	Orders Shipped On Time Total Orders				
On-Time Delivery	Orders Delivered On Time Total Orders				
Order Fill	Orders Shipped Complete Total Orders				
Product Availability	Cases Shipped Cases Ordered				
Customer Complaints	Number Received				
Cost Per Case Shipped	Total Labor $ Cases Shipped				
Cost Per Order Shipped	Total Labor $ Orders Shipped				

Figure 13-a: Sample of Monthly Performance Report

251

KIMBERLY-CLARK'S THIRD-PARTY REPORT CARD

Orders shipped	234	
Transfer orders received	29	
Total	263	

	YES	NO
1. Orders shipped on time	234	0
2. Orders confirmed out on time, accurate	233	1*
3. Transfers confirmed in on time, accurate	29	0
4. Picking/loading accuracy	234	0

Total errors	1
Total correct orders and transfers	262
Total orders and transfers	263

Subtotal score	99.62%
Less billing accuracy	0
Less report of damaged product	0

FINAL SCORE	**99.62%**

* Shipment 22-957880, shipped 9/8, confirmed 9/13.

EXPLANATION OF PERFORMANCE CRITERIA

1. Orders shipped on time – Distribution centers are evaluated based on their ability to ship orders not only on the ship day, but also at the time the carrier arrives to pick up the freight, without delaying the carrier.

2. Orders confirmed out on-time, accurate – Distribution centers are required to confirm orders as having shipped from the distribution center within 24 hours of the shipment. This category also tracks the accuracy of the DC to record product quantity changes on the order.

3. Transfers confirmed in on-time/accurate – DCs must confirm product received at the DC within 24 hours of receipt.

4. Picking/loading errors – DCs are scored on their ability to fill orders correctly, load trailers correctly by delivery schedule, and palletize and shrink wrap according to instructions. Backorders created when product is available are reported as a pick error.

5. Billing timeliness and accuracy – DCs are evaluated on their ability to correctly invoice for storage, handling and accessorial charges. Invoices must be sent timely. Failure in this category will result in the deduction of one percentage grade point from the total score received from categories 1 – 4.

6. Report of damaged product – All DCs are required to report monthly the damaged items in inventory and the quantity.

Figure 13-b: Report card and performance criteria used by Professional Health Care Sector of Kimberly-Clark Corporation to monitor performance of its third-party logistics providers. Partners receive their own monthly report card as well as those of four other facilities used by PHC. (Reprinted with permission from Outsourced Logistics Report, copyright 1995. Harrington-Harps Associates)

with that of others, thus facilitating ongoing measurement and benchmarking within the entire system.

Having said all this, neither the outsourcing firm nor the provider should lose sight of the fact that improved performance is most impacted by the installation of improved processes. In the words of Kate Vitasek, Michael Ledyard, et.al., "While it is true that performance metrics are a necessary and irreplaceable element in performance management, it is essential to combine your business measurement efforts with qualitative process analysis and viable improvement efforts on core businesses." [8]

Motivation and Reward

One of the most important aspects of managing the outsourcing relationship is that of motivation and reward. Too often, good performance is simply taken for granted; and many tend to forget that approval and recognition are basic human needs. Ralph Waldo Emerson said, "The reward for a thing well done is to have done it;" but even when we take pride in our own performance, we take even more pride when it is acknowledged by others.

A number of firms have come to recognize that compliments and acknowledgement of effort are proven motivators, and have established formal programs for doing so. Kimberly-Clark, for example, uses its Third Party Report Card as a basis for identifying a "Warehouse of the Year." All employees of the selected operation are taken out to lunch.

Becton Dickenson has a similar procedure for its warehouse of the year selection, and Nabisco Foods used its 1000-Point Audit as the basis for its annual presentation.

Sam's Club selects a "Distribution Center of the Year" based on certain administrative and operating criteria, and this award is coveted highly by both management and hourly personnel of the logistics service providers in the Sam's network.

The Pillsbury Company has a comprehensive award program for both carriers and distribution centers, measuring performance in such areas as on-time shipping, damage-free shipments, sanitation inspection scores, warehouse damage and case fill.

Almost thirty years ago, a major food manufacturer developed a program that has served it well over time. Each year the company holds a two-day meeting of its logistics service providers. The sessions consist of presentations by both the company and its providers, and offer guidance on topics of mutual interest and importance. Any upcoming changes in policies and procedures are discussed in this forum, and input is sought from the providers.

Each provider is represented by its senior manager, as well as the manager responsible for the account.

The meeting, which includes a good balance of social and business activities, is in itself an excellent motivator; but the high point of the two days is always the presentation of the "Award for Logistics Excellence." Based on criteria very similar to those of the Nabisco 1000-Point Audit, one provider is chosen each year to hold and exhibit this crystal trophy.

Within thirty days of this meeting, the client relationship manager and other key personnel visit the provider's location and "re-present" the trophy at a dinner for all employees associated with the account. Each person attending is given a gift commemorating the event.

Still another firm has a different, but practical approach to rewarding its providers. Again, based on criteria such as customer satisfaction, order fulfillment, and other operational performance, it simply pays out cash bonuses to its providers. These bonuses are paid twice annually, and the management of the company receiving such a cash incentive is strongly urged to share it with the personnel involved with the account.

Whatever method for motivating and rewarding is selected, it is important to remember that recognition must be ongoing and frequent. Do not make the mistake of establishing a wonderful once-a-year program, then ignore good performance for the remainder of the year.

Finally, make certain that the recognition is properly directed. Do not recognize a manager for an outstanding effort of one of the hourly employees. A well-placed, complimentary letter sometimes can be a better motivator than an increase in salary.

Everyone needs recognition for his accomplishments, but few people make the need known quite as clearly as the little boy who said to his father, "Let's play darts. I'll throw and you say, "Wonderful!""

(from *The Best of Bits and Pieces*)

Conclusion

The basic premise of outsourcing is that a firm is selecting a service provider that is well qualified to perform the logistics functions, and one that will do so in a satisfactory manner acting on its own initiative. While at the outset, this may seem inconsistent with the discussions in this chapter, it is not.

It should not be necessary to manage the operations of the provider, but the *relationship* must be managed by knowledgeable, thoughtful client representatives. The provider must be communicated with, monitored, evaluated, motivated, and rewarded. This will be the measure of success in the outsourcing relationship.

In the words of Fost, "Profit is the product of labor plus capital multiplied by management. You can hire the first two. The last must be inspired."

Chapter 14

Be a Good Partner

I'm very loyal in a relationship. Any relationship. When I go out with my mom, I don't look at other moms. I don't go, "Oooh, I wonder what her macaroni and cheese tastes like."

- Gary Shandling

Up until now, the discussions have revolved around the providers; i.e., how they are identified, selected, managed, motivated, and rewarded. But the outsourcing firm constitutes the other critical half of these relationships, and it is equally important that its performance be managed and measured as well. In the previous chapter, the role of the relationship manager was discussed; but in order to manage most effectively, he/she should measure the performance and contribution of his/her own firm.

Measuring Performance

While policies and procedures already have been agreed upon, if the client is truly interested in continuous improvement, it will develop a formal process for determining the provider's perceptions of the client's own performance.

Some companies have done so. All should.

There are numerous ways the client will impact on the performance of the provider, either positively or negatively; and the more important of these should be identified and dealt with on a continuing basis. This is best done with a written survey of providers so there will be little room for misunderstanding or misinterpretation. It need not be lengthy, but should address those issues that are important to the specific relationship.

Relevant questions might include:

- Is your contact readily available to you?
- Are telephone calls returned promptly?
- When problems are presented, does the person contacted deal with them effectively?
- Are changes in procedures communicated clearly and on a timely basis?
- Are shipment projections provided?
- Are they accurate?
- Is documentation on inbound shipments provided prior to arrival?
- Is it accurate?
- Is there sufficient lead time on outbound orders?
- Are inventory levels managed according to plan?
- What do we need to do to make your operation more efficient?

Whatever questions are appropriate to your operations, make sure they are asked and the answers acted upon.

The more the provider and the client work together toward a solution, the more effective it will be.

Honesty is The (Only) Policy

While it is not being suggested that the logistics industry is in a state of complete moral decay, there is no doubt that there has been a decrease in the ethics and integrity with which business people deal with each other. Andrew Carnegie said, "As I grow older, I pay less attention to what men say." This probably still is timely, albeit unfortunate, advice. People who profess to maintain a keen sense of integrity in their personal lives (and often do) at times are unable or unwilling to apply that some code of ethics to a business situation.

A case in point:

> "Your handling invoice is in Accounts Payable, but a lot of them have been out of the office at a meeting."

> "It should be coded today, and put through for payment tomorrow."

> "I approved it last week, but Bill has to approve it, as well. He is on vacation; but as soon as he returns, we will FedEx it to you."

> "I am sorry, but we have a policy of not expediting checks."

The translation of course is, "We have a company policy of paying invoices in forty-five days, not the fifteen we agreed to in the contract, and I am reluctant to admit that to you."

Or consider the situation when a contract is due for a rate review:

> "We have consultants in looking at our entire network and can't really do anything until they have completed the study."

259

This can be a very effective comment, and is designed to do two things; i.e., buy the client a sixty- to ninety-day delay in the price increase and intimidate the provider into keeping silent about it.

To some, these examples will seem somewhat exaggerated; but to most, there will be a hint of familiarity.

In a well-publicized book, *Is Lying Sometimes the Right Thing for an Honest Person to Do?*, author Quinn McKay, consultant and an adjunct professor of business ethics at the University of Utah, draws an interesting distinction between "personal ethics" and "gaming ethics." Under the rules of personal ethics, McKay says, "most of us generally would agree that it's wrong to deliberately mislead or deceive another person…" In gaming ethics, however, "deliberately misleading and deceiving others is not only allowed, it's an essential skill for winning." [1] These are the ethics that encourage running a play over the weak side of the line in a football game, raising the bet on a worthless poker hand, or taking advantage of an opponent's chess move.

Most business executives practice gaming ethics in the routine discharge of their responsibilities, but these actions usually are directed at competitors or adversaries. They should not be practiced in outsourcing relationships. The provider is a partner, or at least an ally, striving for similar goals. It is not the enemy, and most certainly is not a competitor.

"I ran the wrong kind of business, but I did it with integrity.
- Sydney Biddle Barrows [2]

Honor Your Commitments

Perhaps one of the most disturbing attributes of some client representatives is their failure to honor commitments, and the unwillingness of their companies to reinforce them. Often, a logistics service provider will be a small- to medium-sized business; and a breach of commitment can be quite harmful.

One warehouse company was asked by an existing client to lease an additional 200,000 square feet of warehouse space for a new product introduction. Since time appeared to be critical, the provider, in an effort to be responsive, did so based on a request received by facsimile. Although no contract with the client was drawn up, the facility was prepared for occupancy at a great deal of time and expense; but the new product was not forthcoming.

Finally, the client representative who had made the request offered an apology for the fact that the introduction had been cancelled, and there would be no need for the additional space. He went on to say that he had no authority to approve reimbursement for lease and preparation costs.

Obviously, the provider quickly appealed to the senior logistics executive, only to be told that the requesting individual had no authority to approve such a transaction in the first place.

Fortunately for the provider, the prompt initiation of legal proceedings resulted in a satisfactory settlement.

Unfortunately, there are too many similar examples in logistics outsourcing. Promises of decisions on contract extensions, rate increases, product receipts, and other critical aspects of the operations are routinely broken. Obviously, this does nothing to enhance the relationships, and over time only serves to undermine them.

Loyalty

Finally, be loyal to the providers you have chosen. Much effort and time have gone into the consummation of these relationships; and they should be nurtured until there is good reason not to do so.

Some clients feel that keeping a provider concerned about the future of the relationship is the best way to manage it. They believe that constant, subtle threats to cancel the agreement or move to another location will make the provider strive harder for perfection. While this may be effective over the short term, eventually the arrangement will fail.

261

In other cases, some clients will seek new proposals every time a contract nears expiration, even when the provider is providing good service. More often than not, the last thing they want to do is relocate the operations, but believe that such a strategy will force the provider to keep his skills and service honed to a razor sharp edge.

What it actually does is reduce what should be a long-term, continuously improving relationship to a series of short-term planning cycles. A provider never will feel a true commitment to a client who views it as a short-term associate with *possible* renewal options.

Conclusion

There is nothing unique about these four guiding principles. *Self-evaluation* is an exercise all of us should practice on occasion. How are we doing in our relationships? Ask those who know.

Be honest. It is the easiest course of action. If you always tell the truth, you are not burdened with the process of trying to remember what you said under various circumstances.

Honor your commitments. The reputation for not doing so is one to which no business person should aspire. It can destroy not only a relationship, but a career.

Loyalty is perhaps the most important attribute of all; but do not expect it from others if you do not practice it yourself.

For an outsourcing relationship, indeed any relationship, to succeed, it must be based on a keen sense of mutual trust and respect.

Chapter 15

Ending the Relationship

If well thou hast begun, go on; it is the end that crowns us, not the fight.

- Herrick

Inevitably, most business relationships eventually will come to an end. According to a survey conducted by the Outsourcing Institute, fifty-five percent of all "third-party partnerships" fail within five years. Too often, however, this basic premise is ignored in the initial outsourcing contract; and what should be a business-like agreement between the parties to move ahead separately, sometimes turns into an adversarial struggle which, at worst, ends up in court, and at best, results in operational disruptions for both parties.

As discussed in Chapter 9, there should be specific contractual provisions for termination, both for a normal expiration and for service or performance deficiencies. Even when the appropriate language is in place, however, the manner in which the terminations are handled can lead to the same unpleasantness.

Strategic Terminations

There are several strategic reasons for an outsourcing relationship to end, none of which are a result of disagreements or failure to meet expectations. Even successful alliances sometimes are terminated when the interests and focus of the parties themselves change.

Mergers and Acquisitions

Mergers and acquisitions almost have become more the rule than the exception, and can result in a combined firm having more distribution locations than it needs. This is particularly true when the merged companies have product lines in the same or compatible industries.

One major U.S. firm operated within a range of twelve to fourteen distribution centers for over twenty years, then within two years found itself with over two hundred facilities as a result of three major acquisitions. Fortunately, most of the operations were outsourced, providing ample flexibility for reducing the size of the network. On the other hand, well over one hundred fifty contracts had to be terminated. In a large number of the contracts, provisions had been included for such an eventuality; but in others, they had not.

Because of the full disclosure and courtesy with which the firm conducted these termination negotiations, however, there was little difficulty. Some providers even agreed to early terminations without penalties. Most providers will understand and accept the necessity for change in these circumstances if they are dealt with fairly.

Change in Corporate or Logistics Strategy

Another very legitimate reason for ending an outsourcing relationship is a change in corporate or logistics strategy. This can result from realignments of product offerings, target markets, or ordering and shipping philosophy. For example, if a firm has been marketing a product line shipped in less-than-truckload quantities from regional distribution centers, and changes its marketing strategy to provide UPS shipments of smaller quantities ordered through the Internet, it will require significantly different distribution facilities, equipment, and techniques. It may be forced to use different providers to obtain the services it needs.

Discontinuance of Products and Market Withdrawals

Less strategic, but no less final, is the discontinuance of product lines or the withdrawal from certain markets. This, of course, can result in the complete elimination of distribution facilities through no fault of the provider.

Bankruptcies and Shutdowns

Total shutdowns or bankruptcies can lead to the dissolution of entire networks in one fell swoop. Usually, however, this can be predicted; and in these cases, the provider must take extra precautions to ensure that it is not left with unpaid invoices or other liabilities.

Communications

In all the above and similar instances, if the contracts are drawn properly, there should be provisions covering the orderly termination of the operations. But as discussed earlier, if one of the parties to the agreement has less-than-honorable intentions, the opportunity for abuse still is present and likely to be taken advantage of. There is nothing that can be written here that will change that.

If, however, the client is sincerely interested in orderly transitions and amicable suspensions of operations, it will find that full disclosure, good communications, and common courtesy will almost guarantee them.

First of all, major strategic decisions are not made in a week. The planning cycle for changes in product offerings, geographic distribution, or marketing strategies often can be as long as six months to a year. As soon as the *strong possibility* of a discontinuance or curtailment becomes apparent, the information should be shared with the provider. The operative words here are *strong possibility*. Before deciding on further study of viable logistics options, no doubt hundreds of ideas may be advanced; and it would be disruptive and unfair to cause provider concern over each and every one of these. When the possibility of a significant change becomes apparent, however, it is unfair *not* to communicate this to the provider management.

The provider has a right to an opportunity to develop its own contingency plans. It must have ample time to compensate for the possibility of empty space, excess labor, and unutilized equipment. Given enough time and information, most can do so.

A popular client argument against full disclosure is that it will result in a deterioration in the service performance of the provider. Certainly, this is a possibility. If it does happen, there are legal remedies; but more important is the fact that if the provider was selected properly, for the right reasons, and has been treated fairly, this should not be a problem.

Some merger or acquisition transactions will move more quickly, and for a variety of other reasons must be kept confidential. This will shorten the timeframe for notice to the affected providers, but make it all the more important to notify them as quickly as it is practical to do so. More often than not, it will take as much as a year from the closing date of the transaction to achieve any significant consolidations or synergies.

There is almost always time to put alternative plans in place, provided the communications are timely and ongoing.

Bankruptcies and total shutdowns are more difficult to deal with; but fortunately, these occurrences are less frequent. Contracts should provide for this eventuality; but usually, the bankruptcy court will control the actions of the parties. Even here, however, good communications and complete candor will go a long way toward making a difficult situation a little more tolerable.

New Providers

Usually, with terminations in these categories, if the operations are continued at all, they will be combined with those of other providers. In such cases, it will be helpful to have the old and new providers work together on the transition. It even may be possible for displaced employees to be hired by the firm acquiring the additional volume. At a minimum, experienced employees can assist in training new ones.

As unfortunate as these terminations might be for the providers, they should not be adversarial; and a spirit of cooperation should be encouraged and even rewarded financially where appropriate. The payment of bonuses for smooth transitions could be a very good investment.

Performance Related Terminations

The most difficult relationship terminations are those that result from the actual or perceived failure of the provider to perform in a satisfactory manner. In spite of thorough planning and careful implementation, a large number of arrangements will fail due to real or alleged poor performance by the provider. While some of the fault usually lies with the client, most of the problems manifest themselves at the provider level.

There are any number of reasons for this, but the major underlying cause of logistics outsourcing failure involves a firm that contracted for, and a provider that agreed to, the provision of services that neither party clearly understood. This lack of understanding precludes effective management of the relationship and will steadily undermine the operation until the day it is terminated.

Presumably, by the time a client decides to end an outsourcing relationship, there have been numerous attempts to correct deficiencies, probationary periods, and other unpleasant discussions. The attitudes of the parties toward each other usually are adversarial, and an amicable settlement is difficult to envision.

As the popular song indicated, breaking up is hard to do;[1] or more accurately, breaking up can be ugly. One example involved a chain of retail stores that for a number of years had outsourced its store replenishment operations to a qualified logistics service provider. The provider received the products from various sources, stored them, processed orders, and made deliveries to the individual retail outlets. For the most part, service had been satisfactory.

The client decided it wanted to move the operations to a building which it owned in another city, and asked the provider to move its replenishment operation to this new location. The provider agreed, a plan was developed for the transfer of activities from one building to another, and the transition began.

For reasons that were unclear, however, the client decided to accelerate the schedule and mandated that the entire move be completed in a very compressed timeframe. So compressed that over the final weekend, in excess of one hundred fifty trailer loads of product were moved to the new facility. Shipments to stores were scheduled to begin the following Tuesday.

It was at precisely this point the failure die was cast. In the provider's haste to get product into the building, little attention was paid to placement of product or the stock locator system. Items were placed wherever space was available, and record keeping received little attention. In brief, everything was in the warehouse; but no one was sure exactly where.

As store shipments began, most orders were incomplete since the product simply could not be located. Out-of-stock conditions quickly developed at the store level, and there was a significant deterioration in consumer satisfaction. In an effort to improve the situation, the client placed some of its own personnel in the operation; but most really were not qualified to help and only confused things further.

At the beginning of the relationship, the two parties had executed an agreement that stated if the provider's performance became unacceptable, the contract could be cancelled. Written notice was required, and the provider would be given three days to correct the deficiencies. If it was unable to do so to the client's satisfaction, the agreement could be cancelled on two weeks' notice. Within two weeks after the new operation started up, the client rendered the written notice of unacceptability. Obviously, under the best of circumstances, three days is insufficient time to correct any major deficiencies; and in this case, it was an impossibility. In spite of the provider's plea for more time, the client terminated the agreement.

Suits and counter suits quickly followed. The provider wanted to be paid for the life of the contract and its relocation expenses, and the client quickly countered with a multi-million dollar demand for compensation for lost sales. The dispute was submitted to arbitration and just before testimony was to begin, the parties reached a confidential settlement.

Interestingly enough, and to some, somewhat suspicious, was the fact that another provider was ready to step in and assume the operation. This could suggest that planning for such an event may have begun even before the relocation began.

In essence, this operation failed because it was the product of a bad relationship. Several things were wrong. At the outset, the client should not have insisted on the unreasonable three-day correction timeframe; and the provider should not have agreed to it. The client should not have insisted on a transfer of product so accelerated that the chances of successfully doing so were slim. Most certainly, the provider should not have agreed. Finally, the unwillingness of the client to continue the relationship under circumstances it helped to create suggests a serious lack of commitment to its partner.

Unfortunately, there are other stories like this. Another major retailer, Office Max, wound up in court or arbitration three times, each time with a different logistics service provider. [2] Obviously, in these situations, neither party wins. Such disputes are harmful to the client, to the provider and to the industry. While it would be naïve to suggest that litigation may not or should not take place, it should be avoided wherever possible.

There are two basic methods of terminating a relationship for performance deficiencies; i.e., simply failing to renew an agreement on its expiration date, and terminating an agreement early under the failure to perform provisions.

Contract Expiration

If at all practical, it is best to see an agreement through to its normal expiration date. The major advantage to this course of action is that it makes it unnecessary to *prove* performance deficiencies and eliminates the possibility of termination penalties and legal proceedings.

Even so, for the client, this is a difficult situation. The provider will know the client is not pleased with its performance; and as the contract notice date approaches, it should presume it will not be renewed. This should be confirmed by the client, however, at the time and in the manner prescribed by the contract, if not sooner. While such notice may result in a further deterioration in performance, it is the client's legal and moral responsibility to give it.

In many cases, if the relationship has gotten bad enough, the provider will find a great sense of relief in the fact that the experience finally is coming to an end. It may have found itself in a situation well beyond its expertise and competency and will welcome the opportunity to move ahead in other areas, or for other clients.

In other situations, the provider will rationalize the performance problems into client deficiencies, and convince itself that it would be better off out of the relationship. Such thought processes favor the client, and it may well find that the level of cooperation is quite satisfactory, considering the circumstances. The ideal situation is for the parties to agree that the existing arrangement simply is no longer in either of their best interests, and work together to cut their individual losses.

Early Termination

As indicated earlier, when a provider's performance is unsatisfactory, it should be well aware of it. Unfortunately, however, many clients will fail to communicate the extent of their dissatisfaction; and while providers realize there are problems, they do not realize the problems are terminal. It is important therefore for the relationship manager to keep the provider well informed about problem areas and the consequences of not getting them resolved. By the time a probationary period is declared, it should come as no surprise.

The contract should be clear as to how the notice of dissatisfaction should be rendered and allow a reasonable time for the correction of the deficiencies. If they are not corrected within the given timeframe, it will be necessary to give the provider a notice of termination.

Ending a relationship in this manner is much more difficult than simply failing to renew a contract. An early cancellation constitutes a rejection of the provider, its management, and operations, and in almost all cases will be resented. Resentment usually does not foster cooperation, and the client should be prepared for any contingency. A well-defined transition plan will be an absolute necessity.

While every situation will be different, there are six basic principles that should be remembered when terminating a relationship early.

271

First and foremost, *do not act impulsively.* Before the first notice of unsatisfactory performance is rendered, a contingency plan should have been developed and communicated to appropriate managers within the client firm. Do not become so frustrated that an arrangement is terminated before its replacement is ready.

Include the new provider in the planning process. If the operations being terminated are being transferred to another provider, it is very important to involve the new provider early in the planning process. Timetables for the assumption of various aspects of the operations should be developed. Include a timeframe for an orderly transition, but also, as part of the contingency plan, determine exactly how much volume could be transferred on shorter notice.

Ideally, the two providers would work together on the transition, cooperating in areas such as order processing and employee training; but the client and the new provider should be prepared for that not to happen. At best, the cooperation, if it is present at all, could be minimal and uninspired.

Develop alternative distribution points. If for some reason a total breakdown occurs before the new provider is ready to assume the operations, there should be optional shipping points available. Other distribution centers can handle additional volume over the short term, and contingency plans should be developed for doing so. Be sure that adequate labor, equipment, and inventories are available.

Communicate internally. Keep marketing, sales, and other managers informed of developments. Often they can help minimize customer and other issues if they are kept abreast of the developments in the transition. No one likes to admit to mistakes, but it is important for logistics management to acknowledge that a relationship has gone bad, but that appropriate contingent and corrective action is being taken.

Try not to become emotional. By this time, frustration levels will be high, tempers will be frayed, and general unpleasantness will surround the entire situation. The client manager should try to maintain as much equilibrium in the relationship as possible and handle the myriad of details in a professional manner. He or she will find that client behavior, more often than not, is mirrored by the provider.

Break clean. When it's over, it's over. Do not spend an inordinate amount of time relying on past sins as excuses for later mistakes. At this point, nothing is to be gained by continuing recriminations or second-guessing. Learn from the mistakes that were made, and carry on, determined to make the new relationship successful where the other failed.

Emotional Terminations

Some logistics outsourcing relationships are terminated when there are no good business reasons for doing so. Occasionally, this will happen with changes in client logistics management. A new manager may feel more comfortable with a provider he/she has dealt with previously or a friend who is in the business.

In other instances, provider managers may change firms, and clients will want to follow them to their new affiliations. Since these managers are well acquainted with the operations and cost of the arrangement, they are in a position to make attractive proposals for change.

Such terminations are not encouraged; but if a client feels it must make such a change, it should be confronted honestly. Do not try to make poor performance a reason for making a change if in fact it does not exist. This will only lead to hard feelings and possible litigation.

In situations such as this, expect the worst. From a provider perspective, such a termination is akin to a husband leaving his wife for another woman; and a number of providers have reacted accordingly. In some cases, the new provider has been sued; but there also is a potential for being caught up in disputes between employers and employees.

One case in point involved two executives who left J.B. Hunt to work for Cardinal Freight Carriers.[3] Both left Hunt of their own accord, and neither had signed a non-compete agreement. They had, however, signed a confidentiality agreement. In filing suit, Hunt claimed that the knowledge they took with them about Hunt, its strategy, plans, and operations gave their new employer an unfair competitive advantage. The Arkansas Supreme Court agreed, and prohibited the executives from utilizing in their new positions much of the knowledge and information they had gained at Hunt.

While no specific client was named in this proceeding, such involvement is not unheard of. In another instance, an executive of a national logistics provider was terminated; and shortly thereafter, another manager resigned from the same firm to join him in the formation of a new service provider company. At the time of their employment with their old firm, they had not signed a non-compete agreement, but had executed a confidentiality document.

Their first sales call was on a client that they had been responsible for securing initially for their former employer. The logistics manager at the client firm and the two provider managers had worked together in the past and were friends. The client owned the building in which the distribution operations were being conducted.

The contract was coming up for renewal, and the client gave proper notice that it would not be renewing the arrangement. The incumbent provider suspected that the managers in question may have had a hand in the termination, and without too much effort confirmed that their company would be the new provider.

Armed with that knowledge, the provider filed a suit similar to the Hunt case, but with a different twist. The client logistics manager was joined in the suit as a co-conspirator.

He had done nothing wrong. He simply exercised his contractual right to terminate the arrangement. He even notified the provider early so that employee notifications and other necessary termination steps could be taken with as much lead-time as possible. Essentially, he was a victim of the provider's anger and desire to punish its two ex-employees.

Eventually at least some good judgment prevailed; and the client was dropped from the suit. A settlement was reached with the other two parties, and they were able to begin the new operation.

While everyone should have the right to contract with whomever they choose, the client should be very cautious in entering into transactions where personalities are the determining factor. More often than not, there will be some repercussions; and the outsourcing firm must be willing to deal with the distractions or, at worst, litigation.

Terminations for Cost Reasons

There will be instances when a provider rendering very satisfactory service simply becomes too expensive for the client. The rates do not have to reach an exorbitant level but may simply exceed the client's perception of the value of the service. When this happens, the client may turn the operation over to a new provider or bring it back into its private network.

Since there are no performance issues, these terminations almost always are at the end of the contract term, and are much less adversarial. Before increasing fees to the point that prompted the termination of the relationship, the provider no doubt considered that possibility, and deemed itself willing to live with the consequences.

Such terminations should be considered carefully. Make sure that there are valid comparisons between the acceptance of the existing provider's new increased rate structure and the cost of not accepting it. When the costs of relocations, training, and executive distractions are considered, the rate increase may be the low-cost alternative.

Terminations for Ethical Reasons

As mentioned in Chapter 9, there may be circumstances when the firm will want to terminate for "convenience" when the provider may be meeting contractual obligations but failing in another way. In a broader sense, Global Crossing, Enron, Tyco, WorldCom, Arthur Andersen, and unfortunately too many others are good examples. In the logistics industry several freight bill payment companies have found themselves in similar predicaments.

Provisions should have been included in the contract to cover this eventuality, but it may be a difficult transition. Emotions already will be running high and providers no doubt will be concentrating on other priorities. As with other terminations, however, careful prior planning will make the exit transition as smooth as it can be under the circumstances.

Conclusion

Ending any relationship is not easy, and logistics outsourcing is no exception to the rule. In spite of the client's best efforts, some providers will make the termination very difficult. They will be frustrated, angry, and disappointed. Service may deteriorate.

Others will be cooperative and try to make the best out of a bad situation. This will be the group that, even in the face of adversity, will confirm the validity of your selection process.

Chapter 16

The Ten Suggestions...

Sincere advice may offend the ear but is beneficial to one's conduct.

- Chinese Proverb

To say that logistics outsourcing has grown in popularity in recent years would be a classic understatement. The number of logistics service providers is multiplying almost daily, as is the number of outsourcing agreements.

Logistics outsourcing has become a valuable strategy for many firms, and should at least be considered by most. It is important to remember, however, that the outsourcing of any logistics function requires careful planning, implementation, and management.

Adherence to ten basic rules will go a long way toward ensuring a successful and mutually beneficial outsourcing relationship.

1. **Develop a strategy for outsourcing**. Outsourcing should always be carefully thought out and measured against an in-house solution. This will help identify relative strengths and weaknesses for each alternative. Include the provider in the process from the beginning. While RFP's (Requests for Proposal) make potential agreements easier to evaluate, they can ignore the analysis of the most cost-and service-effective processes.

2. **Establish a rigorous provider selection process**. Check industry sources, existing clients, and financial health. Carefully analyze management depth, strategic direction, information technology capability, labor relations, and personal chemistry and compatibility.

3. **Clearly define your expectations**. A number of outsourcing relationships have been unsuccessful because of unrealistic expectations. Providers are often asked to submit bids based on inadequate information about volume, size, and frequency of shipments. Companies simply lack accurate or detailed knowledge of their own logistics activity. In addition, the cost of providing the service, especially in the information technology area, often is underestimated and/or misunderstood. Such inaccuracies result in providers developing costing for and committing to arrangements that don't reflect reality.

4. **Develop a good contract**. Provide incentives to improve operations and productivity with both parties sharing the benefits. Clearly spell out obligations, expectations, and remedies.

5. **Establish sound policies and procedures**. Give the service provider an operating manual. Ideally, the

manual will be developed together and contain all policies, procedures, and other information necessary for the efficient operation of the outsourcing arrangement.

6. *Identify and avoid potential friction points.* Both parties are usually aware of friction points that may arise. Identify them in advance and develop a procedure for dealing with them.

7. *Communicate effectively with your logistics partner.* Poor communication is second only to poor planning as a cause of outsourcing relationship failure. Communication on all aspects of the operation must be frequent and two-way.

8. *Measure performance, communicate results.* When setting up a relationship, clearly identify, agree upon, and communicate standards of performance. Measure performance regularly.

9. *Motivate and reward providers.* Reward good performance; don't take it for granted. Compliments, recognition, awards, trophies, and dinners are all proven motivators. Do whatever works for your particular circumstances, but do something.

10. *Be a good partner.* Good partnerships are mutually beneficial. Bad ones are not. Your logistics provider's ability to serve you and your customers often can hinge on your own performance or lack thereof.

While this book was written primarily from a client perspective, the issues are really the same for both clients and providers. Providers also should have basic "rules of engagement," and their adherence to ten provider-oriented guidelines will make for more successful and rewarding relationships.

1. ***Encourage strategic thinking and planning.*** Often the outsourcing decision is not carefully thought out and planned by the client. If possible, become a part of the process from the beginning. While Requests for Proposal make potential agreements easier to evaluate, they can ignore the analysis of the most cost- and service-effective processes, as well as unique services you may offer.

2. ***Understand the competitive marketplace.*** The sophisticated potential client will check industry sources, existing clients, and financial health. Carefully examine internal management depth, strategic direction, information technology capability, and labor relations, compared to that of the competition. Capitalize on the differences. *Price on your own costs – not on what others charge or what it will take to close the deal.*

3. ***Insist on clearly defined expectations.*** A number of outsourcing relationships have been unsuccessful because of unrealistic expectations. Providers are often asked to submit bids based on inadequate information about volume, size, and frequency of shipments. Prospective clients simply lack accurate or detailed knowledge of their own logistics activity. In addition, the cost of providing the service, especially in the information technology area, often is underestimated or misunderstood. Such inaccuracies result in providers developing costing for, and committing to, arrangements that don't reflect reality.

4. **Develop a good contract.** Suggest incentives for improvements in operations and productivity with both parties sharing the benefits. Be sure that all obligations, expectations, and remedies are clearly spelled out.

5. **Establish sound policies and procedures.** Strongly urge the client to provide an operating manual. Ideally, the manual will be developed jointly and contain all policies, procedures, and other information necessary for the efficient operation of the outsourcing arrangement. Don't leave home without it.

6. **Identify and avoid potential friction points.** Both parties are usually aware of friction points that may arise. Identify them in advance and develop a procedure for dealing with them.

7. **Communicate effectively with your logistics partner.** Poor communication is second only to poor planning as a cause of outsourcing relationship failure. Communications on all aspects of the operation must be frequent and two-way. Visit your key clients on a regular basis.

8. **Request a performance measurement program.** When establishing a relationship, clearly identify and agree upon standards of performance. Ask for regular performance measurement.

9. **Motivate and reward your personnel.** Ideally, this should be done by the client. But if not, reward good performance; don't take it for granted. Compliments, recognition, awards, days off, and dinners are all

proven motivators. Do whatever works for your particular circumstances, but do something.

10. **Be *a good partner*.** Good partnerships are mutually beneficial. Bad ones are not. Your clients' ability to serve their customers will be dependent on both your performances or lack thereof. Finally, even good partnerships end eventually. When this happens, handle it with dignity and courtesy.

Whether you are a client or a provider, following the respective ten steps will set the right course for your outsourcing relationship. As stated repeatedly in this book, however, for the relationship to truly succeed, it must be based on mutual trust and respect. A high level of integrity will ensure a high level of service and satisfaction.

Chapter 17

In Closing...

History shows that great economic and social forces flow like a tide over communities only half conscious of what is befalling them. Wise statesmen foresee what time is thus bringing, and try to shape institutions and mold men's thoughts and purposes in accordance with the change that is silently coming on. The unwise are those who bring nothing to the process, and who greatly imperil the future of mankind by leaving great questions to be fought out between ignorant change on one hand and ignorant opposition to change on the other.

- John Stuart Mill

As this final chapter is written, I find myself only weeks away from the completion of 46 years in the transportation/physical distribution/logistics/supply chain industry. I signed my first two-paragraph warehouse outsourcing contract 42 years ago, even though the term outsourcing had yet to be invented.

As I reflect on those years, I am reminded that while certain basic steps and processes are critical to any outsourcing arrangement, the most successful ones were implemented by individuals with a high level of integrity who were innovative, creative, and "dared to go where no man has gone before."

These successful individuals also were skilled at building and maintaining relationships. As we move into the era of supply chain management, these skills will be all the more important. In my opinion, the most important chapter in this book is 13, "Managing the Relationship."

The successful supply chain manager will have human relations skills, negotiating expertise, and the ability to foster collaboration and integration among the various supply chain functions, including outsourcing. Success will come only after we truly understand that our business is about relationships, not operations.

Doing things as they have always been done results in the same, albeit safe, mediocre performance. Hopefully, the reader has learned something from this book. If so, take that knowledge and improve on it.

Step off the path.

The Calf Path

One day, through the primeval wood,
A calf walked home, as good calves should;
But made a trail all bent askew,
A crooked trail as all calves do.

Since then two hundred years have fled,
And, I infer, the calf is dead.
But still he left behind his trail,
And thereby hangs my moral tale.

The trail was taken up next day
By a lone dog that passed that way;
And then a wise bellwether sheep
Pursued the trail o'er vale and steep,
And drew the flock behind him, too,
As good bellwethers always do.

And from that day, o'er hill and glade,
Through those old woods a path was made;
And many men wound in and out,
And dodged, and turned, and bent about
And uttered words of righteous wrath
Because 'twas such a crooked path.
But still they followed – do not laugh –
The first migrations of that calf,
And through this winding wood-way stalked,
Because he wobbled when he walked.

This forest path became a lane,
That bent, and turned, and turned again;
This crooked lane became a road,
Where many a poor horse with his load
Toiled on beneath the burning sun,
And traveled some three miles in one.
And thus a century and a half
They trod the footsteps of that calf.

The years passed on in swiftness fleet,
The road became a village street;
And this, before men were aware,
A city's crowded thoroughfare;
And soon the central street was this
Of a renowned metropolis;
And men two centuries and a half
Trod in the footsteps of that calf.

Each day a hundred thousand rout
Followed the zigzag calf about;
And o'er his crooked journey went
The traffic of a continent.
A hundred thousand men were led
By one calf near three centuries dead.
They followed still his crooked way,
And lost one hundred years a day;
For thus such reverence is lent
To well-established precedent.

A moral lesson this might teach,
Were I ordained and called to preach;
For men are prone to go it blind
Along the calf paths of the mind,
And work away from sun to sun
To do what other men have done.
They follow in the beaten track,
And out and in, and forth and back,
And still their devious course pursue,
To keep the path that others do.

But how the wise old wood-gods laugh,
Who saw the first primeval calf!
Ah! Many things this tale might teach –
But I am not ordained to preach.

Sam Walter Foss

End Notes

End Notes

Chapter 1

1. Kenneth B. Ackerman, *Warehousing Profitably – An Update* (Columbus, OH: Ackerman Publications, 2000), p. 2.

2. American Warehousemen's Association, *Traveling the Road of Logistics* (Chicago, IL: American Warehousemen's Association, 1991), p. 7.

3. www.fedex.com/us/about/overview/companies/express/facts.html?link=4.

4. Peter F. Drucker, *Post Capitalist Society* (New York, NY: Harper Business, 1993), p. 95.

5. comScore Networks, "Online Holiday Sales Rise 30 Percent," January 5, 2004.

6. Richard Thompson, "FedEx Home Delivery Has Country Covered," *Memphis Commercial Appeal*, September 18, 2002, p. c2.

7. "Supply Chain Execution Systems," *Logistics Today*, December 2003, p. 29.

Chapter 2

1. See for example, Gary R. Allen, Mark J. Columbo, C. John Langley, Jr., "Third Party Logistics: Results and Findings of the 2003 Eighth Annual Study," Georgia Tech University, 2003.

2. Peter F. Drucker, "Peter Drucker Sets Us Straight," *Fortune*, January 12, 2004, p. 118.

3. "Has Outsourcing Gone Too Far," *McKinsey Quarterly*, December, 2001.

Chapter 3

1. Allen, op. cit.

2. Robert V. Delaney, "The Case for Reconfiguration," Presentation at National Press Club, June 2, 2003, p. 32.

3. U.S. Census Bureau, *2002 Economic Census – Transportation*, December, 2003.

4. Case Studies, www.jbhunt.com.

5. *Locomotive Engineers Journal*, Volume 109, Number 1, Spring, 2001.

6. "Union Pacific, Daimler Chrysler Announces New Logistics Company," *Detroit News*, July 31, 2001.

7. "BNSF Logistics Isn't Your Typical Transportation Company," *Arkansas Democrat Gazette*, November 30, 2003.

8. Chuck Salter, "Surprise Package," *Fast Company*, February 2004, p.62.

9. American Waterways Operators, www.americanwaterways.com.

10. R. V. Delaney, *Guidance Regarding the Outsourcing of Freight Payments*, August 2002, p. 2.

11. Leslie H. Harps, "Outsourcing Bid Package Negotiation Can Help Companies Save Big Dollars," *Outsourced Logistics Report*, February 29, 1996, p. 1.

12. Allen, op.cit.

13. "Why It Pays to Share 'Your 3PL,'" *Logistics Management*, March 2003, p. 46.

14. Dale S. Rogers and Ronald S. Tibben-Lembke, *Going Backwards: Reverse Logistics Trends and Practices* (Reno, NV: Reverse Logistics Executive Council, 1999), p. 2.

15. Jane Roberts, "UPS, Toshiba Team Up," *Memphis Commercial Appeal*, April 28, 2004, p. C-1.

16. Rogers and Tibben-Lembke, op.cit., p. 8.

17. Bruce Caldwell, "Reverse Logistics," *Information Week*, April 12, 1999, pp. 50 – 52.

18. Ken Cottrill, "Reversal of Fortunes," *Traffic World*, June 16, 2003, p. 23.

19. Robert J. Trent, Robert M. Monczka, "Understanding Integrated Global Sourcing," *International Journal of Physical Distribution and Logistics Management*, Vol. 32, No. 7, 2003, p. 607.

20. Paul Page, "Packing Up Logistics," *Traffic World*, April 22, 2004, p.34.

21. David Biederman, "Financing the Chain," *Traffic World*, April 12, 2004, pp. 22 – 23.

Chapter 4

1. Scott Adams, *The Dilbert Principle* (New York, NY: Harper Business, 1996), p. 244.

2. Lisa Harrington, "Dedicated Contract Carriage: Evaluation, Implementation and Management," National Private Truck Council, 1996, p. 7.

3. George A. Steiner, *Strategic Planning* (New York, NY: The Free Press, 1979), p. 344.

Chapter 5

1. Take for example the case of Schneider Logistics, a wholly-owned subsidiary of Schneider National, Inc. Piper Jaffray Equity Research defined Schneider Logistics as "one of the largest asset-based, third party logistics providers…" Others have made similar mistakes.

   Schneider Logistics, however, considers itself to be a non-asset-based provider since the assets it employs in providing client solutions actually are owned by Schneider National or other providers.

2. Peter Bendor-Samuel, Todd Furniss, and Eric Simonson, *Sole Source Outsourcing*, Everest Group, p. 1.

3. Shortly after the copyright announcement, a leading logistics educator claimed to have coined the term years before.

Chapter 6

1. K. B. Ackerman, "Strategic Planning for the Logistics Service Provider," *Warehousing Forum*, January, 2004, pp. 1-2.

2. Mason Cooley, *City Aphorisms, Fifth Selection*, New York, 1988.

3. Ferrell, Fraedrich, Ferrell, *Business Ethics: Ethical Decision Making and Cases*, (Boston, MA: Houghton Mifflin Company, 2002), p. 197.

4. Delaney, op.cit.

5. *UPS Newsletter*, Spring, 1999, p. 9.

6. John Goff, "The Discreet Chain of the SMB," *CFO*, March, 2004, p. 76.

7. "Mercedes Partners with Connextions to Meet the e-Commerce Supply-chain Challenge," *Global Logistics and Supply Chain Strategies*, August 2003, p. 36.

Chapter 9

1. Kenneth B. Ackerman, *Ackerman Warehousing Forum*, September 1996, p. 1.

2. Thomas W. Speh, *Contract Warehousing: How It Works and How to Make It Work Effectively* (Oak Brook, IL: WERC, 1993), p. 7.

3. Brad L. Peterson, "Seven Key Questions for Drafting Exit Provisions," *Outsourcing Journal* (Internet), August 2002.

4. National Arbitration Forum, *Drafting Mediation and Arbitration Clauses*, August, 2003, p.2.

5. Ibid, p. 2.

6. Ibid, p.15.

Chapter 12

1. Lisa Harrington, "Building a Better 3PL Relationship," *Transportation & Distribution*, June 2003, p. 50.

Chapter 13

1. Marc Liebman, "Outsourcing Relationships: Why Are They Difficult to Manage?," Everest Group, Inc., 1999.

2. Peter Bendor-Samuel, "A Pact for Differences," *Outsourcing Journal*, November 1999, p. 1.

3. Leslie Hansen Harps, "Selecting 3PL Partners," *Inbound Logistics*, July 1999, p. 50.

4. Matthew E. Brunson, *The Wisdom and Teachings of the Dalai Lama* (New York, NY: Penguin Group, 1997), p. 175.

5. Leslie Hansen Harps, "Manufacturer's Report Card Sparks Peak Performance From Third Party Providers," *Outsourced Logistics Report*, Preview Issue, 1994.

6. Kate Vitasek and Steve Geary, "Metrics and Management," Traffic World, February 24, 2003, p. 33.

7. Ackerman, op. cit.

8. Kate Vitasek, Michael Ledyard, et.al., *Logistics and Supply Chain Management Process Standards*, Council of Logistics Management, 2004.

Chapter 14

1. Quinn G. McKay, *Is Lying Sometimes the Right Thing for an Honest Person to Do?* (Provo, UT: Executive Excellence Publishing, 1997), pp. 142 – 143.

2. Marian Christy, "Mayflower Madam Tells All," *Boston Globe*, 1986.

Chapter 15

1. Howard Greenfield, Neil Sedaka, "Breaking Up Is Hard To Do."

2. Ann Saccamano, "Fourth Time Around," *Traffic World*, July 27, 1998, p. 31.

3. Steven E. Salkin, "Breaking Up Is Hard To Do," *Logistics Management*, April 1999, p. 76.

Appendices

.

WAREHOUSE MANAGEMENT SYSTEM
RFP Template
© HighJump Software ®

Reprinted with permission of and thanks to

**HighJump Software ®
a 3M company**

The 2004 WMS RFP Template

The decision to purchase a warehouse management system (WMS) is a critical initiative for your company's future success. The 2004 WMS RFP Template is an important tool that empowers you to objectively grade prospective vendors on the solutions they offer – and the positive or negative impact those solutions may have on your operations. There are several worksheets included in this document, each providing detailed best practices information compiled from surveys and interviews with hundreds of logistics professionals and consultants across a variety of industries.

Once you've completed this tool, you will be empowered to determine any prospective WMS solution's breadth and depth of functionality, as well as its flexibility to meet your specific needs. To avoid unexpected delays and unbudgeted costs in the future, it is critical to know this information *before* you purchase any solution. As importantly, you will know which capabilities will require demonstration during a vendor presentation. These demonstrations are critical to your ability to separate exaggerated vendor claims from those that can actually be proven.

In-depth knowledge of what a WMS offers in terms of functionality and flexibility arms you with the decision-making criteria you require to complete a true evaluation of each solution you are considering. Ultimately, this knowledge will allow you to determine a system's ability to quickly and cost-effectively meet changing customer and business requirements (key to maintaining competitive advantage), generate strong return on investment (ROI), and provide the lowest total cost of ownership (TCO).

Company: This section allows you to capture detailed information about your prospective vendor and the type of support they are capable of offering.

Functionality: This comprehensive listing of functionality shows what you should expect a vendor to provide in their base product offering. There are also columns asking you to address the cost and time involved in changing this standard functionality, and whether the ability to modify the system quickly and inexpensively can be proven in a vendor demonstration.

Technology: In addition to the details of your general technology requirements, the Technology tab asks you to consider the configuration approach and upgradeability of the system you are evaluating. It is important to remember that only a solution with a flexible platform will allow you to complete system modification sand upgrades quickly and inexpensively.

Adaptability: This section provides you with a set of sample changes that might need to be incorporated in your operations either during implementation or in the future (e.g. a new customer requirement). The concept of adaptability does not refer simply to the notion that your system can be changed. The true question you are addressing here is the impact on your business in terms of the cost and time involved.

The 2004 WMS RFP Template: Company

Requirement	Response
General Information	
1. Company name	
2. Company address (corporate)	
3. Company telephone	
4. Company fax	
5. Website	
6. Year company founded	
7. Company CEO and years with company	
8. Senior management team (names, titles, years with company)	
Contact Information	
1. Proposal contact name	
2. Title	
3. Contact address	
4. Contact telephone	
5. Contact e-mail address	
6. Contact mobile phone	
Financials	
1. Public or private (if private, skip to 3; if public, go to 2)	
2. Stock exchange and ticker symbol	
3. Describe ownership structure (attach additional information if required)	
4. Month in which fiscal year ends	
5. YTD Results (2004)	
5.1 Revenue	
5.2 Profit	
5.3 Software revenue	
5.4 Service revenue	
5.5 Hardware revenue	
5.6 Support/maintenance revenue	
6. 2003 Results	
6.1 Revenue	
6.2 Profit	
6.3 Software revenue	

6.4 Service revenue	
6.5 Hardware revenue	
6.6 Support/maintenance revenue	
7. 2002 Results	
7.1 Revenue	
7.2 Profit	
7.3 Software revenue	
7.4 Service revenue	
7.5 Hardware revenue	
7.6 Support/maintenance revenue	
8. Current Balance Sheet Information	
8.1 Cash and cash equivalents	
8.2 Other current assets	
8.3 Current liabilities	
8.4 Quick ratio (current assets − current liabilities)	
8.5 Total amount of debt	
9. Litigation	
9.1 Any litigation pending?	
9.2 Number of lawsuits in history of company?	
Employee Information	
1. Total number	
2. Number by function	
2.1 Sales	
2.2 Marketing/alliances	
2.3 Professional services	
2.4 Technical support	
2.5 Research and development	
2.6 G&A	
2.7 Other	
Support	
1. Warranty	
1.1 Standard warranty period	

1.2 What is included? (attach if necessary)	
1.3 Location of customer support offices	
2. Maintenance	
2.1 Standard maintenance policy (attach if necessary)	
2.2 Patches included?	
2.2.1 How are patches distributed?	
2.3 Upgrades	
2.3.1 How often are new releases available?	
2.3.2 How long does it take the average customer to complete an upgrade (Including re-application of system modifications)?	
2.3.3 From start to finish, what was the longest time taken by any customer to complete an upgrade?	
2.3.4 What is the average cost to complete an upgrade?	
2.3.5 What is the greatest cost ever incurred by a customer during an upgrade?	
2.3.6 Must custom code always be re-applied during upgrade?	
2.3.7 Do you guarantee your upgrade price?	
3. Support	

3.1 Standard support policy (attach if necessary)	
3.2 Price based upon sold price or current price?	
3.3 Price increases in last 5 years?	
3.4 Provided by vendor or 3rd party?	
3.5 Support location?	
3.6 Escalation policy (attach if necessary)	
3.7 How far back releases supported?	
3.8 24/7 available?	
3.8.1 24/7 staffed or beeper?	
3.9 Web support	
3.9.1 Provided?	
3.9.2 Patches available?	
3.9.3 Create new call?	
3.9.4 Check call status?	
3.10 Support computer hardware?	
3.11 Support RF hardware?	
3.12 Do you support customer-modified applications?	
User Group	
1. Do you maintain an active user group?	
2. Year established?	
3. Meet how often?	
4. Date of last conference?	
5. Number of attendees last conference?	
Customer Base	
1. Total number of WMS customers?	
2. Active number of WMS customers?	
3. Number of WMS sites (across all customers)?	
4. Number of WMS customers on maintenance?	
5. Number of WMS customers that have upgraded?	

6. New WMS customers	
6.1 YTD	
6.2 Last year	
7. Number of WMS customers on latest release?	
Training	
1. Describe the overall approach of your training program (attach additional information if required)	
2. Classroom training available?	
2.1 Classes offered (attach if necessary)?	
2.2 Describe the pricing for classes	
2.3 What is schedule for upcoming classes?	
2.4 Where are the classes held?	
2.5 What is the maximum and minimum class size?	
2.6 What is your cancellation policy?	
2.7 Describe the credentials of your instructors	
2.8 Do you have online registration?	
3. Online training available via the Web?	
3.1 Courses offered (attach if necessary)	
3.2 Describe the pricing for the online courses	
3.3 Online testing available?	
3.4 What are the connectivity requirements?	
4. Do you offer customized or onsite training?	
5. What types of media/activities are employed in training?	
5.1 Written materials	
5.2 Audio/visual	
5.3 Hyperlinked reference materials	
5.4 Hands-on workshops	

The 2004 WMS RFP Template: Functionality

Functionality	R-Required D-Desired F-Future	S-Standard Configuration M-Source Code Mod N-Not Possible	If (M) is required, what is the cost?	Com- ments
Receiving				
1. RF Receiving				
1.1 Receive against a PO				
1.2 ASN receiving				
1.3 Blind receipts				
1.4 Unknown receipts (no item or PO available)				
1.5 Damage identification on receipt				
1.6 Quality sampling and auditing				
1.7 Receive against a generic license				
1.8 Receive and generate smart license				
1.9 Receive without a license				
1.10 Receive returns				

1.11 Receive returns vs. a disposition				
1.12 Receive transfers without orders				
1.13 Prompt for open POs upon receipt				
2. Receivers				
2.1 Option to create. receiver by PO				
2.2 Option to create receiver by load				
2.3 Option to preprint receiving labels				
3. Check				
3.1 Reconcile PO lines w/receipts				
3.2 Multiple operators on a single receipt				
3.3 Capture lot upon receipt				
3.4 RF display special instructions				

3.5 Attach graphic of exceptions				
3.6 RF capture user-defined license attributes (i.e., catch weight, owner)				
3.7 Verify/audit product in staging				
4. Reports				
4.1 Receiving exceptions				
4.2 Receiver list				
4.3 Productivity by user				
4.4 O/S/D report by PO by load				
4.5 Vendor report card				
4.6 Open POs				
5. Yard and appointments				
5.1 Appointment scheduling				
5.2 Dock door assignments				
5.3 Project labor required to unload				
5.4 Ability to unload trailer w/out details				

5.5 Ability to RF-direct yard moves				
5.6 Ability to track demurrage by owner				
5.7 Ability to systematical-ly assign docks				
5.8 Ability to systematical-ly assign yard locations				
5.9 Full trailer visibility				
5.9.1 Trailer posi-tioning yard or dock				
5.9.2 Trailer con-tents				
5.9.3 Pending trailer moves				
Quality Control				
1. QC status				
1.1 License plate holds in non-QC location				
1.2 Hold and release by item				

1.3 Hold and release by lot				
1.4 Hold and release by location				
2. Reports				
2.1 QC inventory visibility				
2.2 Vendor performance statistics				
Put-away				
1. Select best location based upon user-defined rules				
2. Allow user to override				
3. Record overrides in exception log				
4. Put-away at the multiple units of measure				
5. System directs second put-away after override				
6. Put-away				
6.1 To quality control				
6.2 To random storage				
6.3 To forward pick – if open replenish-ment				
6.4 To staging				
6.5 Cross-dock receipt to single order				

6.6 Cross-dock receipt to multiple orders				
6.7 To returns by vendor class				
6.8 Storage logic association to UOM				
6.9 Ability to split a single license plate receipt between replenish-ment and put-away				
6.10 Ability to store by owner				
Location Mapping				
1. Location mapping				
1.1 Zones				
1.2 Special require-ments (e.g., freezer)				
1.3 Mapping of acceptable vehicles by zone				
1.4 Configurable forward pick				
1.5 Multiple forward picks per item				

1.6 Ability to relieve inventory based upon merchandise verification to a certain location type				
1.7 Ability to define aisle contention criteria by vehicle				
2. Reports				
2.1 Productivity by user				
2.2 Full location report				
2.3 Empty location report				
2.4 Warehouse location utilization report				
Picking				
1. Planning				
1.1 Create waves through pre-defined criteria				
1.2 Accept pre-determined waves via download				
1.3 Automatical-ly build waves based on rules				

1.4 Manually override priority of an order				
1.5 Ability to cartonize on order import				
1.6 Ability to pre-manifest pick containers				
1.7 Ability to include orders in waves				
1.8 Ability to include order lines in waves				
1.9 Ability to include order line quantities in waves				
1.10 Ability to wave for specific trailer sizes				
1.11 Ability to define reservation rules by customer				
1.12 Ability to calculate metrics on simulated wave				
1.13 Ability to release waves by pick type (i.e., pallets first)				
1.14 Ability to release waves by zone				

1.15 Ability to auto-create work orders for wave shortages upon release				
1.16 Ability to wave by pick method (i.e., batch pick)				
1.17 Ability to wave by owner				
2. Kitting				
2.1 Bill of material (BOM) capability				
2.2 Kits exploded during release				
2.3 Directed assembly				
2.4 Multi-level BOM support				
2.5 Ability to backflush consumed parts				
2.6 Ability to identify scrap				
2.7 Ability to un-kit				
2.8 Ability to track WIP in assembly				
2.9 Ability to associate cost to assembly				

2.10 Ability to request kitting from an RF terminal				
3. Monitor the progress of a wave				
3.1 Workload monitoring by wave by order by item				
3.2 Visibility of required wave replenishments				
3.3 Calculations of remaining time by wave				
3.4 Calculations of new work vs. existing work				
4. Replenishment				
4.1 Created by min/max				
4.2 Created based upon released orders				
4.3 Created based upon day's demand				
4.4 Created via RF request				
4.5 Replenishment picks in reverse put-away sequence				
4.6 Support cascading replenishments				
4.7 Ability to hold allocation-based replenishments				
4.8 Pick work queues held until replenishment work done				
5. Stock rotation				
5.1 User-configurable rotation rules				
5.2 FIFO				
5.3 LIFO				
5.4 FEFO				
5.4.1 LEFO				

5.5 Select stock by lot number				
5.6 Customer-specific rules				
6. Pick option				
6.1 Single-order picking				
6.2 Batch picking (multiple orders per picker, separated at pick location)				
6.3 Pick and pass across zones				
6.4 Bulk picking (multiple orders per picker, separated at pack or conveyor/sort)				
6.5 Configurable number of pickers per order				
6.6 Equipment-based picking				
6.7 Zoned picking				
6.7.1 Wave picking				
6.8 Use combination of the above options on same order				
7. Picking approach				
7.1 RF-directed				
7.2 Pick confirm by exception on PC				
7.3 Pick to list				
7.4 Pick by label				
7.5 Display special picking instructions				
7.6 Honor item mixing rules (i.e., haz mat)				
7.7 Ability to dynamically change pick transaction priorities				
8. Unpick option				
9. Pick sequencing				
9.1 In location flow				

9.2 In user-defined flow				
9.3 Honoring aisle contention				
Packing/Shipping				
1. Cartonization				
1.1 Determine optimal carton size				
1.2 Determine optimal carton contents				
1.3 Graphically display carton packing orientations				
2. Support system-directed packing				
3. Display special packing instructions				
4. Loading				
4.1 Direct loading regardless of order continuity				
4.2 Direct truck loading by order integrity				
4.3 Direct loading by route/stop integrity				
5. Parcel manifesting				
5.1 Support for UPS				
5.2 Support for FedEx				
5.3 Other support (list)				
5.4 Print compliant labels				
5.5 Rate shopping				
5.6 Support for bundling				
5.7 Support for LTL rating				
5.8 Support online carrier communications				
5.9 Support for 100,000+ parcels/day/site				

5.9.1 Pre-manifesting support				
5.9.2 Support for zone skipping				
6. Reports				
6.1 Bill of lading				
6.2 Packing lists				
6.3 Customer-specific paperwork				
6.4 Hazardous material manifest				
6.4.1 International documenta-tion				
7. Unship option				
Other Functions				
1. Warehouse definition				
1.1 Support multiple warehouses on single application				
1.2 Support facility-specific item master				
2. Cycle count				
2.1 Generate counts through errors				
2.2 Generate counts by A/B/C				
2.3 Download counts from host				
2.4 Create counts by ranges of items, locations and price				
2.4.1 Opportunistic cycle count during picking				
3. Value-added services				
3.1 Configurable categories				
3.2 Configurable messaging				

3.3 Available for all warehouse processes (i.e., receiving, picking, shipping, etc.)				
4. Integrated alerts and messaging				
4.1 E-mail alerts/messages				
4.2 Pager alerts/messages				
4.3 Fax alerts/messages				
4.4 Create XML/FTP messages				
4.5 Built-in escalation profiles				
4.6 Built-in resolution strategies				
4.7 Ability to automatically change process flow upon exceptions				
5. Wireless PDAs				
5.1 Support full WMS application UI on PDA				
5.2 Support full WMS RF function on PDA				
6. Integrated delivery confirmation				
6.1 Support batch delivery confirmation				
6.2 Support RF delivery confirmation				
6.3 Support pick-ups (i.e., returns)				
6.4 Driver and odometer logging				
6.5 Signature capture				
6.6 Detailed audit trail				

6.7 Reason codes for missed deliveries				
7. Interleaving				
7.1 Interleave any directed task				
7.2 Interleave by priority				
7.3 Interleave by proximity				
8. Time standards				
8.1 Static standards by function				
8.2 Dynamic standards by function				
8.3 Comparison of standards vs. actuals				
9. Audit history				
9.1 Timestamp start/stop for all tasks				
9.2 Visibility by employee(s)				
9.3 Visibility by transaction(s)				
10. Equipment maintenance visibility				
10.1 Visibility to required maintenance by vehicle				

10.2 Alerts based on required vehicle maintenance				
11. Integrated activity-based costing				
11.1 Costing by owner				
11.2 Costing by transactions by owner				
11.3 Costing by space by owner				
11.4 Costing by time by owner				
11.5 Ability to calculate costing based on combinations of above				
12. RF messaging				
12.1 Ability to send RF message to specific end-user				
12.2 Ability to send RF message to specific group				
12.3 Ability to recipient to respond to message				
RFID				
1. Does the system support RFID technology?				

1.1 What technology is integrated into your system to support RFID?				
1.2 What manufac- turers of RFID tags, readers and printers do you support?				
1.3 Can your RFID capabilities be demon- strated?				
1.4 How does the system accommo- date changes in RFID tag data such as data elements, structures and identifiers?				
2. Can the same operations be performed by RFID that are already being performed with barcodes?				
2.1 What additional modifications are needed to "swap" barcode input to RFID input?				

2.2 Can the RFID equipment be used in both hand-held and fixed applications?				
2.3 Does your product meet the RFID require-ments set by Wal-Mart and the DoD?				
2.4 How will your product meet future specifications and require-ments of RFID? (i.e., How can your product be modified to comply with new mandates and support new RFID standards?)				
2.5 Hardware restrictions				
2.6 Are you a member of EPCglobal?				
2.7 Do you provide RFID solutions that cover manufac-turing?				

2.8 Do you provide RFID solutions for asset tracking?				
2.9 How many years have you been involved in providing true data collection services and expertise? (i.e., There are significant, fundamental differences in the way RFID data is collected and managed vs. traditional barcode methods in warehouse environ-ments.)				

Requirement	Response	Comments
Software Architecture		
1. How many tiers in your architecture?		
1.1 True for all products?		
1.1.1 If not, please list products that differ and how they differ.		
2. How does each tier in your software architecture scale?		
2.1 Application server		
2.2 Database server		

2.3 Web server				
2.4 Integration/Mid-dleware server				
2.5 Presentation server				
2.6 Other				
3. List OS supported by tier:				
3.1 Application server				
3.2 Database server				
3.3 Web server				
3.4 Integration/Mid-dleware server				
3.5 Presentation server				
3.6 Other				
3.7 Client				
4. List databases supported:				
4.1 Do all applications run on same database?				
4.1.1 If not, please indicate which applications run on which database.				
4.2 Can multiple facilities share the same database?				
4.2.1 If not, please describe why.				
Hardware architecture	*Yes*	*No*	*N/A*	
1. Can multiple facilities run from one central location?				
2. Can server functions be combined onto a single machine?				
3. Does the system scale vertically?				
4. Does the system scale horizontally?				
5. Fault tolerance				
5.1 Mirrored disks supported?				
5.2 RAID 5 disks supported?				

5.3 Hot backup system supported?				
5.4 Warm back-up system supported?				
5.5 Database journaled?				
5.6 UPS monitoring?				
5.7 Redundant power supply?				
5.8 Transaction protection via rollback supported?				
User Interface	**Yes**	**No**	**N/A**	
1. Workstation user interface?				
1.1 Please list supported OS(s)				
1.2 Browser-based client available?				
1.2.1 Is Citrix or some other legacy application bridging product required for Web deployment?				
1.3 Menus vary depending on user ID?				
1.4 User interface supports multiple window views?				
1.5 User can print any screen?				
1.6 Users may have multiple sessions at the same time?				
1.7 Screen content may vary depending on user ID?				
1.7.1 Can configure which fields are displayed?				
1.7.2 Can configure field headings/titles?				
1.7.3 Can configure computed fields?				
1.7.4 Can configure charts and graphs?				
1.7.5 Can make fields display-only?				

1.8 Provides event-driven navigation to take the user directly to related information?				
1.8.1 If yes, can the "links" to related information be configured?				
1.9 Pictures/graphical/multi-media data displayed to user?				
1.10 Can be configured to display information from other business systems such as ERP, OMS, etc?				
1.11 Provides pull-down menus?				
1.11.1 If yes, can the content of any pull-down menu be configured?				
2. RF terminal user interface (graphical/character)?				
2.1 Please list supported RF models				
2.2 Menus vary depending on user ID?				
2.3 Screen content may vary depending on user ID?				
2.3.1 Can configure which fields are displayed?				
2.3.2 Can configure field prompts/names?				
2.4 If supported by the RF gear, pictures/graphical/multi-media data displayed to user?				
2.5 Can be configured to display information from other business systems such as ERP, OMS, etc.?				

RFID	Yes	No	N/A	
1. Does the system support RFID technology?				
1.1 What technology is integrated into your system to support RFID?				
1.1.1 What brand of RFID equipment do you support?				
1.1.2 How do you accommodate RFID brands/frequencies/ types that are not already integrated?				
1.2 What different types of RFID tags may be used with your system?				
1.3 What programming or custom code is required to accommodate RFID?				
1.4 Can your RFID capabilities be demonstrated?				
1.5 What criteria is used when selecting and providing RFID equipment?				
1.6 How does the system accommodate changes in RFID tag data, such as data elements, structures and identifiers?				
2. Can the same operations be performed by RFID that are already being performed with bar codes?				
2.1 What additional modifications are needed to 'swap' bar code input to RFID input?				
2.2 Can the RFID equipment be used in both hand-held and fixed applications?				

Security	Yes	No	N/A	
1. Must workstation and RF users log in with a user ID and password?				
1.1 Is a password history maintained to prevent users from recycling passwords?				
1.1.1 Is the number of remembered passwords configurable?				
1.2 Can users be forced to change their passwords periodically?				
1.2.1 Is the password age configurable?				
1.2.2 Can the system prompt for a new password when the current password is nearing expiration?				
1.3 Can a password minimum length be configured?				
1.4 Can password complexity be enforced?				
1.5 Can users be locked out after a number of failed login attempts?				
1.5.1 Can the number of failed attempts that trigger a lockout be configured?				
1.5.2 Can the amount of time that a user is locked out be configured?				
1.6 Can idle users be required to log back in?				
1.6.1 Is the idle time configurable?				
2. Can security be managed at a group level?				

	Yes	No	N/A	
3. Can the system be configured to require the user to re-enter the password before critical updates?				
4. Audit Trails				
4.1 Is an audit trail maintained for all activities?				
4.2 Is an audit trail maintained for exceptions?				
Configuration	**Yes**	**No**	**N/A**	
1. Is some functionality data-driven?				
1.1 Do changes to data-driven functionality require source code modifications?				
1.2 Do changes to the database schema require source code modifications?				
1.3 Are source code modifications required to associate existing functionality to different data elements?				
2. Does the system support user-configurable rules?				
2.1 Do changes to rule-driven functionality require source code changes?				
2.2 Are source code modifications required to develop new rules?				
2.3 Are source code modifications required to support new rule conditions?				
2.4 Are source code modifications required to associate existing functionality to new rules?				

3. Is some functionality activated or deactivated by application "switches," "flags" or "settings?"				
3.1 Do changes to the functionality activated by a "switch" require source code modifications?				
3.2 Are source code modifications required to introduce new "switches," "flags" or "settings?"				
4. Are business process workflows configurable?				
4.1 Can database data be selected, inserted or deleted as part of the workflow?				
4.1.1 Are source code modifications required to change the way the data is selected, inserted or deleted?				
4.1.2 Can data be accessed from other systems/sources?				
4.2 Can user interactions (prompts) be inserted or deleted from a workflow?				
4.2.1 Are source code modifications required to create new interactions or modify existing ones?				
4.3 Can third-party software components be invoked as part of a workflow?				
4.3.1 Can COM objects be called?				
4.3.2 Can executables be called?				
4.3.3 Can DLLs be called?				

4.3.4 Can command (batch) files be called?				
4.4. Can calculations be part of a workflow?				
4.4.1 Are source code modifications required to reference new variables?				
4.4.2 Are source code modifications required to create new calculations?				
4.5 Do workflows support conditional flow control logic?				
4.5.1 Is branching supported?				
4.5.2 Is looping supported?				
4.5.3 Are "child" workflows supported (workflows within workflows)?				
4.6 Are interfaces to printers supported?				
4.6.1 Bar code label printers?				
4.6.2 Page printers (dot matrix and laser)?				
4.7 Are interfaces to other devices supported?				
4.7.1 Can a message from a device automatically trigger a workflow?				
4.7.2 Are source code modifications required to change the message content to and from a device?				
4.8 Can e-mail be sent from a workflow?				

Bar Code Label Printing	Yes	No	N/A	
1. Are bar code labels user-configurable?				
2. Is a third-party tool used for label design?				
3. Can labels be printed via Web browser?				
Reports/Documents/ Queries	**Yes**	**No**	**N/A**	
1. Reports				
1.1 Is a third-party tool used for reporting?				
1.2 Reports viewed without printing?				
1.2.1 Reports viewable in Web browser?				
1.3 Can reports be printed automatically on a schedule?				
1.4 Can reports be printed on-demand from a workstation?				
1.4.1 From a Web browser?				
2. Shipping Documents (Bill of Lading, Packing List)				
2.1 Are source code modifications required to change the sequence of data on shipping documents?				
2.2 Are source code modifications required to add or remove a field to or from a shipping document?				
2.3 Are source code modifications required to compute and print a sub-total, total or grand total?				
2.4 Are source code modifications required to print a graphic or logo on a shipping document?				

2.5 Are source code modifications required to print different formats of shipping documents for different customers?				
3. Queries				
3.1 Can queries be constructed against any system data?				
3.1.1 If not, please explain.				
3.2 Can queries be constructed against external data (from other systems such as ERP, OMS, etc.)				
3.3 Can queries be exported to a text file?				
3.4 Can queries be exported to a spreadsheet?				
Internationalization/ Localization	**Yes**	**No**	**N/A**	
1. Do the RF terminals display screens in different languages, depending upon the user?				
2. Do workstation screens display in different languages, depending upon the user?				
3. Is documentation available in multiple languages?				
4. Are dates and times displayed in the appropriate localized format?				
5. Is decimalization displayed in the appropriate localized format?				
6. Do you provide translation tools for translating screens from one language to another?				
6.1 Do new translations require source code modifications?				

Host Interfaces	Yes	No	N/A	
1. Is a third-party tool used for interfacing to host (ERP, OMS) business systems?				
2. Please list all standard interfaces provided:				
3. Interface protocols				
3.1 Do you support TCP/IP messaging?				
3.2 Do you support IBM MQ Series?				
3.3 Do you support FTP?				
3.4 Do you support XML messaging?				
3.5 Do you support ODBC?				
4. Do transactions automatically queue if connection fails?				
4.1 Are queued transactions submitted automatically when connection restored?				
4.2 Are queued transactions submitted in FIFO order?				
5. Are source code modifications required to introduce new interface points or messages?				
6. Are source code modifications required to change the content or format of a message?				
Upgrades	Yes	No	N/A	
1. Must some source code changes be re-applied to the new version during the upgrade process?				

1.1 If source code modifications were made to data-driven functionality, will these modifications need to be re-applied?				
1.2 If source code modifications were made to support database schema changes, will these modifications need to be re-applied?				
1.3 If source code modifications were required for changes to rule-driven functionality, will these modifications need to be re-applied?				
1.4 If source code modifications were required to develop new rules, will these modifications need to be re-applied?				
1.5 If source code modifications were required to support new rule conditions, will these modifications need to be re-applied?				
1.6 If source code modifications were required to associate existing functionality to new rules, will these modifications need to be re-applied?				
1.7 If source code modifications were required to make changes to the functionality activated by a "switch", will these modifications need to be re-applied?				

1.8 If source code modifications were required to introduce new "switches," "flags" or "settings," will these modifications need to be re-applied?				
2. Are configured workflows preserved during the upgrade process?				
2.1 If source code modifications were required to change the way that data is selected, inserted or deleted within a workflow, will these modifications need to be re-applied?				
2.2 If source code modifications were required to create or modify user interactions, will these modifications need to be re-applied?				
2.3 If source code modifications were required to reference new variables within a workflow, will these modifications need to be re-applied?				
2.4 If source code modifications were required to create new calculations within a workflow, will these modifications need to be re-applied?				
2.5 If source code modifications were required to change the message content to and from a device within a workflow, will these modifications need to be re-applied?				

3. Are shipping document layouts preserved during the upgrade process?				
4. Are bar code label formats preserved during the upgrade process?				
5. Are user-configured queries preserved during the upgrade process?				

The 2004 WMS RFP Template: Adaptability

Description of Common Changes	Resource Needed V-Vendor I-In-house Resource C-Consultant	Source Code Change (Y/N)?	Can This Be Shown in a Demo?	Cost of Change	Comments
Business Processes					
1. Expand the length of the item number field in the system.					
2. Expand the length of the serial number field in the system.					
3. Expand the length of the location ID field in the system.					
4. Add an RF prompt to capture Julian production date for goods received from manufacturing.					

5. Add an RF prompt to capture special pricing information during picking for select customers.				
6. Within an RF prompting sequence, generate a compliance label under certain conditions (i.e., less than case pick).				
7. Within an RF-directed packing sequence, generate a personalized marketing letter to top-tier customers.				
8. Within and RF-directed pick, interface with a counting scale to verify accuracy of picking counts.				
9. Add a prompt to the RF log-on sequence to capture some labor tracking information.				
10. Add a new put-away rule that is not in the base package.				

11. Notify warehouse manager if an expected purchase order is late by automatically generating an e-mail alert.					
12. Within the RF-directed picking process, get real-time customer-specific pick instructions from the host and display them to the picker.					
13. Add a new version of your ASN receiving process to handle validating item quantities on every Nth ASN receipt, but keep the original ASN receiving process intact, because the process used will vary depending on an unpredictable set of conditions.					
Decision Support/ Reporting					
1. Add an item image to the item master screen (page).					

2. Create a new link from an existing screen to another screen.					
3. Create a screen that presents data from an outside data source.					
4. Create a screen that hyperlinks to a Web page from another application or outside Web site.					
5. Create a Web page that allows the user to edit a subset of fields within the page.					
6. Change field headings on a screen to match your nomenclature.					
7. Change colors and fonts of screens to match your corporate identity.					
8. Add a field to an existing screen to display a piece of data critical to your operation.					
9. Add additional search criteria to an existing look-up screen.					

Appendix 6-1
Page 45

10. Add a graph to a screen.					
11. Configure user-defined metrics within wave release utility based upon data elements critical to the operation (i.e. number of order lines belonging to a specific item family).					
12. Add graphical images to batch/load/ wave release utility (i.e., add flame image to rush orders).					

Appendix 7-1

SAMPLE
COST COMPARISON
IN-HOUSE VS. OUTSOURCED
LOGISTICS OPERATION

Account	In-House Last Year	Provider Pro Forma	Provider Better/Worse
Salaries			
Overtime			
Part-time			
Salary Continuation			
Moving Allowance			
Moving Expense			
Travel			
Meals & Entertainment			
Tuition			
Training			
Incentives			
Physical Exams			
Outside Services			
Consultant Fees			
Meetings			
Contributions			
Telephone			
Fax			
Software			
Computer Expense			
Maintenance & Supplies			
Rent – Land & Building			
Property Taxes			
Insurance – Workers Comp			
Insurance – Prop'y Damage			
Hardware Maintenance			
Depreciation			
Repair – Office			
Dues and Subscriptions			
Messenger			
Office Supplies			
Postage			
Duplication			
Fuel			
Storage			
Sundry Expense			
Freight – Customer Returns			

**COST COMPARISON
IN-HOUSE VS. OUTSOURCED
LOGISTICS OPERATION**

Account	In-House Last Year	Provider Pro Forma	Provider Better/Worse
Reconditioning			
Laundry & Uniforms			
Stretch Wrap			
Pallets			
Slipsheets			
Fringe Benefits			
Transferred Expense			
Hourly Payroll – Straight			
Hourly Vacation & Holiday			
Illness/Accident Benefits			
Hourly Payroll – Misc			
Repairs – Materials			
Repairs – Labor			
Painting Supplies			
Water			
Purchased Electricity			
Detention			
Misc Tools and Supplies			
Car Preparation			
Cleaning Supplies			
Maintenance – Grounds			
Demurrage			
Plant Cartage			
Fumigants			
Plant Protection			
Employee Activities			
Miscellaneous			
Total			

Appendix 7-2

COMPARISON OF IN-HOUSE VS. CONTRACT CARRIER COSTS

This is a pro forma costing structure used by one company to track transportation operation expenses. This company assigns responsibility for completing the form to the controller, distribution, transportation and human resource managers. The completed information is used to compare against vendor bids.

	Previous Year Actual	YTD	YTD Annualized	Outsourcing Pro Forma	Outsourcing Better/Worse
Miles Operated ex Drayage					
Internal Cost per Mile					
Drayage Cost per Mile					
Total Cost per Mile					
For Hire Revenue					
Back Haul Revenue					
Net 3rd Party Revenue					
Inter-Div Hauling Income					
Total Truck Revenue					
Truck Wages/Benefits					
Supervision Salaries					
Clerical Wages					
Driver Wages					
Backhaul Unload Wages					
Restricted Duty Wages					
Other Wages					
Union Pension Fund					
Health & Accident Ins – Union					
Health & Accident Ins – Group					
Long-term Disability					
Quality Fund					
Other Associate Welfare					
Work Comp Admin Cost					
Work Comp Est Unpd Losses					
FICA & Unemployment Tax					
Total Truck Wages/Benefits					

Reprinted with permission from Dedicated Contract Carriage: Evaluation, Implementation, & Management, *by Lisa Harrington. Published by National Private Truck Council, Alexandria, Virginia; 1996.*

TRANSPORTATION OPERATING EXPENSES

	Previous Year Actual	YTD	YTD Annualized	Outsourcing Pro Forma	Outsourcing Better/Worse
Supplies					
Dry Ice					
Other Supplies					
Parts					
Tire					
Fuel					
Oil & Grease					
Total Supplies					
Garage Wages/Benefits					
Restricted Duty Wages					
Garage Wages					
Union Pension Fund					
Hlth & Accident Ins — Union					
Hlth & Accident Ins — Group					
Union Admin Group Ins					
Long-term Disability					
Quality Fund					
Other Associate Welfare					
Work Comp Paid Losses					
Work Comp Est Unpd Losses					
FICA & Unemployment Tax					
Total Garage Wages/Benefits					
Garage					
Garage Supplies					
Garage Parts					
Repairs Due to Accident					
Other Repairs					
Other Garage Expenses					
Total Garage Expenses					
Other Expenses					
Travel/Entertainment					
Training					
Miscellaneous					
Mdse Damage					
Mdse Short					
Backhaul Short/Damage					
Salvage Sales/Recoup					
Total Other Expenses					

TRANSPORTATION OPERATING EXPENSES

	Previous Year Actual	YTD	YTD Annualized	Outsourcing Pro Forma	Outsourcing Better/Worse
Fixed Expenses					
Licenses					
Truck Leasing Expenses					
Less: Interest Expense on Leased Equipment					
Outbound Drayage					
Inbound Drayage					
Road Taxes					
USFT Superfund					
Truck Liability					
Vehicle Physical Damage					
Cargo Liability					
Other Insurance					
Depreciation/Amort					
InterCo Expense					
Total Fixed Expenses					
Total Truck Expenses					
Total Truck Operations					

Appendix 9-1

RATE QUOTATION AND CONTRACT
PUBLIC WAREHOUSE COMPANY

_____

_____

Proposal Date _____

Subject to the attached Terms and Conditions, _____ quotes rates for storage, handling and other services as follows:

PRODUCT DESCRIPTION (Type, Container, Size, Weight)	STORAGE RATE Per _____	HANDLING RATE Per _____

The information contained on the "Service Specifications" page of this contract was used to develop the rates for those products covered by this contract. Should the handling, storage or other characteristics of the products covered by this contract change materially, _____ may revise this rate accordingly.

All goods stored and handled in accordance with the Standard Contract Terms and Conditions for Merchandise Warehousemen incorporated into this agreement.

> ALL CHARGES ARE DUE AND PAYABLE UPON RECEIPT OF WAREHOUSEMAN'S INVOICE.
> CHARGES, CLAIMS WILL NOT BE DEDUCTED FROM WAREHOUSEMAN'S INVOICES.

ROUTING INSTRUCTIONS: Shipments to be consigned to yourself in care of _____.

Destination _____ Delivering Carrier _____
Bill of Lading and Manifest of contents are to be received by warehouse before arrival of shipment.

SERVICE SPECIFICATIONS

_____ (Location)

PRODUCT INFORMATION:

Description:	Type Container	Dimensions L x H x W	#	Units per Pallet	Pits High	Inv. Level	

COMMENTS:	Damaged Goods Instructions: ☐ Refuse ☐ Accept

STORAGE DATA:

PALLET SIZE	TOTAL SKU'S	EST. TURN/YR.	RACKING YES ☐ NO ☐	STORAGE LIFE	SPACE REQUIRED
TEMP. LEVEL	HUMIDITY LEVEL	SANITATION YES ☐ REPORTS NO ☐	EST. DEAD SPACE	EST. Hon.Cb.	HAZARDOUS OTHER ☐ POISON ☐ FLAM ☐

INBOUND HANDLING DATA:

RAIL %	TRUCK %	TOFC %	PALLETIZED/UNIT YES ☐ NO ☐	UNLOADED BY WH ☐ DRIVER ☐	MAX PALLETS/UNIT PER LIFT	SPACE REQUIRED
LINE ITEMS PER INBOUND	RAIL	TRUCK	ORDER PER RAIL TRUCK INBOUND		ARRIVAL MAIL ☐ CARRIER ☐ NOTICE PHONE ☐ OTHER ☐	

OUTBOUND HANDLING DATA:

ORDERS/DAY	LINES/ORDER	UNITS/LINE	PALLET/LIFT YES ☐ NO ☐	LOADED BY WH ☐ DRIVER ☐	PALLET %	PICK %	TRUCK RAIL % %
CUSTOMER TRUCK	COMMON CARRIER		WILL CALL	TOFC	ROUTING INSTRUCTIONS	YES ☐ NO ☐	

CUSTOMER SERVICE & ORDER PROCESSING:

ORDERS RECEIVED BY	PHONE ☐ FAX ☐ MAIL ☐ OTHER ☐	BACK ORDER	YES ☐ NO ☐	BILL OF LADING	WH ☐ SPECIAL ☐	MARK AND STENCIL	YES ☐ NO ☐
INVENTORY CONTROL	OTHER ☐ SPREAD SHEET ☐ SPECIAL FORM ☐	INVENTORY REPORTING		DAILY ☐ MONTHLY ☐	OTHER ☐		
CODE DATE RECORDING	YES ☐ NO ☐	PAPERWORK DISTRIBUTION	SALES OFFICE ☐ DISTRIBUTION ☐	TRAFFIC DEPT. ☐ SPECIAL ☐	See instructions		

CONTACTS:

DISTRIBUTION	PHONE	INVENTORY	PHONE		PHONE
TRAFFIC	PHONE	SALES/DISTRIBUTOR	PHONE		PHONE

SUPPLEMENTAL SERVICES

Clerical Services:

1. Clerical Labor ....
2. Overtime Clerical Labor ....
3. Withdrawal Order ....
4. Preparation of Export Forms ....
5. Inventory Reporting Charge ....
6. Preparation of O, S & D Reports ....
7. Photocopy Preparation ....
8. Back Orders ....
9. Communications Expense ....
10. Collection of COD's ....
11. UPS Order Charge ....
12. Same Day Service Charge ....
13. Additional Report ....

Warehouse Services:

1. Extra Labor ....
2. Overtime Labor   HANDLING ....
3. Sunday & Holiday EQUIPMENT ....
    Overtime Labor   INCLUDED ....
4. Reporting Serial Numbers of Markings ....
5. Stenciling ....
6. Export Stenciling ....
7. Minimum Handling Inbound ....
8. Minimum Storage Inbound ....
9. Minimum Monthly Billing Storage ....
10. Minimum Monthly Billing Handling ....
11. Special Handling DF Car ....
12. Dunnage, Bracing or Packaging Material ....
13. Sorting Mixed Freight – Rail or Truck ....
14. Trash Removal ....
15. Car Cleaning Charge ....
16. Recoopering ....
17. Will Call Charge ....
18. Minimum Recurring Storage per SKU ....
19. UPS Processing Charge ....
20. Loose Case Unloading Exceeding Profile ....
21. Case Picking Exceeding Profile ....

For demurrage and detention purposes _____ shall be responsible for handling _____ rail cars and/or _____ trucks per day or their equivalent.

All warehouse overtime requires foreman to supervise. This time will be charged at the rates listed above.

Damaged or uncrated goods shall be assessed storage charges of 1½ times the applicable storage rate in the event these goods are not removed or reconditioned within 48 hours of receipt of notification by the depositor.
Physical inventories will be performed upon depositor REQUEST at the hourly rates established above. Book balances will be adjusted at the time of inventory.

Service charges are based upon requirements listed on the Service Specifications listing.

Any services not specified above will be charged at the hourly rate.

Standard Contract Terms and Conditions for Merchandise Warehousemen
(Approved and promulgated by American Warehouse Association, October 1968; revised and promulgated by International Warehouse Logistics Association, January 1998)

ACCEPTANCE – Sec. 1
(a) This contract and rate quotation including accessorial charges endorsed on or attached hereto must be accepted within 30 days from the proposal date by signature of depositor on the reverse side of the contract. In the absence of written acceptance, the act of tendering goods described herein for storage or other services by warehouseman within 30 days from the proposal date shall constitute such acceptance by depositor.
(b) In the event that goods tendered for storage or other services do not conform to the description contained herein, or conforming goods are tendered after 30 days from the proposal date without prior written acceptance by depositor as provided in paragraph (a) of this section, warehouseman may refuse to accept such goods. If warehouseman accepts such goods, depositor agrees to rates and charges as may be assigned and invoiced by warehouseman and to all terms of this contract.
(c) This contract may be canceled by either party upon 30 days written notice and is canceled if no storage or other services are performed under this contract for a period of 180 days.

SHIPPING – Sec. 2
Depositor agrees not to ship goods to warehouseman as the named consignee. If, in violation of this agreement, goods are shipped to warehouseman as named consignee, depositor agrees to notify carrier in writing prior to such shipment, with copy of such notice to the warehouseman, that warehouseman named as consignee is a warehouseman and has no beneficial title or interest in such property and depositor further agrees to indemnify and hold harmless warehouseman from any and all claims for unpaid transportation charges, including undercharges, demurrage, detention or charges of any nature, in connection with goods so shipped. Depositor further agrees that, if it fails to notify carrier as required by the preceding sentence, warehouseman shall have the right to refuse such goods and shall not be liable or responsible for any loss, injury or damage of any nature to, or related to, such goods.

TENDER FOR STORAGE – Sec. 3
All goods for storage shall be delivered at the warehouse properly marked and packaged for handling. The depositor shall furnish at or prior to such delivery, a manifest showing marks, brands, or sizes to be kept and accounted for separately, and the class of storage and other services desired.

STORAGE PERIOD AND CHARGES – Sec. 4
(a) All charges for storage are per package or other agreed unit per month.
(b) Storage charges become applicable upon the date that warehouseman accepts care, custody and control of the goods, regardless of unloading date or date of issue of warehouse receipt.
(c) Except as provided in paragraph (d) of this section, a full month's storage charge will apply on all goods received between the first and the 15th, inclusive, oF a calendar month; one-half month's storage charge will apply on all goods received between the 16th and the last day, inclusive, of a calendar month, and a full month's storage charge will apply to all goods in

351

storage on the first day of the next and succeeding calendar months. All storage charges are due and payable on the first day of storage for the initial month and thereafter on the first day of the calendar month.

(d)   When mutually agreed by the warehouseman and the depositor, a storage month shall extend from a date in one calendar month to, but not including, the same date of the next and all succeeding months. All storage charges are due and payable on the first day of the storage month.

TRANSFER, TERMINATION OF STORAGE, REMOVAL OF GOODS – Sec. 5

(a)   Instructions to transfer goods on the books of the warehouseman are not effective until delivered to and accepted by warehouseman, and all charges up to the time transfer is made are chargeable to the depositor of record. If a transfer involves rehandling the goods, such will be subject to a charge. When goods in storage are transferred from one party to another through issuance of a new warehouse receipt, a new storage date is established on the date of transfer.

(b)   The warehouseman reserves the right to move, at his expense, 14 days after notice is sent by certified or registered mail to the depositor of record or to the last known holder of the negotiable warehouse receipt, any goods in storage from the warehouse in which they may be stored to any other of his warehouses; but if such depositor or holder takes delivery of his goods in lieu of transfer, no storage charge shall be made for the current storage month. Warehouseman will store the goods at, and may without notice move the goods within and between, any one or more of the warehouse buildings which comprise the warehouse complex identified on the front of this warehouse receipt.

(c)   The warehouseman may, upon written notice to the depositor of record and any other person known by the warehouseman to claim an interest in the goods, require the removal of any goods by the end of the next succeeding storage month. Such notice shall be given to the last known place of business or abode of the person to be notified. If goods are not removed before the end of the next succeeding storage month, the warehouseman may sell them in accordance with applicable law.

(d)   If warehouseman in good faith believes that the goods are about to deteriorate or decline in value to less than the amount of warehouseman's lien before the end of the next succeeding storage month, the warehouseman may specify in the notification any reasonable shorter time for removal of the goods and in case the goods are not removed, may sell them at public sale held one week after a single advertisement or posting as provided by law.

(e)   If as a result of a quality or condition of the goods of which the warehouseman had no notice at the time of deposit the goods are a hazard to other property or to the warehouse or to persons, the warehouseman may sell the goods at public or private sale without advertisement or reasonable notification to all persons known to claim an interest in the goods. If the warehouseman after a reasonable effort is unable to sell the goods, he may dispose of them in any lawful manner and shall incur no liability by reason of such disposition. Pending such disposition, sale or return of the goods, the warehouseman may remove the goods from the warehouse and shall incur no liability by reason of such removal.

HANDLING – Sec. 6

(a) The handling charge covers the ordinary labor involved in receiving goods at warehouse door, placing goods in storage, and returning goods to warehouse door. Handling charges are due and payable on receipt of goods.

(b) Unless otherwise agreed, labor for unloading and loading goods will be subject to a charge. Additional expenses incurred by the warehouseman in receiving and handling damaged goods, and additional expense in unloading from or loading into cars or other vehicles not at warehouse door will be charge to the depositor.

(c) Labor and materials used in loading rail cars or other vehicles are chargeable to the depositor.

(d) When goods are ordered out in quantities less than in which received, the warehouseman may make an additional charge for each order or each item of an order.

(e) The warehouseman shall not be liable for demurrage or detention, delays in unloading inbound cars, trailers or other containers, or delays in obtaining and loading cars, trailers or other containers for outbound shipment unless warehouseman has failed to exercise reasonable care.

DELIVERY REQUIREMENTS – Sec. 7

(a) No goods shall be delivered or transferred except upon receipt by the warehouseman of complete written instructions. Written instructions shall include, but are not limited to, FAX, EDI, TWX or similar communication, provided warehouseman has no liability when relying on the information contained in the communication as received. However, when no negotiable receipt is outstanding, goods may be delivered upon instruction by telephone in accordance with a prior written authorization, but the warehouseman shall not be responsible for loss or error occasioned thereby.

(b) When a negotiable receipt has been issued, no goods covered by that receipt shall be delivered, or transferred on the books of the warehouseman, unless the receipt, properly endorsed, is surrendered for cancellation, or for endorsement of partial delivery thereon. If a negotiable receipt is lost or destroyed, delivery of goods may be made only upon order of a court of competent jurisdiction and the posting of security approved by the court as provided by law.

(c) When goods are ordered out a reasonable time shall be given the warehouseman to carry out instructions, and if he is unable because of acts of God, war, public enemies, seizure under legal process, strikes, lockouts, riots and civil commotions, or any reason beyond the warehouseman's control, or because of loss or destruction of goods for which warehouseman is not liable, or because of any other excuse provided by law, the warehouseman shall not be liable for failure to carry out such instructions and goods remaining in storage will continue to be subject to regular storage charges.

EXTRA SERVICES (SPECIAL SERVICES) – Sec. 8

(a) Warehouse labor required for services other than ordinary handling and storage will be charged to the depositor.

(b) Special services requested by depositor including, but not limited to, compiling of special stock statements; reporting marked weights, serial numbers or other data from packages; physical check of goods; and handling transit billing will be subject to a charge.

(c) Dunnage, bracing, packing materials, or other special supplies may be provided for the depositor at a charge in addition to the warehouseman's cost.
(d) By prior arrangement, goods may be received or delivered during other than usual business hours, subject to a charge.
(e) Communication expense including postage, teletype, telegram or telephone will be charged to the depositor if such concern more than normal inventory reporting of if, at the request of the depositor, communications are made by other than regular United States Mail.

BONDED STORAGE – Sec. 9
(a) A charge in addition to regular rates will be made for merchandise in bond.
(b) Where a warehouse receipt covers goods in U.S. Customs bond, such receipt shall be void upon the termination of the storage period fixed by law.

MINIMUM CHARGES – Sec. 10
(a) A minimum handling charge per lot and a minimum storage charge per lot per month will be made. When a warehouse receipt covers more than one lot or when a lot is in assortment, a minimum charge per mark, brand, or variety will be made.
(b) A minimum monthly charge to one account for storage and/or handling will be made. This charge will apply also to each account when one customer has several accounts, each requiring separte records and billing.

LIABILITY AND LIMITATION OF DAMAGES – Sec. 11
(a) THE WAREHOUSEMAN SHALL NOT BE LIABLE FOR ANY LOSS OR INJURY TO GOODS STORED HOWEVER CAUSED UNLESS SUCH LOSS OR INJURY RESULTED FROM THE FAILURE BY THE WAREHOUSEMAN TO EXERCISE SUCH CARE IN REGARD TO THEM AS A REASONABLY CAREFUL MAN WOULD EXERCISE UNDER LIKE CIRCUMSTANCES AND WAREHOUSEMAN IS NOT LIABLE FOR DAMAGES WHICH COULD NOT HAVE BEEN AVOIDED BY THE EXERCISE OF SUCH CARE.
(b) GOODS ARE NOT INSURED BY THE WAREHOUSEMAN AGAINST LOSS OR INJURY HOWEVER CAUSED.
(c) THE DEPOSITOR DECLARES THAT DAMAGES ARE LIMITED TO _____, PROVIDED, HOWEVER, THAT SUCH LIABILITY MAY AT THE TIME OF ACCEPTANCE OF THIS CONTRACT AS PROVIDED IN SECTION 1 BE INCREASED UPON DEPOSITOR'S WRITTEN REQUEST ON PART OR ALL OF THE GOODS HEREUNDER IN WHICH EVENT AN ADDITIONAL MONTHLY CHARGE WILL BE MADE BASED UPON SUCH INCREASED VALUATION.
(d) WHERE LOSS OR INJURY OCCURS TO STORED GOODS, FOR WHICH THE WAREHOUSEMAN IS NOT LIABLE, THE DEPOSITOR SHALL BE RESPONSIBLE FOR THE COST OF REMOVING AND DISPOSING OF SUCH GOODS AND THE COST OF ANY ENVIRONMENTAL CLEAN UP AND SITE REMEDIATION RESULTING FROM THE LOSS OR INJURY TO THE GOODS.

NOTICE OF CLAIM AND FILING OF SUIT – Sec. 12
(a) Claims by the depositor and all other persons must be presented in writing to the warehouseman within a reasonable time, and in no event longer than either 60 days after

delivery of the goods by the warehouseman or 60 days after depositor of record or the last known holder of a negotiable warehouse receipt is notified by the warehouseman that loss or injury to part or all of the goods has occurred, whichever time is shorter.

(b) No action may be maintained by the depositor or others against the warehouseman for loss or injury to the goods stored unless timely written claim has been given as provided in paragraph (a) of this section and unless such action is commenced either within nine months after date of delivery by warehouseman or within nine months after depositor of record or the last known holder of a negotiable warehouse receipt is notified that loss or injury to part or all of the goods has occurred, whichever time is shorter.

(c) When goods have not been delivered, notice may be given of known loss or injury to the goods by mailing of a registered or certified letter to the depositor of record or to the last known holder of a negotiable warehouse receipt. Time limitations for presentation of claim in writing and maintaining of action after notice begin on the date of mailing of such notice by warehouseman.

LIABILITY FOR CONSEQUENTIAL DAMAGES – Sec. 13
Warehouseman shall not be liable for any loss of profit or special, indirect, or consequential damages of any kind.

LIABILITY FOR MISSHIPMENT – Sec. 14
If warehouseman negligently misships goods, the warehouseman shall pay the reasonable transportation charges incurred to return the misshipped goods to the warehouse. If the consignee fails to return the goods, warehouseman's maximum liability shall be for the lost or damaged goods as specified in Section 11 above, and warehouseman shall have no liability for damages due to the consignee's acceptance or use of the goods whether such goods be those of the depositor or another.

MYSTERIOUS DISAPPEARANCE – Sec. 15
Warehouseman shall not be liable for loss of goods due to inventory shortage or unexplained or mysterious disappearance of goods unless depositor establishes such loss occurred because of warehouseman's failure to exercise the care required for warehouseman under Section 11 above. Any presumption of conversion imposed by law shall not apply to such loss and a claim by depositor of conversion must be established by affirmative evidence that the warehouseman converted the goods to the warehouseman's own use.

RIGHT TO STORE GOODS – Sec. 16
Depositor represents and warrants that depositor is lawfully possessed of the goods and has the right and authority to store them with warehouseman. Depositor agrees to indemnify and hold harmless the warehouseman from all loss, cost and expense (including reasonable attorneys' fees) which warehouseman pays or incurs as a result of any dispute or litigation, whether instituted by warehouseman or others, respecting depositor's right, title or interest in the goods. Such amounts shall be charged in relation to the goods and subject to warehouseman's lien.

ACCURATE INFORMATION – Sec. 17
Depositor will provide warehouseman with information concerning the stored goods which is accurate, complete and sufficient to allow warehouseman to comply with all laws and regulations concerning the storage, handling and transporting of the stored goods. Depositor will indemnify and hold warehouseman harmless from all loss, cost, penalty and expense (including reasonable attorneys' fees) which warehouseman pays or incurs as a result of depositor failing to fully discharge this obligation.

SEVERABLILITY AND WAIVER – Sec. 18
(a) If any provision of this receipt, or any application thereof, should be construed or held to be void, invalid or unenforceable, by order, decree or judgment of a court of competent jurisdiction, the remaining provisions of this receipt shall not be affected thereby but shall remain in full force and effect.
(b) Warehouseman's failure to require strict compliance with any provision of the Warehouse Receipt shall not constitute a waiver or estoppel to later demand strict compliance with that or any other provision(s) of the Warehouse Receipt.
(c) The provisions of this Warehouse Receipt shall be binding upon the depositor's heirs, executors, successors and assigns; contain the sole agreement governing goods stored with the warehouseman; and cannot be modified except by a writing signed by warehouseman.

SAMPLE
WAREHOUSING AGREEMENT

THIS AGREEMENT is made and entered into this _____ day of _____,
20__, by and between _____, a _____ corporation
("Client"), and _____, a _____ corporation ("LSP").

WITNESSETH:

WHEREAS, Client is in the business of _____ and desires to
engage LSP to provide _____;

WHEREAS, LSP can provide _____.

NOW, THEREFORE, in consideration of the mutual agreements, covenants and
conditions contained herein, the parties agree as follows:

1. LSP agrees to provide _____ square feet of warehouse space located
in the building at _____. These facilities will be used
exclusively for the storage and handling of Client goods and operation of Client
account.

Alternative Language

> *1. LSP agrees to provide the services covered by this agreement in the
> building Client is leasing from LSP located at _____.
> This facility will be used exclusively for the storage and handling of
> Client goods and operation of Client's account in accordance with the
> terms and conditions of this Agreement and the corresponding
> Warehouse Lease Agreement attached hereto as Exhibit ___.*

2. The products that will be stored and handled pursuant to this Agreement are
listed in Exhibit A. Client represents and warrants that he has the right and
authority to store them with LSP.

Client represents and warrants that there are no known potential health, safety, and/or environmental hazards associated with its products or the storage and handling thereof.

3. LSP agrees to handle Client's merchandise, as a public warehouseman, including: inbound and outbound handling, warehousing and order filling, adequate supervision and clerical services, maintaining inventory records and supplying daily reports listing quantities received, quantities shipped, and balance on hand. All goods and merchandise warehoused for Client by LSP hereunder shall be stored pursuant to IWLA customary form of Warehouse Receipt, which is hereto attached as Exhibit B and shall be in compliance with Client's reasonable policies hereinafter covered by this Warehousing Agreement, the corresponding Warehouse Lease Agreement (Exhibit C) (*if any*) and/or covered in Client policy and procedure manuals.

4. LSP agrees that it will not use or permit anyone else to use the premises for any purpose which by reason of odor or otherwise would be harmful to Client's products.

5. LSP agrees to receive and ship sufficient railroad cars and trucks (provided same are available to LSP) to satisfy Client shipping schedules, provided advance notice is given.

6. Client shall provide current policy and procedure manuals and shall provide all orders and shipping papers and forms for daily reports.

7. Client shall provide specifications for papering, dunnage, and doorway and product protection for outbound rail cars and trucks and will either provide the materials therefor or reimburse LSP for same.

8. All demurrage, detention, or overtime labor charges resulting from conditions beyond the control of LSP shall be paid by client.

9. Client agrees to pay LSP the rates and charges set forth in Exhibit D, attached to this agreement and made a part hereof. Invoices will be prepared _____ and will be payable within _____ ( ) days of their receipt by

Client. Rates and charges for handling will be subject to review annually on the anniversary of the contract, subject to the provisions of Section _____.

10. The term of this Agreement shall commence on _____, and shall continue in full force and effect through _____ unless terminated earlier as hereinafter provided.

11. This Agreement may be terminated by the parties as follows:

(a) LSP may terminate this Agreement during the aforesaid term, if it shall have previously given at least ninety (90) days written notice that the then existing handling rates as set forth above are reasonably deemed by LSP to be inadequate and no agreement concerning a substituted handling charge shall have been reached and put into effect by the parties within the ninety (90) day period. LSP may not render such notice during the first 12-month period that this Agreement is in effect and render such notice only once during any calendar year thereafter.

(b) Client may terminate this Agreement during the aforesaid term should LSP fail to perform satisfactorily the services required hereunder. However, prior to terminating for unsatisfactory performance, Client shall give written notice to LSP at least ninety (90) days prior to its exercising said right, and shall in said notice set forth the reasons for said termination. If LSP corrects the conditions giving rise to the unsatisfactory performance within said ninety (90) days to Client's satisfaction, the Agreement shall not terminate provided, however, that Client's satisfaction with LSP's corrective efforts shall not be unreasonably withheld.

(c) Notwithstanding the prior provisions of this Section 4, if LSP does not maintain the premises so that they reasonably comply with all applicable laws, rules, and regulations pertaining to the warehousing of _____ products, including those of the _____ and of Client, Client may terminate this Agreement on ninety (90) days written notice. However, Client shall notify LSP of such failure to comply and

359

shall allow thirty (30) days for LSP to correct such inadequacies specified in such notice.

(d) If, during the term of this Agreement, the warehouse in which space is leased or assigned to Client located at _____ is damaged by fire or other cause so as to interfere substantially with the storage of Client's products therein, then, if the warehouse shall not be repaired within one hundred and eighty (180) days thereafter, unless failure to make such repairs is due to causes beyond LSP's control, such as strikes, work stoppages, weather conditions, inability to obtain materials, etc., this Agreement may be terminated at the option of either party by written notice to the other.

Alternative Language (Add if lease agreement exists.)

*(e)   The termination of this Agreement under either of the foregoing
        Sections (a) and (b) of
    Paragraph 11 shall not affect the Warehouse Lease Agreement
between LSP and Client.*

12. It is agreed that LSP's services hereunder shall be rendered as a merchandise warehouseman in the State of _____ and as an independent contractor and in no wise partner or agent of Client.

13. LSP agrees to hold Client harmless from any and all claims asserted by any parties whomsoever insofar as the same shall arise because of the fault or negligence, actual or alleged, of LSP, its agents, servants, or employees occurring on the premises described in the Agreement.

14. In no event shall LSP's duties to Client under this Agreement exceed that of a reasonable prudent warehouseman under _____ state law. LSP shall not be liable for any loss or injury to goods stored, however caused, unless such loss or injury resulted from the failure of LSP to exercise such care in regard to the goods as a reasonably careful man, owning similar goods, would exercise under like circumstances.

15. LSP does not insure Client's goods against loss or injury however caused.

16. Client agrees to hold LSP harmless from any and all claims asserted by any parties whomsoever, insofar as the same shall arise because of the fault or negligence, actual or alleged, of Client, its agents, servants, or employees.

17. Except as otherwise stated herein, if requested, each of the parties hereto shall advise the other of all applicable insurance coverage.

18. LSP shall maintain at its expense such insurance as will fully protect it from claims under Workers' Compensation and Occupation Disease Acts and from claims for damage for bodily injury, including death, and for property damage, which may arise from operations under this Agreement, whether such operations by LSP or by any subcontractor or anyone directly or indirectly employed by either of them.

LSP also agrees that such insurance shall include the following:

(a) Workers' Compensation Insurance in compliance with the Workers' Compensation Act of _____ if such act requires part of all of liability to employees for occupational accidents or diseases to be satisfied by such insurance, or insurance in a State Fund, for liability to employees for occupational accidents or diseases and pay all premiums and taxes required by the Workers' Compensation Act of _____ if such Act requires insurance of part or all of LSP's liability with the State Fund.

(b) Employer's Liability Insurance on all employees not covered by a Workers' Compensation Act, for occupational accidents or disease with limits of liability of not less than _____ for any one accident or disease.

(c) Comprehensive General Liability Insurance with limits not less than _____ combined single limit bodily injury and property damage per occurrence.

Certificates of Insurance showing compliance with the foregoing requirements shall be furnished by LSP when it returns the signed Agreement to Client. Certificates shall state the policy or policies will

361

not be cancelled nor altered without at least ten (10) days prior written notice to Client.

If Client shall so request, LSP shall furnish Client for its inspection and approval such policies of insurance with all endorsement, or confirmed specimens of proof thereof, certified by the insurance company to be true and correct copies.

Maintenance of such insurance and the performance by LSP of its obligations under the foregoing paragraph shall not relieve LSP of liability under its indemnity agreement set forth in this Agreement.

19. Physical inventories will be taken and reconciliation made once each _____. LSP shall also conduct weekly cycle count inventories at Client's request.

Once each year, after the end of the fourth quarter, if there are inventory losses and warehouse damages in excess of inventory overages which exceed _____ of _____ percent of the total case volume handled by LSP during such year, LSP shall pay Client upon presentation of an invoice therefor an amount equal to such amount in excess of _____ of _____ percent times Client's production and inbound transportation costs.

20. Neither party shall be responsible for delays, failure, or omissions due to any cause beyond its reasonable control, wheresoever arising and not due to its own negligence or intentional misconduct and which cannot be overcome by the exercise of due diligence, including, but not limited to labor disturbances, riots, fires, earthquakes, floods, storms, lightning, epidemics, war, disorders, hostilities, expropriation of confiscation of properties, interference by civil or military authorities or acts of God.

21. LSP acknowledges that in the course of rendering warehousing services under this Agreement, Client may disclose to LSP, or LSP may come into the possession of information as a result of its relationship with Client under this Agreement, respecting the business and affairs of Client, including data pertaining to Client's products and customers. LSP acknowledges that such information is confidential and proprietary to client, and covenants and agrees to

keep such information in the strictest confidence, and to take all necessary steps to assure that its employees will keep in the strictest confidence all information and not disclose any such information to any third party without the prior written consent of client. This covenant shall survive the termination or expiration of this Agreement.

22. Client and LSP acknowledge and agree that the personnel employed by each company in the performance of or in connection with the activities of the parties contemplated by this are important assets of their respective companies. Therefore, without the prior written consent of the other, neither Client nor LSP shall solicit for employment the employees or the officers of the other (or any of their subsidiaries or their affiliates) for employment by them or any affiliate or subsidiary of either of them. Such non-solicitation shall be for a period of this Agreement and for a period of six (6) months after the termination of this Agreement.

Client and LSP further agree and acknowledge that a monetary remedy for a breach of this provision would be inadequate and may be impractical and extremely difficult to prove, and such a breach would cause each of the companies irrevocable harm. In the event of a breach of the provisions hereof, each of the parties will be entitled, in addition to any monetary damage it may subsequently prove, to temporary and permanent injunction relief. Including temporary restraining orders, preliminary injunctions and permanent injunctions. This provision of the paragraph shall survive the termination of this Agreement.

LSP shall not pay any salaries, commissions, fees, or make any payments or rebates, to any employee or officer of Client or to any designee of any such employee or officer, or favor any employee or officer of Client or any designee of any such employee or officer, with gifts or entertainment or significant cost or value with service of goods sold at less than full market value.

23. Client agrees to repair at its own cost any damage or injury done to the warehouse of LSP which results because of the negligence of Client, its agents or employees, except any damage or injury caused by fire, the elements, and any other causes outside the control of LSP.

24. LSP and its agents, servants, employees, invitees, and licensees shall faithfully keep and observe in every respect all federal, state, and local laws and regulations including the standards of the National Board of Fire Underwriters.

25. This Agreement shall inure to the benefit of and be binding upon the successors and assigns of the parties hereto, provided, however, neither party to this Agreement shall assign or sublet its interest or obligations herein, including, but not limited to, the assignment of any monies due and payable, without the prior written consent of the other party, which consent shall not be unreasonably withheld. Notwithstanding the aforesaid, Client shall not need the prior consent of LSP in the event Client assigns this Agreement to a parent, subsidiary, affiliate or a company into which Client is merged or with which Client is consolidated.

26. This Agreement shall be governed by, construed and enforced in accordance with the laws of the State of _____.

27. Any notice or demand required or permitted hereunder shall be given in writing and shall be considered as having been given by either party to the other party upon the facsimile transmission confirmed by the mailing thereof to such other party at the following addresses or to such other address as such other party may from time to time specify in writing:

    If to LSP:

        _____
        _____
        _____

    If to Client:

        _____
        _____
        _____

Alternative Language

The parties agree that any claim or dispute relating to this Agreement, or any other matters, disputes or claims between us, shall be subject to non-binding mediation if agreed to by the parties within 30 days of either party making a request to the other by letter. Any such mediation will be held in _____ and shall be conducted according to the mediation rules of the National Arbitration Forum.

The parties to this Agreement agree to arbitrate all disputes, controversies, or differences that may arise between the parties with respect to any of the provisions of this Agreement. Either party may give written notice to the other of its decision to arbitrate any dispute. The notice shall specify the issue(s) to be arbitrated. The parties may agree on one arbitrator but if agreement cannot be reached then each party shall select one (1) arbitrator and the third arbitrator shall be appointed by mutual consent of the parties. In the event the parties cannot agree upon such third arbitrator, the two arbitrators shall jointly select a third arbitrator. The parties agree to arbitrate in accordance with arbitration rules and procedures. The decision of the arbitrator or majority of such three arbitrators, including but not limited to assessment of the cost of the arbitration, shall be final and binding.

28. This Agreement, together with all exhibits and attachments, constitutes the entire agreement between the parties, and there are no other terms and conditions.

29. This Agreement may not be amended or varied except by the written agreement of the parties hereto, and all waivers of any rights must be in writing to be effective.

IN WITNESS WHEREOF, the parties have caused this Agreement to be executed by their authorized representatives as of the day and year first above written.

LOGISTICS SERVICE PROVIDER

By _____

Title _____

CLIENT

By _____

Title _____

EXHIBIT A

**LIST AND DESCRIPTION OF PRODUCTS
TO BE HANDLED**

EXHIBIT B

NON-NEGOTIABLE WAREHOUSE RECEIPT

(Reprinted with permission of International Warehouse Logistics Association)

Original
NON-NEGOTIABLE
WAREHOUSE RECEIPT

(Warehouse) claims a lien for all lawful charges for storage and preservation of the goods; also for all lawful claims for money advanced, interest, insurance, transportation, labor, weighing, coopering, and other charges and expenses in relation to such goods, and for the balance on any other accounts that may be due. The property covered by this receipt has NOT been insured by this Company for the benefit of the depositor against fire or any other casualty.

THIS IS TO CERTIFY THAT WE HAVE RECEIVED the goods listed hereon in apparent good order, except as noted herein (contents, condition, and quality unknown). SUBJECT TO ALL TERMS AND CONDITIONS INCLUDING LIMITATION OF LIABILITY HEREIN AND ON THE REVERSE HEREOF. Such property to be delivered to THE DEPOSITOR upon the payment of all storage, handling, and other charges. Advances have been made and liability incurred on these goods as follows:

DOCUMENT NUMBER
DATE
CUSTOMER NUMBER
CUSTOMER ORDER NO.
WAREHOUSE NO.

RECEIVED FROM

FOR ACCOUNT OF

DELIVERING CARRIER	CARRIER NUMBER	PREPAID/COLLECT	SHIPPERS NUMBER

International Warehouse
Logistics Association

QUANTITY	SAID TO BE OR CONTAIN (CUSTOMER ITEM NO., WAREHOUSE ITEM NO., LOT NUMBER, DESCRIPTION, ETC.)	WEIGHT	RATE	CODE	STORAGE RATE / HANDLING RATE	DAMAGE & EXCEPTIONS
	TOTALS					

NO DELIVERY WILL BE MADE ON THIS RECEIPT EXCEPT ON WRITTEN ORDER

BY _____
AUTHORIZED SIGNATURE

Appendix 9-2
Page 13

Standard Contract Terms and Conditions for Merchandise Warehousemen

(Approved and promulgated by American Warehouse Association, October 1968; revised and promulgated by International Warehouse Logistics Association, January 1998)

ACCEPTANCE – Sec. 1

(a) This contract and rate quotation including accessorial charges endorsed on or attached hereto must be accepted within 30 days from the proposal date by signature of depositor on the reverse side of the contract. In the absence of written acceptance, the act of tendering goods described herein for storage or other services by warehouseman within 30 days from the proposal date shall constitute such acceptance by depositor.

(b) In the event that goods tendered for storage or other services do not conform to the description contained herein, or conforming goods are tendered after 30 days from the proposal date without prior written acceptance by depositor as provided in paragraph (a) of this section, warehouseman may refuse to accept such goods. If warehouseman accepts such goods, depositor agrees to rates and charges as may be assigned and invoiced by warehouseman and to all terms of this contract.

(c) This contract may be canceled by either party upon 30 days written notice and is canceled if no storage or other services are performed under this contract for a period of 180 days.

SHIPPING – Sec. 2

Depositor agrees not to ship goods to warehouseman as the named consignee. If, in violation of this agreement, goods are shipped to warehouseman as named consignee, depositor agrees to notify carrier in writing prior to such shipment, with copy of such notice to the warehouseman, that warehouseman named as consignee is a warehouseman and has no beneficial title or interest in such property and depositor further agrees to indemnify and hold harmless warehouseman from any and all claims for unpaid transportation charges, including undercharges, demurrage, detention or charges of any nature, in connection with goods so shipped. Depositor further agrees that, if it fails to notify carrier as required by the preceding sentence, warehouseman shall have the right to refuse such goods and shall not be liable or responsible for any loss, injury or damage of any nature to, or related to, such goods.

TENDER FOR STORAGE – Sec. 3

All goods for storage shall be delivered at the warehouse properly marked and packaged for handling. The depositor shall furnish at or prior to such delivery, a manifest showing marks, brands, or sizes to be kept and accounted for separately, and the class of storage and other services desired.

STORAGE PERIOD AND CHARGES – Sec. 4

(a) All charges for storage are per package or other agreed unit per month.

(b) Storage charges become applicable upon the date that warehouseman accepts care, custody and control of the goods, regardless of unloading date or date of issue of warehouse receipt.

(c) Except as provided in paragraph (d) of this section, a full month's storage charge will apply on all goods received between the first and the 15th, inclusive, of a calendar month; one-half month's storage charge will apply on all goods received between the 16th and the last day, inclusive, of a calendar month, and a full month's storage charge will apply to all goods in storage on the first day of the next and succeeding calendar months. All storage charges are due and payable on the first day of storage for the initial month and thereafter on the first day of the calendar month.

(d) When mutually agreed by the warehouseman and the depositor, a storage month shall extend from a date in one calendar month to, but not including, the same date of the next and all succeeding months. All storage charges are due and payable on the first day of the storage month.

TRANSFER, TERMINATION OF STORAGE, REMOVAL OF GOODS – Sec. 5

(a) Instructions to transfer goods on the books of the warehouseman are not effective until delivered to and accepted by warehouseman, and all charges up to the time transfer is made are chargeable to the depositor of record. If a transfer involves rehandling the goods, such will be subject to a charge. When goods in storage are transferred from one party to another through issuance of a new warehouse receipt, a new storage date is established on the date of transfer.

(b) The warehouseman reserves the right to move, at his expense, 14 days after notice is sent by certified or registered mail to the depositor of record or to the last known holder of the negotiable warehouse receipt, any goods in storage from the warehouse in which they may be stored to any other of his warehouses; but if such depositor or holder takes delivery of his goods in lieu of transfer, no storage charge shall be made for the current storage month. Warehouseman will store the goods at, and may without notice move the goods within and between, any one or more of the warehouse buildings which comprise the warehouse complex identified on the front of this warehouse receipt.

(c) The warehouseman may, upon written notice to the depositor of record and any other person known by the warehouseman to claim an interest in the goods, require the removal of any goods by the end of the next succeeding storage month. Such notice shall be given to the last known place of business or abode of the person to be notified. If goods are not removed before the end of the next succeeding storage month, the warehouseman may sell them in accordance with applicable law.

(d) If warehouseman in good faith believes that the goods are about to deteriorate or decline in value to less than the amount of warehouseman's lien before the end of the next succeeding storage month, the warehouseman may specify in the notification any reasonable shorter time for removal of the goods and in case the goods are not removed, may sell them at public sale held one week after a single advertisement or posting as provided by law.

(e) If as a result of a quality or condition of the goods of which the warehouseman had no notice at the time of deposit the goods are a hazard to other property or to the warehouse or to persons, the warehouseman may sell the goods at public or private sale without advertisement on reasonable notification to all persons known to claim an interest in the goods. If the warehouseman after a reasonable effort is unable to sell the goods he may dispose of them in any lawful manner and shall incur no liability by reason of such disposition. Pending such disposition, sale or return of the goods, the warehouseman may remove the goods from the warehouse and shall incur no liability by reason of such removal.

HANDLING – Sec. 6

(a) The handling charge covers the ordinary labor involved in receiving goods at warehouse door, placing goods in storage, and returning goods to warehouse door. Handling charges are due and payable on receipt of goods.

(b) Unless otherwise agreed, labor for unloading and loading goods will be subject to a charge. Additional expenses incurred by the warehouseman in receiving and handling damaged goods, and additional expense in unloading from or loading into cars or other vehicles not at warehouse door will be charged to the depositor.

(c) Labor and materials used in loading rail cars or other vehicles are chargeable to the depositor.

(d) When goods are ordered out in quantities less than in which received, the warehouseman may make an additional charge for each order or each item of an order.

(e) The warehouseman shall not be liable for demurrage or detention, delays in unloading inbound cars, trailers or other containers, or delays in obtaining and loading cars, trailers or other containers for outbound shipment unless warehouseman has failed to exercise reasonable care.

DELIVERY REQUIREMENTS – Sec. 7

(a) No goods shall be delivered or transferred except upon receipt by the warehouseman of complete written instructions. Written instructions shall include, but are not limited to, FAX, EDI, TWX or similar communication, provided warehouseman has no liability when relying on the information contained in the communication as received. However, when no negotiable receipt is outstanding, goods may be delivered upon instruction by telephone in accordance with a prior written authorization, but the warehouseman shall not be responsible for loss or error occasioned thereby.

(b) When a negotiable receipt has been issued no goods covered by that receipt shall be delivered, or transferred on the books of the warehouseman, unless the receipt, properly endorsed, is surrendered for cancellation, or for endorsement of partial delivery thereon. If a negotiable receipt is lost or destroyed, delivery of goods may be made only upon order of a court of competent jurisdiction and the posting of security approved by the court as provided by law.

(c) When goods are ordered out a reasonable time shall be given the warehouseman to carry out instructions, and if he is unable because of acts of God, war, public enemies, seizure under legal process, strikes, lockouts, riots and civil commotions, or any reason beyond the warehouseman's control, or because of loss or destruction of goods for which warehouseman is not liable, or because of any other excuse provided by law, the warehouseman shall not be liable for failure to carry out such instructions and goods remaining in storage will continue to be subject to regular storage charges.

EXTRA SERVICES (SPECIAL SERVICES) – Sec. 8

(a) Warehouse labor required for services other than ordinary handling and storage will be charged to the depositor.

(b) Special services requested by depositor including but not limited to compiling of special stock statements; reporting marked weights, serial numbers or other data from packages; physical check of goods; and handling transit billing will be subject to a charge.

(c) Dunnage, bracing, packing materials or other special supplies, may be provided for the depositor at a charge in addition to the warehouseman's cost.

(d) By prior arrangement, goods may be received or delivered during other than usual business hours, subject to a charge.

(e) Communication expense including postage, teletype, telegram, or telephone will be charged to the depositor if such concern more than normal inventory reporting or if, at the request of the depositor, communications are made by other than regular United States Mail.

BONDED STORAGE – Sec. 9

(a) A charge in addition to regular rates will be made for merchandise in bond.

(b) Where a warehouse receipt covers goods in U.S. Customs bond, such receipt shall be void upon the termination of the storage period fixed by law.

MINIMUM CHARGES – Sec. 10

(a) A minimum handling charge per lot and a minimum storage charge per lot per month will be made. When a warehouse receipt covers more than one lot or when a lot is in assortment, a minimum charge per mark, brand, or variety will be made.

(b) A minimum monthly charge to one account for storage and/or handling will be made. This charge will apply also to each account when one customer has several accounts, each requiring separate records and billing.

LIABILITY AND LIMITATION OF DAMAGES – Sec. 11

(a) THE WAREHOUSEMAN SHALL NOT BE LIABLE FOR ANY LOSS OR INJURY TO GOODS STORED HOWEVER CAUSED UNLESS SUCH LOSS OR INJURY RESULTED FROM THE FAILURE BY THE WAREHOUSEMAN TO EXERCISE SUCH CARE IN REGARD TO THEM AS A REASONABLY CAREFUL MAN WOULD EXERCISE UNDER LIKE CIRCUMSTANCES AND WAREHOUSEMAN IS NOT LIABLE FOR DAMAGES WHICH COULD NOT HAVE BEEN AVOIDED BY THE EXERCISE OF SUCH CARE.

(b) GOODS ARE NOT INSURED BY THE WAREHOUSEMAN AGAINST LOSS OR INJURY HOWEVER CAUSED.

(c) THE DEPOSITOR DECLARES THAT DAMAGES ARE LIMITED TO ____________, PROVIDED, HOWEVER, THAT SUCH LIABILITY MAY AT THE TIME OF ACCEPTANCE OF THIS CONTRACT AS PROVIDED IN SECTION 1 BE INCREASED UPON DEPOSITOR'S WRITTEN REQUEST ON PART OR ALL OF THE GOODS HEREUNDER IN WHICH EVENT AN ADDITIONAL MONTHLY CHARGE WILL BE MADE BASED UPON SUCH INCREASED VALUATION.

(d) WHERE LOSS OR INJURY OCCURS TO STORED GOODS, FOR WHICH THE WAREHOUSEMAN IS NOT LIABLE, THE DEPOSITOR SHALL BE RESPONSIBLE FOR THE COST OF REMOVING AND DISPOSING OF SUCH GOODS AND THE COST OF ANY ENVIRONMENTAL CLEAN UP AND SITE REMEDIATION RESULTING FROM THE LOSS OR INJURY TO THE GOODS.

NOTICE OF CLAIM AND FILING OF SUIT – Sec. 12

(a) Claims by the depositor and all other persons must be presented in writing to the warehouseman within a reasonable time, and in no event longer than either 60 days after delivery of the goods by the warehouseman or 60 days after depositor of record or the last known holder of a negotiable warehouse receipt is notified by the warehouseman that loss or injury to part or all of the goods has occurred, whichever time is shorter.

(b) No action may be maintained by the depositor or others against the warehouseman for loss or injury to the goods stored unless timely written claim has been given as provided in paragraph (a) of this section and unless such action is commenced either within nine months after date of delivery by warehouseman or within nine months after depositor of record or the last known holder of a negotiable warehouse receipt is notified that loss or injury to part or all of the goods has occurred, whichever time is shorter.

(c) When goods have not been delivered, notice may be given of known loss or injury to the goods by mailing of a registered or certified letter to the depositor of record or to the last known holder of a negotiable warehouse receipt. Time limitations for presentation of claim in writing and maintaining of action after notice begin on the date of mailing of such notice by warehouseman.

LIABILITY FOR CONSEQUENTIAL DAMAGES – Sec. 13

Warehouseman shall not be liable for any loss of profit or special, indirect, or consequential damages of any kind.

LIABILITY FOR MISSHIPMENT – Sec. 14

If warehouseman negligently misships goods, the warehouseman shall pay the reasonable transportation charges incurred to return the misshipped goods to the warehouse. If the consignee fails to return the goods, warehouseman's maximum liability shall be for the lost or damaged goods as specified in Section 11 above, and warehouseman shall have no liability for damages due to the consignee's acceptance or use of the goods whether such goods be those of the depositor or another.

MYSTERIOUS DISAPPEARANCE – Sec. 15

Warehouseman shall not be liable for loss of goods due to inventory shortage or unexplained or mysterious disappearance of goods unless depositor establishes such loss occurred because of warehouseman's failure to exercise the care required of warehouseman under Section 11 above. Any presumption of conversion imposed by law shall not apply to such loss and a claim by depositor of conversion must be established by affirmative evidence that the warehouseman converted the goods to the warehouseman's own use.

RIGHT TO STORE GOODS – Sec. 16

Depositor represents and warrants that depositor is lawfully possessed of the goods and has the right and authority to store them with warehouseman. Depositor agrees to indemnify and hold harmless the warehouseman from all loss, cost and expense (including reasonable attorneys' fees) which warehouseman pays or incurs as a result of any dispute or litigation, whether instituted by warehouseman or others, respecting depositor's right, title or interest in the goods. Such amounts shall be charges in relation to the goods and subject to warehouseman's lien.

ACCURATE INFORMATION – Sec. 17

Depositor will provide warehouseman with information concerning the stored goods which is accurate, complete and sufficient to allow warehouseman to comply with all laws and regulations concerning the storage, handling and transporting of the stored goods. Depositor will indemnify and hold warehouseman harmless from all loss, cost, penalty and expense (including reasonable attorneys' fees) which warehouseman pays or incurs as a result of depositor failing to fully discharge this obligation.

SEVERABILITY and WAIVER – Sec. 18

(a) If any provision of this receipt, or any application thereof, should be construed or held to be void, invalid or unenforceable, by order, decree or judgment of a court of competent jurisdiction, the remaining provisions of this receipt shall not be affected thereby but shall remain in full force and effect.

(b) Warehouseman's failure to require strict compliance with any provision of the Warehouse Receipt shall not constitute a waiver or estoppel to later demand strict compliance with that or any other provision(s) of this Warehouse Receipt.

(c) The provisions of this Warehouse Receipt shall be binding upon the depositor's heirs, executors, successors and assigns; contain the sole agreement governing goods stored with the warehouseman; and, cannot be modified except by a writing signed by warehouseman.

Appendix 9-2
Page 14

EXHIBIT C

WAREHOUSE LEASE AGREEMENT

(if any)

EXHIBIT D

RATES AND CHARGES FOR ALL SERVICES

SAMPLE
WAREHOUSE LEASE AGREEMENT

This Warehouse Lease made and entered into this _____ day of
_____, 20___ by and between Client, a Corporation (hereinafter
referred to as "Lessee") and LSP, a Corporation (hereinafter referred to as
"Lessor").

In consideration of the mutual agreements and covenants herein contained, and
for other goods and valuable consideration, _____ and _____ do
hereby agree and subscribe to the Warehouse Lease as follows:

LEASE AGREEMENT

1. Lessor hereby leases to Lessee and Lessee hereby leases from Lessor
_____ square feet of warehouse space located at
_____ together with proper
access thereto, including use of necessary docks, rail sidings, truck doors, and
parking facilities (hereinafter referred to as the Leased Premises").

2. The term of this lease shall commence on the _____ day of
_____, 20___, and shall terminate on the _____ day of
_____, 20___. As rental for the Leased Premises, Lessee agrees
to pay Lessor $_____ per month in advance of the first day of each month
until _____.

As additional rent, Lessee agrees to pay a pro rata portion of the following
charges per square foot based on the portion of Leased Premises used:

(a)	Property Taxes	$_____
(b)	Building Insurance	_____
(c)	Building and Grounds Maintenance	_____
(d)	Utilities	_____
(e)	Security and Alarm	_____
(f)	Supplies and Miscellaneous	_____
	Total	$_____

These charges will be based on the best information available, and will be payable in monthly installments at the rate of _____ due in advance of the first day of each month until _____. At the conclusion of each year of the rental term or extended term, these costs shall be reviewed and adjusted to reflect actual expenses incurred. Any adjustment shall be reflected in the charges payable for the lease year commencing on each anniversary date of this Agreement during the term and any extended term of this Agreement. The term "property taxes" includes any special assessment levied on the owner of the property (Lessor or its assigns) in its capacity as owner of the property, but in all events excluding income taxes.

3. If Lessor does not maintain the Leased Premises so that they reasonably comply with all applicable laws, rules, and regulations pertaining to the warehousing of _____ products, including those of _____, and other federal, state, or local government agencies, and Lessee, Lessee may terminate this Agreement on one hundred eighty (180) days' written notice. However, prior to termination for any of the reasons set forth in this subparagraph, Lessee shall give written notice to Lessor at least thirty (30) days after receipt of same within which to correct said violations. In the event said violations are corrected by Lessor, Lessee shall not terminate this Agreement pursuant to this clause.

4. Lessee shall have the option to renew this lease for three (3) years commencing _____, and terminating on _____, provided that notice is given prior to _____. Terms and conditions for such renewal period shall be the same terms and conditions herein stated except that the warehouse space under contract and rate shall be negotiated.

5. The Leased Premises shall be used and occupied for the receiving, storing, shipping, and delivering of Lessee's products and for such other activities and business as may be connected therewith or incident thereto, provided that the Leased Premises shall not, without Lessor's prior written consent, be used for manufacturing, processing, or packing, other than product repacking and reconditioning damaged merchandise.

6. Lessee agrees to take good care of the Leased Premises and suffer no waste and, at the end or expiration of the term hereof, to surrender the Leased Premises to Lessor in as good order and condition as the Leased Premises are

at the beginning of such term, natural deterioration, reasonable and ordinary wear, tear, and use, and damage by fire and the elements and by any other cause outside of the control of Lessee excepted. It is also understood between the parties that Lessor has caused fire and extended coverage to be issued on the Leased Premises and Lessor agrees to furnish to Lessee waivers of subrogation by the insurance company or companies under such policy or policies. It is further understood and agreed by the parties hereto that all risk of loss, while said Leased Premises are in Lessee's control and possession, for any damage to the Leased Premises due to fire, the elements, any other cause outside the control of Lessee and such perils as are covered by said insurance policy or policies shall be borne by Lessor.

Lessee agrees to repair at its own cost any damage or injury done to the Leased Premises which results because of negligence of Lessee, its agents or employees, except any damage or injury caused by fire, the elements, any other causes outside the control of Lessee and such perils as are covered by fire and extended insurance policies of Lessor referred to above or any other insurance carrier by Lessor on Leased Premises.

7. Lessee shall have the right to place and maintain signs or marks on the Leased Premises or on the property stored therein that may be necessary or desirable to indicate the tenancy of Lessee in and to property stored therein, provided that the size, design, and location of such signs shall be subject to the prior written approval of Lessor which approval shall not be unreasonably withheld, and the appropriate city and county bodies.

8. If during the terms of this lease, the Leased Premises are damaged by fire, or other cause, so as to interfere substantially with Lessee's use thereof, then, if the Leased Premises shall not be repaired within one hundred and eighty (180) days thereafter, this lease may be cancelled at the option of either party by written notice to the other, and rent shall be payable only to the date of such fire or other cause. In the event any such damage is so repaired within any such time when the Leased Premises are substantially unusable by Lessee, and if only a portion of the Leased Premises shall be rendered substantially unusable by Lessee, then there shall be only a proportional abatement in the rent during the period that such portion is substantially unusable by Lessee.

9. Lessor shall ensure that the Leased Premises will at all times be in such condition as is suitable for the proper storage of Lessee's products, and Lessor shall be under no obligation to repair any defect within the Leased Premises unless and until Lessee gives Lessor written notice of the existence of such defect.

10. Lessee shall not assign this Agreement or sublet the Leased Premises or any part thereof, or make any alterations in the Leased Premises without the prior written consent of Lessor which shall not be unreasonably withheld, and Lessee shall not occupy or permit or suffer the Leased Premises to be occupied for any purposes deemed extra hazardous on account of fire or which fail to comply with deed or zoning restrictions.

11. Lessee agrees to and shall indemnify and hold harmless Lessor from any and all claims of loss, injury, or damage to any persons or property asserted by any parties whomsoever, insofar as the same shall arise because of the fault or negligence, actual or alleged, of Lessee, its agents, and employees. Lessor agrees to and shall indemnify and hold harmless Lessee from any and all claims of loss, injury, or damage to any persons or property, whatsoever, arising from the fault or negligence of Lessor, its agents, or employees.

12. Each of the parties hereto shall advise the other of all applicable insurance coverage, and each party agrees to secure from its insurers waivers of such insurers' rights of subrogation against the other party hereto with respect to fire and extended coverage. If requested, each of the parties hereto shall advise the other of all applicable insurance coverage.

13. In the event that Lessor is adjudicated bankrupt or files by petition or answers any pleading seeking reorganization or other relief under bankruptcy or other debtor relief law, or makes a voluntary assignment for the benefit of its creditors or in the event that a receiver of Lessor is appointed, then at the option of Lessee and upon five (5) days' notice to Lessor, Lessee will either provide management personnel to operate the Leased Premises under the Lease Agreement for the duration of the Agreement, or

provide written notice that this lease shall cease and terminate. The penalties provided under Paragraph 3 shall not apply to a termination by Lessee under this paragraph.

14. In the event Lessee is adjudicated bankrupt or files by petition or answers any pleading seeking reorganization or other relief under the bankruptcy or other debtor relief law, or makes a voluntary assignment for the benefit of its creditors, or in the event that a receiver of Lessee be appointed, then at the option of Lessor and upon five (5) days' notice to Lessee, this lease shall cease and terminate.

15. Any notice required or permitted under terms hereof may be given by either party to the other by registered mail, addressed to the party to whom the notice is to be given at the address as follows:

Lessee:

_____

_____

_____

Lessor:

_____

_____

_____

And unless received earlier, such notice shall be deemed to have been received three (3) days after the mailing thereof by first class registered mail. Either party may change its address for the purpose of receiving notices by giving written notice to the other party of such change.

16. If Lessee pays the rent therein provided for and performs the covenants of this lease on its part to be performed, Lessee shall be entitled to hold, occupy, and enjoy the Leased Premises peaceably and quietly without any let, hindrance, or molestation by any person or persons whomsoever.

17. The covenants and agreements herein contained shall be binding upon the parties hereto and upon their respective successors and assigns.

18. This lease contains all the terms and conditions of the Agreement between the parties hereto and may not be modified except by instrument in writing, signed by the parties hereto or their respective successors in interest.

19. After execution of the Agreement, Lessor shall obtain from all those mortgagors of the Leased Premises whose mortgage interests predate the date that the Agreement was executed, a non-disturbance agreement (in a form reasonably satisfactory to Lessee) in favor of Lessee's leasehold interest in the Leased Premises.

IN WITNESS WHEREOF, _____ and _____ have caused this Agreement to be executed, sealed, and attested by their respective officers hereunto duly authorized, as of the day and year first above written.

LOGISTICS SERVICE PROVIDER (Lessor)

By: _____

Title: _____

CLIENT (Lessee)

By: _____

Title: _____

Alternative Language

Partial Cancellation Privilege

*Lessee shall have the right to cancel up to _____ percent (____%)
of the square footage covered by this lease (in _____ square foot
increments) after the ____ (___) and _____ (____) years of the
Agreement, providing that _____ days' notice is given. The earliest
such notice may be given is at the beginning of the fifth year. If such
notice is given, Lessee agrees to pay an on-time penalty cost per
square foot to be determined as follows:*

> *(a) $_____ per square foot times the square footage
cancelled in year six.*
> *(b) $_____ per square foot times the square footage
cancelled in year seven.*

*The penalty will be paid in _____ (___) monthly installments,
commencing _____ (___) months prior to the date of termination.*

*It is further agreed between Lessor and Lessee that any portion of the
Leased Premises previously cancelled may be reinstated in
_____ (_____) square foot increments, if available, at the
then current storage rate in effect, with _____ (___) days' advance
notification. Further, the penalty per square foot will abate pro rata on
the Leased Premises restored at the time Lessee resumes occupancy.*

Option to Purchase

*_____ ("Lessor" or "Seller") Lessor agrees that _____
("Lessee" or "Buyer") Lessee shall have an option to purchase the
Leased Premises on the _____ (___), _____ (___), and _____
(___) anniversary date of this Agreement. The purchase price for the
Leased Premises, which are the subject of this Option Agreement, shall
be determined by the following procedures. Upon proper exercise of
said option by Buyer within a period no later than ninety (90) days prior
to the option exercise dates specified above, the Seller shall select a*

disinterested qualified commercial real estate appraiser who shall be "MIA" certified and licensed in the State of _____ as a commercial real estate appraiser ("Seller's Appraiser"). Seller's Appraiser shall appraise the premises at the full cash fair market value as of the date of the exercise of said option by Buyer. The cost of said appraisal shall be shared equally by Buyer and Seller. In the event Buyer objects to the valuation of Seller's Appraiser, Buyer may, within ten (10) days after receipt of Seller's appraisal and at its own cost, hire a disinterested qualified commercial real estate appraiser, who shall be "MAI" certified and licensed in the State of _____ as a commercial real estate appraiser ("Buyer's Appraiser"). Buyer's Appraiser shall appraise the Leased Premises at the full cash fair market value as of the date of the exercise of said option by Buyer. In the event Seller objects to Buyer's appraisal within ten (10) days after receipt thereof, Seller and Buyer agree that Seller's Appraiser and Buyer's Appraiser shall, by mutual agreement, and with the cost of said appraisal to be shared equally by Buyer and Seller, choose a third disinterested appraiser with the same qualifications as outlined above for Buyer's and Sellers' appraisers, who shall appraise the Leased Premises at the full cash fair market value as of the date of the exercise of said option by Buyer. The valuation of the Leased Premises as determined by said third appraiser shall be binding on both Buyer and Seller. The purchase price for the Leased Premises shall be the full cash fair market value as finally determined by the appraisal, but in no case less than the outstanding debt on the building and will not include any amount for commissions or other costs that would be incurred in selling through brokers or agents. Any transfer or transaction tax imposed in connection with sale of the Leased Premises pursuant to this paragraph shall be equally shared by the Seller and Buyer. Upon such purchase by Buyer, this Lease Agreement shall be terminated and all responsibilities of each party herein.

Appendix 9-4

SAMPLE
CONTRACT FOR MOTOR CARRIAGE

Contract Number _____ (Provided by carrier)

THIS CONTRACT is made and entered into this _____ day of _____,
20__, by and between _____, hereinafter referred to as
Company and _____, hereinafter referred to as Carrier.

WHEREAS, Carrier is engaged in the business of transporting property for
hire by motor vehicle, is duly authorized by the appropriate state and federal
regulatory authorities to operate as a motor carrier transporting the property
hereinafter described, within the territories hereinafter described, and
desires to serve Company as a contract carrier by motor vehicle; and

WHEREAS, Company, having authority to choose the Carrier for
transportation of freight to be tendered under this Agreement, desires to
enter into an Agreement with Carrier providing for transportation of such
quantities of Company's property as it, its suppliers and consignors may
tender to Carrier for shipment, between designated origins and destinations;

NOW THEREFORE, in consideration of the mutual promises herein
contained, the parties hereto agree as follows:

1. SCOPE OF AGREEMENT - Carrier shall transport between origins and
destinations designated by Company, products named in Schedule A
attached hereto, under such terms and conditions and at such rates and
charges as set forth in Schedule B attached hereto, as the same may be
supplemented or amended pursuant to Sections ___ and ___ hereof.

Shipments made under this Contract shall be subject to the rules and
regulations attached as Schedule C. This Contract shall supersede any
conflicting bill of lading or tariff provision. Amendments to rules must be
made in the manner described in Sections ___ and ___ hereof to be
effective as to transportation provided under this Contract.

2. PAYMENT OF FREIGHT CHARGES - Payment of freight charges shall be the responsibility of the Company, consignee, or other party as set forth by the bill of lading. Payments shall be due within ____ days following receipt of invoice by Company. However, a late payment will not alter the application of discounts, rates and charges. Shipments must be invoiced as soon as practicable after delivery, but in no event more than ____ days thereafter; failure to bill charges to Company within the said ____ days shall waive forever any right of Carrier to bill to or collect from Company charges for any shipment not billed, regardless of any rule, regulation or understanding to the contrary.

3. MINIMUM VOLUME COMMITMENT - Company agrees to tender to Carrier and Carrier agrees to transport for Company a minimum of ____ shipments of Company's freight during the initial term of this Contract, and during each subsequent renewal hereof. Should this Contract be terminated at any time other than the conclusion of the initial term hereof or the end of any subsequent renewal period, the minimum quantity of freight provided in this section as applying to the final partial term hereof shall be reduced by the proportion the unexpired portion of the term bears to one year.

Should Shipper fail to tender or to have tendered to Carrier the minimum volume set forth in this Section, such failure shall not change in any respect the rates or charges due Carrier for shipments which Shipper did tender or have tendered for movement.

4. RATE AND RULE CHANGES - Rates and charges in the Contract shall not be increased during the term of this Contract, and rules shall not be changed, except by mutual written agreement of Company and Carrier. Unless otherwise agreed in writing, no rate increase by Carrier shall take effect on less than ____ days' notice to Company.

Rate reductions (including cancellation of a proposed increase) may be made on ____ days' notice to Company.

5. LOSS AND DAMAGE - Carrier will be liable for loss or damage to the Goods only while in the care and control of the Carrier, and when it results from the negligence or intentional acts of the Carrier, its employees, subcontractors, or

agents. In no event will the Carrier be liable for concealed damage or where the loss or damage is caused by an act of God, the public enemy, and act of Company or its employees or agents, a public authority or the inherent nature of the Goods. Carrier's liability to Company for any loss or damage to the Goods shall not exceed the direct cost to the Company of the Goods involved, including transportation to the point of loss or damage, less its salvage value, if any.

A claim under this contract for loss, damage, injury or delay to a shipment shall be made in writing or electronically within ___ days after delivery or tender of delivery of the shipment, or, if it is not delivered or tendered for delivery, within ____ months after a reasonable time for delivery has elapsed. If shipment is made at a released value, it will be declared on the Bill of Lading.

Any action at law or suit in equity pertaining to a shipment transported by Carrier shall be commenced within ___ years from the date Company receives written notice from Carrier that Company's claim or any part thereof has been disallowed.

Company shall have the immediate right to offset freight or other charges owed to Carrier against claims for loss, damage or delay, or for overcharge and duplicate payment claims, unless Carrier disputes such claims.

6. UNDERCHARGES AND OVERCHARGES - Any action or proceeding by the Carrier to recover charges alleged to be due hereunder, and any action or proceeding by Company to recover overcharges alleged to be due hereunder, shall be commenced no more than ____ (___) days after delivery or tender of delivery of the shipment with respect to which such charges or overcharges are claimed. To the extent permitted by applicable law, the expiration of the said ____-day period shall be a complete and absolute defense to any such action or proceeding, without regard to any mitigating or extenuating circumstance or excuse whatever. Undercharge claims may not be collected unless notice is received by company within ___ days of the original freight bill date.

7. DISTINCT NEEDS OF THE SHIPPER - A company may want to ensure that the carrier meets the continuing needs and requirements of the company. In the ever-changing environment of the twenty-first century this could be a very

important provision. Examples of important considerations are shown in Schedule D of the contract in Appendix 9-4.

Carrier agrees that it will provide service to Company as a contract carrier by motor vehicle, which is and will be designed to meet the distinct needs of Company. Carrier shall tailor its service to meet those needs more particularly set forth in Schedule D attached hereto, as well as those indicated elsewhere in this Agreement. There shall be a review on an ongoing basis on the requirement to alter or amend the service standards from those initially needed by Company, so as to make certain that the distinct needs of Company continue to be met. Carrier agrees to train its personnel who provide and will provide service to Company to ensure that Company receives that service which meets and will continue to meet Company's distinct needs.

8. INSURANCE - Carrier, at its own expense, agrees to carry and keep in force at all times public liability, property damage, cargo, and workmen's compensation insurance with such reliable insurance companies and in such amounts as Company may from time to time approve and such as will meet the requirements of federal and state regulatory bodies having jurisdiction of Carrier's operations under this Contract. Certificates of insurance showing Carrier's compliance with the provisions of this section shall be furnished to Company prior to any transportation under this Contract and whenever Carrier changes or renews its insurance coverage.

9. INDEPENDENT CONTRACTOR - It is the specific intention of the parties that this Contract not be construed to make Carrier or any of its agents or employees in any sense a servant, employee, agent, partner or joint-venture participant of or with Company, and Carrier is not authorized or empowered by this Contract to obligate or bind Company in any manner whatsoever. Carrier shall conduct operations hereunder as an independent contractor, and as such shall have control over its employees and shall retain responsibility for complying with all federal, state and local laws pertaining in any way to this Contract. Said responsibilities include, but are not limited to, provision of safe equipment appropriate to haul Company's property tendered under this Contract, assumption of full responsibility for payment of all state and federal taxes for unemployment insurance, old age pensions, or any other social security law or laws as to all employees or agents of Carrier engaged in the performance of this

Contract. Carrier shall not display Company's name on any motor vehicle equipment it provides under this Contract without specific authorization to do so from Company.

10. INDEMNIFICATION - Carrier agrees to indemnify and hold Company harmless from any and all claims for death or injury to persons, and loss or damage to property of any nature arising from Carrier's transportation of property for Company. Carrier further agrees to comply with all applicable federal and state statures, rules and regulations, including judicial interpretations thereof, and to also indemnify and hold Company harmless from any and all claims or fines arising from Carrier" transportation of property of Company in violation of any such statute, rule or regulation.

11. FORCE MAJEURE - Neither Company nor Carrier shall be liable for failure to perform caused by acts of God, public authority, revolutions or other disorders, wars, strikes, fires or floods.

12. NOTICES - All notices required or permitted to be given under this Contract shall be in writing and shall be deemed to have been sufficiently given when received if delivered in person, when deposited at the telegraph office if transmitted by telegraph, or when deposited in the mails of the United States Postal Service, certified, return receipt requested, postage and other charges prepaid, and addressed to the respective parties at the following addresses:

CARRIER: COMPANY:

_____   _____

_____   _____

_____   _____

_____   _____

13. CONFIDENTIALITY - Neither party shall disclose the terms of this Contract to any third party except: (1) to a parent, affiliate or subsidiary corporation; (2) as

may be required by law; (3) to any attorney, auditor or consultant who has a need for the Contract in the performance of professional services for a party.

14. TERM - This Contract shall remain in full force and effect for ___ (__) year(s) from the date hereof (herein referred to as the initial term of this Contract), (and from year-to-year thereafter,) subject to the right of termination by either party at any time on ____ (__) days' notice to the other party sent by certified mail, return receipt requested.

15. AMENDMENT - This Contract shall not be amended or altered except in writing and signed by authorized representatives of both parties.

16. ASSIGNMENT - Without the prior written approval of Company, Carrier shall not assign this Contract, and shall not assign any rights under this Contract to a third party. Any unapproved attempted assignment shall be null, void, and of no force or effect; should it be attempted, Carrier agrees to pay to Company any expenses including reasonable attorneys' fees that Company may incur in defending against any action or conduct related thereto. This Contract shall be binding upon each party's heirs, successors and assigns, if any, including any successor or assign by operation of law.

IN WITNESS WHEREOF, the parties have executed this Contract on the day and year first herein written.

CARRIER:

By: _____

Title: _____

COMPANY:

By: _____

Title: _____

SCHEDULE A
TRANSPORTATION CONTRACT

PRODUCTS COVERED BY CONTRACT

SCHEDULE B
TRANSPORTATION CONTRACT

REPRESENTATIVE TERMS, CONDITIONS, RATES, CHARGES ETC.

1. The provisions of this schedule apply on interstate and intrastate LTL shipments handled direct and joint line between points in the USA served by the Carrier, and to any additional direct or joint line points added during the period of this Contract.

2. Classification: Shipments must be on the bill of lading and shipping orders by commodity in accordance with the National Motor Classification. However, all outbound and inbound shipments will be subject to FAK class ___ for all class 50 through ___, FAK ___ for all commodities carrying class rating in excess of ___ and commodities less than class ___ will be rated at actual class rates less the discounts shown herein. These classes will likewise apply to all inbound collect shipments and third-party billing.

3. Rates: Except as otherwise specifically provided herein, all shipments will be subject to the provisions of the National Motor Freight Classification, ICC NMF 100 Series, and class rates and/or minimum charges as determined from Czar-Lite base January 1, 1996 rates.

4. Discount: Except as otherwise specifically provided herein, minimum charges and charges resulting from the application of
class rates subject to weight groups of less than 20,000 pounds as provided in paragraph 3 above will be reduced (discounted) by:

    A. Discount ____% on outbound direct shipments and ____% on joint line shipments.

    B. Discount ____% on inbound direct shipments and ____% on joint line shipments.

In no case will the freight charges applicable to any shipment be reduced or discounted below $_____.

5. Shipments tendered to Carrier hereunder may, at Carrier's discretion, be randomly selected for verification of weight and inspection as to the commodity description and its being in compliance with the National Motor Classification descriptions.

6. Waiver of Increase: Rates will be frozen for one year of signed agreement by both parties to this Contract. In the event of circumstances arising affecting the cost of transportation, the terms of this Contract will be renegotiated.

7. Third-party billing provisions will apply on any bill paid by Company.

8. Carrier agrees to waive single shipment charges.

9. Carrier agrees to waive linear foot rule.

10. Carrier agrees to waive any charges for bill of lading or delivery receipts copies.

11. Carrier agrees to waive any applicable cubic minimum charges.

12. Carrier agrees to waive notification charges.

13. Carrier agrees to waive sorting and segregating charges.

14. Carrier agrees to waive inside delivery charges.

SCHEDULE C
TRANSPORTATION CONTRACT

FUEL ADJUSTMENT SCHEDULE (EXAMPLE)

The base fuel price shall be $_____ per gallon based on the national average published on Monday of each week in *Transport Topics*.

The surcharges based on deviations from this price will be as follows:

This surcharge will appear on the freight bill as a separate line item, and is not subject to discount.

The surcharge will be adjusted each Monday, depending on the published cost of fuel.

SCHEDULE D
TRANSPORTATION CONTRACT

DISTINCT NEEDS OF SHIPPER (EXAMPLE)

- Appointment time provisions

- Schedules

- Type of equipment

- Unique delivery requirements

SAMPLE
FREIGHT BILL PAYMENT SERVICE AGREEMENT

THIS SERVICE AGREEMENT ("Agreement") is made and entered into as of the ___ day of _____ 20__, by and between _____ ("Client"), a _____ corporation, and Freight Bill Payment Company ("FBPC"), a _____ corporation.

WHEREAS FBPC is in the business of handling pre-audit and payment of freight bills. _____ desires to hire FBPC to perform pre-audit, data capture, freight payment and management information services for carriers used by _____ (the "Carriers"). The parties desire to enter into this Agreement and to fully set forth their understanding of the terms, commitments and conditions of their relationship.

NOW THEREFORE, in consideration of the promises hereof and the mutual commitments and conditions hereinafter set forth and other good and valuable consideration, the receipt and sufficiency of which is hereby acknowledged, the parties hereto, intending to be legally bound, hereby agree as follows:

1. Engagement. _____ hereby engages FBPC and FBPC hereby agrees to perform pre-audit, data capture, freight payment and management information services for _____.

2. Services to Be Provided. FBPC will provide the following services:

   A. Pre-Audit. FBPC will audit freight bills, including but not limited to duplicate payments, rates, classifications, discounts, extensions and verification. However, _____ will be responsible for providing FBPC with updated material regarding any changes in rate agreements with certain Carriers.

   B Data Capture. FBPC will capture data from all freight invoices and accompanying documentation as required by _____.

392

C. <u>Freight Payment</u>. Payment will be performed on a weekly basis, with checks being issued to each Carrier on _____'s behalf. _____ will transfer funds to FBPC each __(day)__ and Carrier checks will be mailed the following __(day)__.

D. <u>EDI Payment</u>. FBPC shall have, and hereby confirms that it does have, the capability to receive electronic billings from such of the Carriers as may be so designated by _____.

E. <u>Reports</u>. FBPC will compile and submit to _____ those standard weekly reports and customized monthly reports listed in Exhibit A, attached hereto.

F. <u>Internet Access</u>. FBPC will provide _____ with secure access to its data through the Internet and will provide _____ with training in the use of such system at no charge to _____.

G. <u>Software and other web services received</u>. FBPC will provide Client with SW and web system maintenance and upgrades for the entire term of this Agreement. Upon termination of this Agreement, Client hereby agrees to return all software and materials and copies thereof, relating to SW. In addition, Client acknowledges that it has no ownership rights in SW.

FBPC represents and warrants that it is the owner of SW and that it has the right and authority to license SW to Client and that there exist no outstanding claims, allegations or requests for license that SW infringes any copyright, patent, trade secret, trademark, service mark or any other intellectual property right of any third party.

FBPC will defend, indemnify and hold harmless Client, its affiliates and subsidiaries and their officers, directors, employees, representatives, agents and subcontractors from and against any and all claims, allegations and requests for a license that SW or its use infringes any US or foreign copyright, trademark, patent or any other intellectual property right of any third party. In the event FBPC or Client is enjoined from using SW, FBPC , at its expense, shall procure for Client the right to used SW or modify SW so it is non-infringing. If it is not commercially reasonable for FBPC to procure such right or to modify SW so it is non-infringing, either party may terminate this Agreement upon 30 days' prior written notice to the other.

3. <u>Errors</u>. In the event of errors by FBPC, FBPC shall file claims to recover incorrect payments at their own expense.

4. <u>Renewal and Termination</u>. The term of this Agreement will be for _____ (__) months from the date first entered above. Except as provided in Paragraph(s) _____, this Agreement will renew on an annual basis until cancelled. Cancellation without cause requires a minimum ___-day prior written notice by either party.

5. <u>Fee Schedule</u>. The fees to be paid to FBPC for the services set forth in Section ___ herein, are listed on Exhibit B attached hereto and are based on the profile by _____ and summarized in Exhibit C. Fees shall be billed and paid weekly. In the event fees are not paid as agreed, FBPC reserves the right to terminate this Agreement upon 30-days' written notice.

If after six (6) months of experience, the profile varies significantly from the profile projected in Exhibit C (+ or – 15%), FBPC reserves the right to reopen the fees for negotiation. This applies not only to total transactions, but also transactions within each category.

If no agreement is reached within 30 days of a request for a modified fee schedule, either party may terminate this Agreement upon 30 days' written notice.

6. <u>On-Site Audit</u>. _____ has the right to perform on-site audits at FBPC on those processes relating to the _____ account.

7. <u>Miscellaneous Provisions</u>.

A. <u>Severability</u>. If one or more of the provisions contained in the Agreement shall for any reason be held invalid, illegal or unenforceable for any reason, such invalidity, illegality or unenforceability shall not affect any other provision of this Agreement, which shall be construed as if such invalid, illegal or unenforceable provision had never been contained herein.

B. <u>Counterparts</u>. This Agreement may be executed in counterparts, each of which shall be deemed an original, but all of which together shall constitute one and the same instrument. This Agreement and all other documents to be executed in connection herewith are hereby authorized to be executed and accepted by facsimile signatures and such facsimile signatures shall be considered valid and binding as original signatures and may be relied upon by the parties hereto.

C. <u>Entire Agreement</u>. This Agreement supersedes all prior understandings, representations, negotiations and correspondence between the parties, constitutes the entire agreement between them with respect to the matters described, and shall not be modified or affected by any course of dealing, course of performance or usage of trade. It may not be changed orally but only by an agreement in writing executed by the parties hereto.

D. <u>Governing Law: Enforcement</u>. This Agreement shall be construed in accordance with the laws of the State of _____, and the rights and liabilities of the parties hereto, including any assignees, shall be determined in accordance with the laws of the State of _____. In any litigation the prevailing party shall be entitled to recover from the losing party reasonable attorneys' fees and other costs and expenses of the litigation.

E. <u>Default</u>. FBPC agrees that institution of, or consent to, any insolvency proceedings constitutes default and may result in cancellation of entire Agreement.

IN WITNESS WHEREOF, the parties have hereunto affixed their names or caused their names to be hereunto affixed by the undersigned officers who are thereunto duly authorized as of the date first above written.

_____

By: _____

Its: _____

FBPC

By: _____

Its: _____

EXHIBIT A

REPORTS TO BE FURNISHED

EXHIBIT B

FEE SCHEDULE

Implementation fee   -------- $

Installation includes all items listed in the fee schedule attached to the
_____ proposal.

Processing and Payment
     EDI Air Bills   -------- $___ per freight bill
     Manual Bills   -------- $___ per freight bill
EDI Motor Bills   -------- $___ per freight bill
Accounting Splits   -------- $___ per split
Bill of Lading Match
     (B/L storage)   -------- $___ per BOL
Coding Freight Bills
     Computer Coded   --------
     Manually Coded   -------- $___ per freight bill
Includes:
   1. Remittance advice to carriers explaining billing amendments
   2. Dual data entry of all bills
   3. Duplicate payment protection using pro number and bill of lading
      number
   4. Returning freight bills in a batch order
   5. Standard weekly reports
   6. Individual carrier checks
   7. All needed monthly reports
Internet Fees
Monthly maintenance fee   -------- $___ per month (one user)
     $__/month for additional passwords.
   Includes:
   1. Mapping and graphing capabilities
   2. Telephone support
   3. Training
   4. _____ database updates

Shipping Cost of Bills and Reports
    Regular U.S. Mail or UPS   --------
    All other modes   --------   At Cost
Rate Negotiations/Consulting   --------   Available upon request
Loss & Damage Claims Processing   -------- $_____ per claim
Special Programming Fees   --------   Determined on a per
                                              project basis as agreed
                                              upon by both parties.

Appendix 9-5
Page 9

EXHIBIT C

ACCOUNT PROFILE

Appendix 13-1

SAMPLE
ANNUAL WAREHOUSE OPERATIONS AUDIT

_____

Date: _____   Location: _____

Contact: _____

HIRING PRACTICES

1.	What is the source of most applicants (i.e., newspaper ads, agencies, off the street, etc.)?	
2.	What are the hiring criteria (i.e., experience, high school diploma, etc.)?	
3.	Do you have a standard interview procedure, or do questions differ for each applicant?	
4.	How many people interview a prospective employee? If more than one interviews, how many people must vote in the affirmative to hire the candidate?	
5.	How much input to the hiring process does the prospective employee's immediate supervisor have?	

6.	Do new employees take a physical exam?	
7.	Are new employees given a drug screen? If so, for which drugs?	
8.	Are references checked?	

TRAINING

1.	What positions require formal training programs for new employees?	
2.	Who conducts the training of new employees?	
3.	Do outside companies participate in the training programs (i.e., forklift training, safety classes)?	

4.	What type of ongoing training is given to veteran employees?	
5.	Is there cross-training?	
6.	Are work rules posted?	

SCHEDULING

1.	When are scheduling meetings held?	
2.	What topics are discussed at the meetings? Who conducts the meetings?	
3.	Are inbound receiving logs kept?	

4.	Is there a separate log for TOFC trailers, containers, railcars, etc.?	
5.	How are inbound/outbound trucks controlled for unloading/loading?	
6.	What criteria are used to determine the number of inbound trucks that can be worked each day?	
7.	Are pieces of equipment (forklifts, etc.) assigned to particular employees?	
8.	Is there a standards program?	
9.	Who updates the standards program and how often?	
10.	Are production standards used in scheduling, personnel reviews, etc.?	

RECEIPTS/SHIPMENTS

1.	What are the receipt procedures?	
2.	Is a tally log kept to record each inbound shipment?	
3.	What information is on the warehouse form (i.e., carrier, trailer #, seal #, shipper #, etc.)?	
4.	When are blind counts used?	
5.	Is the blind tally checked against the packing list? If so, by whom?	
6.	How is inbound damage handled?	

7.	Are there written shipping procedures?	
8.	Is the picking document initialed by the puller and checker?	
9.	Is there a separate staging area for outbound orders?	
10.	What procedures do dock personnel use to ensure that the correct freight is being shipped?	
11.	Are records kept on shipping performance? If so, how is it measured?	

SYSTEMS AND HANDLING

1.	Does an updated Disaster Recovery Plan exist? When is it dated?	
2.	Has a copy of the Plan been forwarded to the client?	
3.	Are backup hard copies of inventory reports and locator reports created on a regular basis and stored securely? How frequently	
4.	Is there a warehouse management system? Does it function efficiently?	
5.	Does the Fixed Asset List match the equipment inventory?	
6.	Is each PC system powered through an Isobar or adequate power surge protection device?	

7.	Are terminals, printers and data communications equipment powered through properly grounded receptacles?	
8.	Is all equipment cleaned or dusted (at least) monthly and all equipment located in dusty areas covered when not in use?	
9.	Are all cables in good repair, head covers attached securely, and connectors securely attached to equipment with screws?	
10.	Are RF scanners in good repair, working properly?	
11.	Are backups of PC systems performed daily, weekly, or on another appropriate schedule?	
12.	Are weekly file backups stored off-site, at least in a building separate from the system(s) site?	

13.	Is user documentation available for each software package used by the facility?	
14.	Are all software packages installed on the PC licensed?	
15.	Are any custom software applications that may exist properly documented with adequate support provisions?	

INVENTORIES

1.	Is there a computerized inventory program?	
2.	Are pre-inventory meetings held to organize the office and the warehouse?	
3.	Is a firm cut-off date for shipments and receipts agreed to with the customer prior to the inventory?	

4.	Are outstanding orders at the time of inventory canceled or confirmed as shipped?	
5.	Who controls an inventory (i.e., general manager, operations manager, office manager, etc.)?	
6.	When a two-count inventory is done, are there different teams completing each count?	
7.	What steps are taken if there is a variance?	
8.	Who reconciles the inventory with the client's books?	
9.	Is there a post inventory meeting to discuss ways of improving the next inventory?	

10.	How often are cycle counts conducted throughout the year, and what are their purpose?	
11.	Are logs kept of the cycle counts and physical counts?	

HOUSEKEEPING

1.	What is the planned housekeeping procedure/schedule?	
2.	Is trash picked up and dumped on a regular basis?	
3.	Are damaged cases put into designated areas?	
4.	What is the general appearance of the stock? Are there damaged cases in stock?	
5.	Is a pest control program in effect? Is it internal or an outside company or both?	

6.	Are the truck dock wells free of debris?	
7.	In food grade warehouses, is an 18" sanitation line being observed next to every wall?	
8.	Are the restrooms in good condition?	
9.	Are the lunch areas in good condition?	
10.	Do the offices give a good, clean, and orderly appearance?	
11.	Is carpeting clean?	

SAFETY

1.	Is there a safety committee and does it meet on a regular basis?	
2.	Are minutes of the meeting kept and what is done with them?	
3.	Is there an emergency organization plan for each facility and is it posted?	
4.	How often are in-house safety inspections conducted?	
5.	Is there a plot plan posted indicting the location of fire exits, hoses, extinguishers, etc.?	
6.	Are fire extinguishers properly labeled and mounted?	

7.	Are all fire lanes clear and clearly marked?	
8.	Are all fire exits clear and clearly marked?	
9.	Are the no-smoking regulations enforced?	
10.	Is the battery charger area clean?	
11.	How often are forklift safety classes held?	
12.	What are the procedures for clean-up of damaged or spilled products?	
13.	What safety equipment is kept in the warehouse (i.e., rubber gloves, masks, respirator, etc.)?	

14.	Is there a fire evacuation plan?	
15.	Are there properly equipped first aid stations? Trained personnel; i.e., CPR, etc.?	
16.	Are trailers chocked or locked?	

MORALE

1.	Are good working conditions provided (i.e., clean work area, clean restrooms, lunch area, etc.)?	
2.	Are the employees provided with uniforms?	
3.	What extra curricular activities are encouraged (i.e., company softball team, bowling, picnics, etc.)?	

4.	Where is turnover rate greatest, in the warehouse or office?	
5.	Is there a problem with tardiness and absenteeism?	
6.	Are employee meetings held, how frequently, and what is discussed?	
7.	Are job evaluations given? If so, how frequently and how are they used?	

FACILITY CONDITION AND MAINTENANCE

1.	What is the general outside appearance of the facility?	
2.	Is the parking lot clean and striped for parking?	

3.	Is the lawn maintained? What is the appearance?	
4.	If dock seals are present, what is their condition?	
5.	Is a planned maintenance program for the air conditioning system in effect?	
6.	Are truck rail doors in good operating condition?	
7.	If automatic dock plates are used, are they in good repair and operating safely?	
8.	Are the signs, gutters and trim on the facility in good condition?	

9.	Is the lighting sufficient for operating?	
10.	What is the condition of the roof? Any leaking problems?	
11.	What is the condition of the warehouse floor, stress cracks, etc.?	
12.	Is floor striped?	
13.	How are bay locations identified?	
14.	What is condition of racks?	
15.	Is interior sprinkler equipment properly protected?	

EQUIPMENT CONDITION AND MAINTENANCE

1.	What is the general appearance and age of the operating equipment?	
2.	Is there a preventive maintenance program in effect? In-house or outside contractor?	
3.	Are forklift batteries maintained and checked on a daily basis?	
4.	Are propane tanks kept in a locked cage outside the facility?	
5.	What is the procedure for the forklift operator on reporting problems with the equipment?	
6.	Are all lifts qualified to meet the safety standards of OSHA and local city and state requirements?	

SECURITY

1.	What type of security alarm is used? Are there problems with setting or after-hour phone calls from the alarm company?	
2.	What are the procedures for non-employee visitors, truck drivers, etc., on entering and leaving the building?	
3.	Are all truck, rail and pedestrian doors checked by designated personnel before leaving the facility for the day and/or throughout the day?	
4.	Are alarm pass cards kept to a minimum and given to necessary personnel only?	
5.	Are keys to the facility controlled and given to necessary personnel only?	
6.	Are locks changed on all access doors when an employee who had keys leaves the company?	
7.	Is his/her pass card canceled on termination?	

8.	Who reviews the opening and closing reports?	

TRANSPORTATION

1.	Is equipment company-owned or are contract operators used?	
2.	What is the condition of equipment?	
3.	What type of routing procedure is used?	
4.	What are the procedures when shortages are reported?	
5.	Are records and manifests kept on file for backup information?	
6.	How are drivers controlled and tracked?	

7.	Are complaints handled by designated personnel?	
8.	Are refused damages and shortages a common occurrence?	
9.	What is the accident rate?	
10.	Is detention a problem with TOFC drayage?	

BILLING

1.	How are receiving records/invoices accounted for?	
2.	How are all tally lists accounted for?	

3.	How are special projects (accessorial) charges accounted for? Are special sheets issued and numerically controlled?	
4.	Is the billing audited?	
5.	Is the billing a separate function or part of the CSR functions?	

CUSTOMER SERVICE LEVELS

1.	How is shipping performance measured?	
2.	How is order processing performance measured?	
3.	How is receiving performance measured?	

4.	Customer feedback – how quick is response?	
5.	What are backup procedures?	

SAMPLE SANITATION AUDIT

A. EXTERIOR PREMISES & SURROUNDING AREA CONDITION:

NO.		YES	NO
1.	Are there nearby structure and establishments such that cooperative control programs with proprietors, or municipal authorities required for adequate control?		
2.	Are there nearby harborages for rodents, insects, and other vermin (dumps, landfills, abandoned buildings, river levees, railroad embankments, open drainage ditches, areas of heavy vegetation or standing water, etc.)?		
3.	Are there grain elevators or feed mills in the vicinity? Nearby sources of airborn contamination (smoke, dust, fly ash, chemicals, etc.)?		
4.	Is the exterior perimeter free of spillage and other miscellaneous accumulations, which might attract and harbor rodents, or other pests?		

NO.		YES	NO
5.	Are exterior perimeters adequately trapped/baited to deter pest entry to the internal premises? Are trap and bait stations in good condition and properly maintained?		
6.	Are external storage areas (if present) for equipment and supplies properly maintained (free of refuse and debris)? Does it provide for off-the-floor storage?		
7.	Is the building above grade on all sides, of good construction, and generally in good physical repair (i.e., windows in good repair, adequately screened, or kept closed; roof void of leaks; doors in good repair, etc.)?		
8.	Does the facility have vehicular ramps leading to the dock platform, and/or central warehouse? Are the ramps guarded by flashing, or self-closing doors with adequate threshold stripping?		
9.	Are doors leading to the interior premises (i.e., dock loading, track well, exit, etc.) kept closed when not in use, or otherwise maintained to deter flying insects, and other pest entry?		
10.	Is there any evidence of rodent activity (i.e., burrowing, gnawing, evidence in bait station, live or dead rodents)?		

NO.		YES	NO
11.	Is there any evidence of bird activity (i.e., nesting or roosting in adjacent trees, under canopies or overhangs, roof wall junctions, or vents)?		
12.	Are pallets stored outside? Are they contaminated by bird or rodent excrement?		
13.	Are there separate storage and disposal facilities for waste? Are the containers covered? Are these waste disposal areas properly constructed and maintained?		
14.	Are rail track and truck dock areas free of debris and spillage; weeds, grass, or shrubbery properly trimmed; hard-surfacing in good repair; all areas properly drained?		
15.	Are the spaces under the leveling platforms at the truck docks easily accessible for cleaning and spraying? Are these spaces properly cleaned and treated to preclude insect breeding/harborage?		
	COMMENTS		

B. INTERNAL PREMISES:

NO.		YES	NO
16.	Is the interior lighting sufficient to allow adequate inspection and cleaning of perimeter and central storage area?		
17.	Does the facility have a scheduled housekeeping inspection program? Insect/pest control program? Is the insect/pest control program administered by a certified pest control operator or under the supervision of a certified operator?		
18.	Are all insecticides, pesticides, fumigants being used approved and registered with the EPA? Are these materials being used in the manner prescribed by law? Are all insecticides, pesticides, and fumigants maintained in separate storage and under lock?		
19.	Are all pipes and similar items which pass through walls, or are attached to walls, properly caulked, etc.? Is there adequate clearance for inspection and cleaning?		

NO.		YES	NO
20.	Are stored products, shipping materials, and equipment arranged so as to facilitate adequate inspection of the perimeter and central storage areas? Are finished products adequately protected from insects, rodents, and other pest, mechanical equipment damage, and the elements?		
21.	Are products stored off the floor, on pallets, or racks? Are damaged products immediately removed from storage or temporarily taped? Are all resultant spillages removed on a timely basis?		
22.	Are shipments of products examined for damage, infestation, contamination, etc., upon receipt? If found to be damaged, infested, and/or contaminated, is the product reworked, destroyed, or otherwise treated with an approved material (i.e., fumigant, etc.) to correct the condition prior to placement in storage? Trade shipment?		
23.	Does the facility maintain a separate area for storage and reconditioning of damaged and returned products? Are damaged products reconditioned and rotated on a scheduled and timely basis?		

NO.		YES	NO
24.	Does the facility store other potentially adulterous products (i.e., fertilizers, soaps, toxic chemicals, etc.)? Are these products appropriately separated from human/pet foods which would be susceptible to odor transfer contamination?		
25.	Are products stacked in the proper pattern and height? Are recommended rotation procedures being followed?		
26.	Are adequate number of rodent control stations (bait and/or trap) present and well placed? Are rodent shields or guards used where necessary (i.e., doors, walls, track well entrance doors, etc.)?		
27.	Was any evidence of rodent activity observed in the warehouse (i.e., excreta or urine stains on product containers, pallets, etc.)?		
28.	Were any live or dead product-infesting insects observed on floors, walls, empty pallets, product containers? Were any seen flying about the warehouse? Were any insect tracks in dust deposits on floors, ledges, etc.?		

NO.		YES	NO
29.	Were numerous non-product-infesting type insects (alive or dead) observed?		
30.	Were any birds seen flying about the warehouse? Were any bird excreta, feathers, nests, or nesting material observed on product containers, ledges, roof supports, etc., within the warehouse?		
31.	Are rail track wells hard surfaced, in good repair, and properly drained? Are the track wells free of debris and product spillage?		
32.	Does the facility perform at adequate intervals space fogging and crack and crevice treatments?		
33.	Are only approved materials and methods used for fogging and crack and crevice treatments?		
	COMMENTS		

C. RECONDITIONING OPERATION:

NO.		YES	NO
34.	Does the facility have a reconditioning operation?		
35.	Is the operation conducted in an enclosed room?		
36.	Is the area adequately maintained in accordance with sanitation guidelines?		
37.	Are conditions in this area adequate to protect the purity and wholesomeness of the finished product pending return to central storage?		
38.	Are recoupered packages coded in accordance with company policy?		
39.	Are light fixtures properly covered and maintained?		
	COMMENTS		

D. CARRIER INSPECTION PRACTICES:

NO.		YES	NO
40.	Are adequately trained personnel available for railcar/truck/container inspection?		
41.	Is all carrier equipment inspected for suitability for use? Sprayed and/or fumigated when necessary?		
42.	Does the facility have an adequate incoming car/truck inspection program?		
	COMMENTS		

E. RESTROOMS, LUNCHROOMS, DRESSING ROOMS, ETC.:

NO.		YES	NO
43.	Are restroom/dressing room facilities clean and properly equipped with plumbing and structure conditions properly maintained and in good repair?		

NO.		YES	NO
44.	Are handwashing signs posted in all appropriate facilities (i.e., restroom, dressing room, etc.)? Are these facilities supplied with soap, hot water, and sanitary towels?		
45.	Are lunchrooms adequately cleaned and maintained on a regular basis?		
	COMMENTS		

Index

Index